AF323616

UNITING EUR★PE
JOURNEY BETWEEN GLOOM AND GLORY

UNITING EUROPE

JOURNEY BETWEEN GLOOM AND GLORY

Albrecht Rothacher

Imperial College Press

Published by

Imperial College Press
57 Shelton Street
Covent Garden
London WC2H 9HE

Distributed by

World Scientific Publishing Co. Pte. Ltd.

5 Toh Tuck Link, Singapore 596224

USA office: 27 Warren Street, Suite 401-402, Hackensack, NJ 07601

UK office: 57 Shelton Street, Covent Garden, London WC2H 9HE

Library of Congress Cataloging-in-Publication Data
Rothacher, Albrecht.
Uniting Europe : journey between gloom and glory / by Albrecht Rothacher.
    p. cm.
  Includes bibliographical references and index.
  ISBN 1860945163 (alk. paper)
   1. European Union. 2. Federal government--European Union countries. 3. European Union
countries--Economic policies. 4. European Union countries--Social policies. 5. European Union
countries--Relations. I. Title.

HC240.R68 2005
337.1'42--dc22

                                                2004065843

British Library Cataloguing-in-Publication Data
A catalogue record for this book is available from the British Library.

Typeset by Stallion Press
Email: enquiries@stallionpress.com

Printed in Singapore.

Very early in this excellent book, Albrecht Rothacher suggests that Europe is standing at a crossroads. What is interesting about this observation is not just how correct it seems at this precise moment, but how often and in how many ways it has been said about the European Union in the past. If Europe is a journey as this book suggests, every enlargement, every treaty, every divided Council and every opinion poll often seems to place us at a crossroads of a kind. The new constitutional treaty agreed at Brussels in 2004, and at the time of writing poised to run the gauntlet of national parliaments and public opinion, is unlikely to change the perception that European Union is a journey, as Rothacher rightly suggests, without a clear destination. Indeed, it is probably the greatest achievement of the EU that it has endured, and added so much to Europe's common life, in the complete absence of any clear consensus among Europeans about what it is for and where it is going.

The fact remains that European Union is both a destination and a way of getting somewhere. It is a *modus vivendi* for a continent with an historic leaning towards armed conflict and military dispute. It is a mechanism for creating a single market that has delivered extraordinary prosperity for Europeans. But it is also the expression of the idea, long latent on the European continent and its offshore islands, that Europe's peoples form a political community of a kind and that they must someday have institutions that express that. If the first two, at least in the current liberal consensus about the value of regulated free markets, seem uncontroversial, the last still has the quality of an existential debate for many in Europe. Decades of failure to properly articulate an objective view of European Union to European citizens — on the part of governments, an increasingly powerful media and the institutions of the EU themselves — has left a deep void of public incomprehension. This in turn has encouraged a tabloid perception that unscrupulous pro-European integrationists have had the better of the past five decades, expanding their sinister project without the burden of too much public scrutiny or comprehension. If the Eurosceptics sometimes sound paranoid and parochial, it is at least in part because defenders of European Union have too often given them little reason to think otherwise. The space between the Philadelphia dreams of Valery Giscard d'Estaing and the more ambitious *conventionels* and the stubborn nostalgia of the British "withdrawalists" is still much too sparsely populated by public debate or media attention. And therein lies a real failure to make the European Union comprehensible to the people it serves. It also suggests that we may find ourselves at the European crossroads for a little while longer.

Part of the problem, as Rothacher points out, lies in the tendency to subordinate the political argument for European Union to the economic one, especially in more euro-wary countries like Sweden and Britain. This creates a debate on Europe that is badly misshapen. Unless we can talk openly about the political instinct that leads many Europeans to the conclusion that the European peoples have (a) a common cultural and political heritage, (b) an inescapable political interdependence in the face of global political, economic and ecological challenges and (c) a responsibility, given Europe's traumatic history, to bind themselves together politically so that they can never again be broken by military conflict or disfigured by dictatorship — both painfully recent memories in much of Europe — the argument for European Union will sound half-baked, and Europe's crisis of identity will persist. If nothing else, we will have no apposite response to those who can and do make the inverse of this argument: that the tribal European nation states can never form any kind of political community, federated, confederated or otherwise.

This intelligent book does not duck that argument, or the questions it raises. Indeed, Rothacher is clear that unless we try to understand Europe as a political problem we will never understand it at all. As important as it may be to understand the neo-functionalist analysis of the inter-institutional dynamic, unless you learn to see the European Union as it looks to a Brussels *fonctionaire*, or an Irish farmer, or a Portuguese businessman or the Prime Minister of Poland, it simply won't make any sense. It won't make a lot of sense when you *do* learn to see it that way — but that is at least partly the point. The fact that this book is leavened with this kind of perspective makes it a refreshing analysis. For all of the ink spilt at the feet of individual Union policies, it is still rare for a writer to consider Europe as a whole, in its many political contexts. Nor does Rothacher confine himself to description, and his prescriptions for the European Union are lucid. Whether you agree or disagree, whether you think Europe's journey tends to gloom or glory, the arguments in this book will make a good companion at the European crossroads.

Graham Watson MEP
Brussels
June 2004

CONTENTS

ACP   African, Carribean and Pacific group of states

CAP   common agricultural policy
CFI   Court of First Instance
CFP   common fisheries policy
COR   Committee of Regions
COREU   European Correspondence
CSFP   common security and foreign policy

DG   Directorate General of the Commission

EBRD   European Bank for Reconstruction and Development
EC   European Commission
ECA   European Court of Auditors
ECB   European Central Bank
ECJ   European Court of Justice
ECS   Economic and Social Committee
ECSC   European Coal and Steel Community
ECTS   European Credit Transfer System
ECU   European Currency Unit
EDC   Euorpean Defense Community
EDF   European Development Fund
EEC   European Economic Coomunity
EIB   European Investment Bank
EIC   Euro Info Centres
EMI   European Monetary Institute
EMS   European Monetary System
EMU   European Monetary Union

EP	European Parliament
EPC	European Political Cooperation
ESCB	European System of Central Banks
ESF	European Social Funds
ETP	Executive Training Programme (in Japan)
EU	European Union
Euratom	European Atomic Energy Community
FVO	Food and Veterinary Office
IGC	inter-governmental conference
ISPA	Instrument for Structural Policies for Pre-Accession
JET	Joint European Torus
LDC	less developed countries
MEA	multilateral environmental agreements
MED	Mediterranean
MEP	Member of the European Parliament
OAD	Offical Aid for Development
QMV	qualified majority voting
SIS	Schengen Information System
TAC	total allowable catches
TEN	Trans-European Networks
UNICE	Union of European Industries
VAT	value added tax
WEU	Western European Union

Some day historians will probably rank Europe's peaceful integration achieved in half a century of sustained efforts among mankind's major achievements. Other parts of the world — East Asia, Latin America, Sub-Saharan Africa, the Arab world — envy our old quarrelsome continent to have accomplished such a remarkable degree of unity, solidarity and common purpose against all odds. There is truly no historical equivalent. Yet, how come that Europe's integration is seen by many, if not most, contemporaries and even quite a few active participants as tedious, wearing and somnific, if not as annoying and threatening the accustomed way of life and of politics proper?

There are, in my view, three major reasons for this perfectly avoidable alienation:

- Europe's current constitution is a messy nightmare. The Council is an executive body which operates as a legislature. The European Parliament to this day enjoys only partial budgetary rights and no right of taxation. Further, Parliament and Commission are mostly in charge of sectoral policies which could often be better decided at national or regional level. At the same time they remain impotent on most high politics issues of internal and external security for which continent-wide decisions and policies would matter most. As a result, the EP is being blamed for all the wrongs of "Brussels", and at each European election voter participation shrinks to ever lower minoritarian levels.

- European decision making is done by intransparent commitology, incomprehensible in its dynamics and workings to anybody but a handful of gray gnomes in the Council and a select few expensive lobbyists. There are precious few heroes left on the European scene, like Jean Monnet or Jacques Delors, to provide both vision and real leadership.

- There is no shortage of earnest panel discussions, thick volumes and sober monographs covering in literally exhaustive detail the minutiae of a vast range of EU policies. Yet at the same time these worthy libraries (to which this author also modestly contributed) exude a spirit of collective ennui and stodginess. A look at student reviews of the major EU textbooks on the net reveals a fairly damning unanimous verdict.

Hence this book attempts to show that Europe is an interesting, fascinating and multi-faceted challenge, where people, provided they have the proper information, can change the course of history for the better. Programmatically it attempts to offer a perspective of federal democracy with a few core competences handled at the European level, and the rest — including the most current EU spending programmes and regulatory policies — in the spirit of subsidiarity, returned ("devoluted") to the national, or often better, regional and local level of decision making.

Karl Marx once claimed his dialectical materialism had put German idealism and Hegelian philosophy standing on their heads back on their feet. European integration has to do the same. The functionalist method of integration through the backdoor has become a victim of its own success and outlived its usefulness. The proliferation of second and third order regulations and of poorly administered funding programmes has eroded popular acceptance and obscured the view for the essentials of constitutional reform in Europe.

There is no shortage of good inspiring federal systems in the contemporary world. They range from Anglo-Saxon models like the US, Canada, Australia, South Africa and Malaysia to continental models like Austria, Germany, Belgium and Switzerland. Probably the Swiss system of a small, effective, multilingual and well controlled executive, with a strong element of direct participatory democracy, is best suited for Brussels.

If Europe's citizens choose not to act and leave decisions on their future to the type of leadership which currently runs the major member states, then the current muddle is very likely to continue. An enlarged Union of 25 member states risks stalemates on all major issues, with more populist summit shows, less real problem resolution, and the erosion of legitimacy and public trust. This might see in consequence the gradual unraveling of Europe's current achievements of integration. The EU, with the functioning internal market and the monetary union at its core, will then become an ever more unmanageable free trade area — with serious risks to our future security and prosperity.

What Europe needs now is a fresh, lively and informed debate on constitutional reform unhindered by the vested interests of national and European bureaucracies. This book wishes to contribute and to be helpful. The time for treaty revisions, which since more than one decade have been following faithfully the laws of diminishing returns and are now repeated at ever quicker intervals, should be over.

The political message of this book is clear. I tried to underpin my case with the gist of more than 20 years of research, teaching, writing and practical work experience on Europe's integration. It goes without saying that all the views expressed here are strictly my own. They certainly do not commit any of the institutions for which I currently work (or ever worked before). They surely have not been influenced by the European Commission's censorship provisions either.

I tried to make EU policies and decisions more comprehensible by sparingly inserting anecdotes and mostly true personal experiences, not with the intention to "kiss and tell", but rather to demonstrate the underreported human side of this great European adventure.

I have to thank my European Studies students at the National University of Singapore for their stimulating questions and presentations. Ten thousand kilometres away from Brussels, the haze of Eurospeak and commitology finally begins to fade. Grandeur and follies of this great enterprise become much clearer. I also owe a lot to hundreds of inspiring debates over the future of Europe which I had with academics, businessmen, politicians, bureaucrats and regular citizens from Stockholm to Budapest, and from Porto to Vilnius. These debates, about the benefits and pitfalls of EU accession, took place in my previous incarnation at the Commission's directorate general for

Enlargement. Prior to this, between 1992 and 1996 I journeyed up and down Austria as a travelling missionary on matters related to EU. This is a lasting experience which was very helpful in putting all EU policies into a common sensical frame of mind, and in finding good, honest and self-critical answers to a lot of good and honest questions. I have to thank my family for permitting me to write yet another book (though it won't be the last I hasten to threat). Therefore this book is dedicated to my children. My deep thanks also go to Jenny Tan for her marvellous typing skills and for deciphering my handwriting, as I remain old-fashionably and incurably addicted to putting my words on paper first.

The title of this book is inspired by the seminal volume *Europe: Journey to an Unknown Destination*, written three decades ago by my academic supervisor at the European University Institute, the late Sir Andrew Shonfield. In the meantime, the destinations available have become clearer. Europe is at the crossroads. *Hic Rhodus, hic salta*. The choice is ours.

Albrecht Rothacher
Singapore
August 2004

Is there a European Identity?

If British and French businessmen meet in Japan they probably discover quickly and with relief, common values, beliefs and ways of behaviour in the difficult bureaucratic and corporate environment of an alien civilisation. On the other hand, if they are off duty on the beaches of Spain, they will probably hardly bother to discover their shared values and roots but rather stick to their own countrymen and friends.

It is obviously easier to find common European ground in view of outsiders and foreign ways than to define quick everyday common denominators within Europe.

National identities for most people today remain strongly held. They represent a combination of many powerful elements: common values, a shared heritage of political and legal norms, a community of learning and of communication with permanent interactions and dialogue, thus assuring a collective understanding of rights, values and norms, a shared language, a community of common destiny and history, which accepts internal and external events as shared challenges, and finally a community of solidarity which protects its weaker members. Clearly tribal or multi-cultural societies, or those with strong social or racial sub-cultures (like the US of the 1960s: "Two nations separate and unequal.") have difficulties in achieving the national identity which modern European nation states and their citizens have developed since more than two centuries. While most of the sound and fury of early 20th century nationalism has been fortunately tuned down, some more recent nation states on the East European scene show them all the more passionately.

If modern European man has a tangible regional and a more or less strongly felt national identity, where is Europe beyond lofty abstraction? Obviously a European people does not exist, but rather a multitude of peoples of Europe.

Historically, "Europe" has always been proclaimed and defined against enemies from beyond and from within. Without such challenges in times of peace and tranquility, the term soon fell into disuse, only to be rediscovered quickly in times of need.

The term "Europeans" was first used by ancient Greece and Macedonia when they felt threatened by the barbaric Persians. The defense of "Europe" was again proclaimed when in the early Middle Ages, Germanic empires and tribes united against powerful invaders from different civilisations and religions. During Karl Martell's defense against the Arabs in Tours and Poitiers in 732, during Charlemagne's campaign against the Awars, and when King Otto I fought against the invading Magyars on the Lechfeld in South Germany in 955. The calls for crusades to liberate the Holy Land from the infidels, like by Pope Urban II in 1095, similarly appealed to a European solidarity and a common Christian civilisation. Well until the 19th century, Turkey and its Ottoman Empire were seen as the major threat which Europe faced. To a lesser extent this role was played by Russia. In the Crimean War, for instance, both Britain and France justified their intervention by claiming to defend Europe's freedom, civilisation and progress against the despotism of the Russian Empire, as *The Economist* put it on April 14, 1855.

"Europe" was also a rallying cry against internal threats to the established order by Democrats, Jacobin revolutionaries, and later Socialists. It was also the code word for solidarity in Europe's coalition politics which upheld the continent's fragile balance of power system, set up in 1648 at the end of the Thirty Years War and lasted effectively until 1914 (in the view of some Tory foreign policy analysts, it still exists). It is no surprise then that the defense of Europe and its values figured prominently in the propaganda of both sides in the Napoleonic wars, in World War I and even in World War II.

More serious and consequential were the concepts which the leaders of the pan-European non-communist resistance against Hitler had developed. They build on the federalist ideas which thinkers like the

Austrian Count Richard Coudenhove-Kalergi and the French and German Foreign Ministers Aristide Briand and Gustav Stresemann had advocated in the inter-war period — then sadly in vain. Basically they had intended a just post-war order of a confederation of equals, not of the victors exploiting the vanquished like the 1919 treaty system which had triggered a round of violent revisionism, from which Europe would not recover. Their ideas came too late and were ineffectual to prevent Hitler, Mussolini, a series of other unsavoury dictators, and WWII. But during the war they gained new currency and credibility among the thinking resistance. With the gentle discreet help of the US and the Vatican, which saw Europe's Christian civilisation threatened by the aggressive atheism of Stalin's expanding empire, this finally led to the creation of the Council of Europe in 1949 and the Treaties of Rome in 1957 and a vastly different post-war order than in 1919.

If Europe was only (and temporarily) united against external threats, wouldn't it now disintegrate once its mightiest external threat, the Soviet empire, had imploded? Well, it has not and since 1989 has rather shown signs of new vitality.

Attempts by federalists to denigrate the nation state in making it responsible for Europe's wars or questioning its ability for problem resolution (from job creation to saving the whale and the ozone layer) are not particularly helpful. Replacing the EU 25 member states with some 700 regions of the size of Luxembourg would rather seem like a nightmarish relapse into medieval tribalism and become as ungovernable as the Holy Roman Empire at its worst.

In times of need, people feel — rightly or wrongly — that it is foremost their nation state which can offer them shelter, help and protection. Even in Italy where national pride — in difference to local and regional pride or pride in Europe — is least pronounced, the nation state due to its irreplaceable functional needs is making a comeback.

Federalists exaggerate when they make nationalism responsible for all military evils of the 20th century. They may be right with regard to most of the first half of that century. But between 1950–1990 mankind's survival was threatened surely not by nationalism but by the antagonism of two multinational superpowers pursuing ideologies with universalist claims.

Some historians, like Ernst Nolte, with some plausibility even claim that the European wars between 1917 (the year of the October revolution) and 1945 constituted essentially a European civil war triggered by the revolutionary agenda of Bolshevist totalitarianism.

The historical fate of most multinational empires equally suggests caution and prudent self-restraint. Over-extension and the rule over foreign subjects, unwilling and/or unable to assimilate, usually led to bloody conflicts over power, culture and resources, ending mostly in a quick and violent collapse of imperial reach.

Europe with its multitude of indigenous national and regional cultures and identities cannot duplicate the melting pot model of the traditional immigrant nations of North America (*"e pluribus unum"*) and Oceania. It should thus make sure that those countries and people who join the Union share a well defined and tangible common European identity on top of the plurality of identities which modern man inherits or acquires by chance or purposeful choice.

These identities in sum determine an individual's self esteem and achievement level. Without them, meaningful social interactions cannot take place. They cover gender, religion, education, family situation, age, social class, ideological beliefs, professional standing, but also in varying strength local, regional, national and continental identities.

Without firm cultural identities there is anarchy and social disintegration — as evident in the multi-cultural slums of Western metropolises. Cultural identity in short implies shared symbols and meanings. Events then are recognised as common challenges requiring a joint reaction, or failing this, are perceived as foreign concerns with no need to act.

What then is the European identity, this elusive staple of summit rhetorics and Euro-prose? In the realm of values there were the traditions of Roman law, which were rediscovered and applied across the continent via church law since the first millennium. During the Middle Ages there was unity of the (West) Roman Church, with Latin as the common scholarly and legal language and artisans, merchants, scholars and monks moving freely and frequently. Changes in architecture, monastic and merchantile styles regularly crossed the continent with little inhibition. For more than three centuries the Hanseatic League enforced common commercial, maritime and municipal laws from Bruges to Nowgorod. Once the reformation ended the linguistic and scholastic unity of the Catholic Church, the critical spirit of the enlightenment, the defense of personal, civic and urban freedom against absolutism, feudal and clerical oppression became pan-European concerns. The spirit of religious, philosophical and practical tolerance was a shared consequence of the decade long religious wars which devastated Europe in the 17th century.

Although the advent of modern nation states following the French Revolution had finally eroded what remained of legal and linguistic unity, until WWI a culture of shared values, civilised standards and a common practice of cross-national experience and continental travel remained the norm in Europe's aristocracy and bourgeoisie, as well as for anybody who wanted to be taken seriously as a scientist, artist or artisan. All of this contributed to the world hegemony of European culture, its administrative, technical and military standards, and its scientific and aesthetic norms. This hegemony ended even before the last major colonies were lost after WWII.

Almost 2,000 years of Christianity created a common view of man and the world. Certainly, there were also significant contributions from Middle Eastern civilisations, and those of Greek, Roman, and later Celtic, Germanic and Slavic origin, which shaped the evolution of Christian thought.

In difference to Byzantium ("East Rome") which stuck to the rigid despotic norms of Caesaropapism, the unity of clerical and worldly rule still prevalent in the Eastern orthodoxy which prevented the enlightenment and liberal traditions from taking root from Moscow to Athens in often painful century-long debates and conflicts, "West Roman" Catholicism finally accepted the division and co-existence of civic ("*temporalia*") and clerical ("*spiritualia*") rule; that is, the separation of politics and religion.

This freedom permitted critical thinking, scientific debate and the development of modern technology. Christian thinking postulated the dignity and uniqueness of the human being, which set the basis for well-defined human rights, constitutional law and a division of power and state-free spheres for civic society to develop. Ultimately the welfare state, with its norms of dignified working and living conditions, basic income guarantees in case of sickness, age and unemployment and social equity during economic development, also has the same Christian roots.

According to Denis de Rougemont, a Swiss writer, three common European virtues resulted: the quest for objective truth, the acceptance of personal responsibility, and the desire for freedom, all elements of a very personalised European ethic. Other attempts at a definition of European identity claim permanent innovation and inter-cultural learning made in the spirit of enlightenment and humanism. This, however, is so vague and politically correct that it could also easily apply to most Asian and African intellectuals.

Abstractly written legal norms have been developed since the late 18th century. During the Renaissance, the rediscovery of the rationalism and individualism of Greek philosophy allowed modern European man to question religious traditions and ultimately, for better or for worse, to dominate nature. In business the use of Arab decimals permitted accounting and thus helped to lay the technical foundations of modern capitalism. Modernity surely made a head start in the Protestant regions of Europe. Whatever is left of the Protestant work ethic has spread since the war to the Catholic areas of Europe. With strong progress in education and welfare systems in consequence, Europe's traditional North/South divide has narrowed perceptively.

National differences have become almost imperceptible in the postnational fun culture of modern youth, however American, dubious and transitory this may appear on occasion. This points to the gravest risks for Europe's fragile identity: the failure of most of its contemporary secondary education systems to teach its historical and intellectual foundations, and the mediatic mass culture made by market-dominating US media conglomerates as the instant, easiest and smallest common denominator for a continent of cultural and linguistic diversity. Obviously this includes the propagation of all current US norms in terms of lifestyle, business culture and political behaviour, correct-speak and correct-think — no doubt at the expense of genuine European creativity, originality and depth of discourse, which is being steamrollered.

For their weak and often disparate common identity (a French definition of European identity will surely be different from the one of a Swede, a Pole or a German), Europeans have nobody but themselves to blame. It is their inability to organise an accountable European political class and a European public outside the charmed circle of some 20,000 Brussels Eurocrats, and their inability to communicate Europe's integration as an achievement of civilisation winning over irrationality, tyranny and violence.

We may then answer our original question: yes, there is a European identity. It mainly concerns a community of values and of common fate — the experience of the great European civil war of 1914–1945, for instance. Due to linguistic divisions, however, there is little of a community of dialogue and communication. A community of common fate, destiny and solidarity is hence still more of an abstraction and has as yet little concrete appeal to rally the peoples of Europe behind their blue 12-star flag or the Commission's President. Europe cannot be built against deeper seated and more strongly felt national or regional identities. They are all, in fact, wonderfully complementary, in their respective degrees, depending on one's personal choice or even mood of the day. With this inevitable diversity, a European's set of identities then represents precisely the individuality and uniqueness of this small, densely settled and diverse half continent which opposes anything smacking of uniformity.

CHAPTER 2

How to Create "Europe": Of Treaties and Men

How are great empires created? You can settle down in more or less empty spaces — like in North America, Australia or in the South and East of Czarist Russia. In feudal days you could marry successfully — as the Hapsburgs famously did. In the modern age, without much empty space or effective marital diplomacy left, military conquest to achieve supremacy was attempted by Napoleon I, Adolf Hitler and Joseph Stalin. Due to the collective resistance of the conquered subjects, these exploitative empires remained very transitory. Most collapsed within a decade. With its more effective repressive mechanisms, only the post-Stalinist empire managed to survive half a century, before it ultimately imploded between 1989 and 1991.

Yet there is a remarkable alternative: the voluntary merger of countries as equals without subjugation to a dominant hegemony.

This approach needs a rethinking of the classical hierarchical world order approach of the great powers. For better or for worse, in post-war Western Europe no great powers were left, only five medium-sized countries licking their wounds and contemplating past policy mistakes and military follies.

The most elegant and straightforward way towards a European federation would have been to call all nations concerned to have their people vote for a constitutional assembly, which then after earnest debate and deliberation would draft a decent federal constitution, defining basically the rights and obligations of its citizens and the delimitation of policy competences between the four constituent layers of the federation: the tasks of the federation itself, those of the constituent nation states, of their regions and of their municipalities, plus a parliamentary-judicial mechanism for conflict resolution. The result would be submitted to popular referendum for approval and — abracadabra — the United States of Europe are created.

Seductive in its elegant simplicity, inspired by Altiero Spinelli, the directly elected European Parliament in 1984 in fact once drafted such a wonderful constitution — only to be ignored by the political classes and the uninterested electorates in all member states — except Italy! This failure has a most honourable tradition. Already the 1848 Paulskirche assembly in Frankfurt had failed to create a German empire based on a constitutional democracy with the same method in the face of revisionist power politics. It took Bismarck's genius and three limited wars to achieve the objective less democratically in form and in substance more than two decades later in 1871.

The European Union's genius was Jean Monnet. Monnet (1888–1979) was born into a Cognac producing family and had no particular education beyond secondary level. As his family's travelling export salesman, with the help of his attractive lubricant, early on he made many useful contacts in high places, notably in London and in North America. This proved helpful when during both world wars he worked for the French government on armament procurement and its financing among the initially nominally neutral Americans. As a trusted adviser with little personal ambition, he made no secret after WWII of his firm conviction that the repetition of the peace conditions of 1919 — massive cessations of territories, crippling reparations, discriminatory production controls and protectionism — would lead to yet another repeat of the catastrophe.

Working through a small elite network of ministers in Western Europe and in the US, he was the personal driving force behind the creation of the European Coal and Steel Community (ECSC) — proposed formally by an originally hesitant Foreign Minister Robert Schuman on May 9, 1950 (since celebrated as St Schuman Day amongst EU officialdom). He made the proposals for a European Army (meaning, like in the Foreign Legion at the time, German soldiers under French officers — yet he was defeated by a not very far-sighted French National Assembly in 1954, as German soldiers ever since are under US-NATO command), and inspired the creation of Euratom, as nuclear power in the mid-fifties was considered to be the future source of limitless cheap energy. Monnet was less engaged in the Messina conference of 1954, which, to the surprise of many, led to the Treaties of Rome of 1957. The new EEC created not just a free trade area, but a customs union (by 1968) with a common external tariff replacing national tariffs and a common agricultural policy (CAP). The CAP was thought to compensate French farmers — then a powerful, if somewhat idyllically backward political force — for the perceived gains of West Germany's rebuilt industry in the common market of the six founding members. This construction was to be sensibly complemented by a common external trade policy and strict competition policies. All were to be managed by a newly created independent executive body, the European Commission. Its policy proposals were to be approved in a Council of Ministers (of the then six) by majority voting.

Monnet's method was clearly not the spectacular federalism of a constitutional assembly, but a much less attractive and unexciting, and also less resistance-inviting, approach, later termed (neo-) functionalism by sharp-thinking academics. It implies that progress in integration through economic success and international administrative networking achieved in one area — like the coal and steel market — would "spill over" into pressure for progress and integrative expansion of other industrial and commodity markets. This in turn would functionally require a host of collateral common regulations: consumer protection, common technical standards, competition rules, environmental and labour protection, a common currency, etc. All of this gradual, imperceptible and irresistible progress was legitimised by economic need and civic success, not by popular referenda or spectacular political quantum leaps. Clearly Monnet, with his unique method, was Europe's most successful and most unsung statesman of the second half of the 20th century. But his achievements came at a price: the price of persistent popular alienation of the integration project.

Jean Monnet was a visionary who made things happen through tireless networking. With little liking for the constraints of bureaucratic politics and routines, he rarely stayed long in the institutions he so skilfully created. For the European Commission, in 1958 a German law professor Walter Hallstein (1901–1982) took the helm. As a Secretary of State and right hand man to Germany's first post-war Chancellor, Konrad Adenauer, he had negotiated the Treaties of Rome and as a good lawyer took its federalist legal norms and objectives at face value. With his fresh-faced new Commission, Hallstein began to implement the EC's customs union, negotiated earnestly the Dillon and the Kennedy Rounds within GATT and in 1962 began to design time tables for an economic and monetary union.

All this greatly annoyed Charles de Gaulle, the French war hero. He, as an ardent nationalist in 1959 had overthrown the Fourth Republic, whose leaders had signed the Treaties of Rome, and of whose federal ambitions he disapproved. In 1963 he vetoed the first accession bid of "les Anglo-Saxons" (UK, Ireland and Denmark), whom he had heartily disliked since his days of exile in London. Then, during 1965–1966, citing the presidential airs of Hallstein (who, though personally unassuming, had dared to step on a red carpet during a visit to Washington DC in 1961), de Gaulle ordered his ministers and officials to stay away from Council meetings and through a policy of "empty chairs" boycotted all proceedings [a policy which another political genius, John Major, replicated for three months in 1996 at the height of the UK's self-inflicted BSE crisis, boycotting (some) Council business].

De Gaulle called off his boycott — a policy not strictly foreseen in the treaties — only after the other member states accepted in a "Luxembourg compromise" that on any major piece of national concern a member state could veto proposals submitted to the Council. De Gaulle was overthrown by the Paris student revolt in 1969, and Hallstein was not reappointed in 1968. But the unanimity principle endorsed in Luxembourg continued to block most significant integration initiatives for the next two decades until the arrival of Jacques Delors in 1995. His predecessor, the former Luxembourg Premier Gaston Thorn, was mostly occupied by mediation of the British budget conflict and in deflecting Mrs Thatcher's handbag attacks ("I want my money back!").

Jacques Delors (1925–), similarly to Jean Monnet, began his remarkable political career with only secondary education. Starting as a lowly clerk in the Banque de France, he rose quickly through the ranks of the Christian trade union movement. In 1981 he became Minister of Finance in Francois Mitterand's first government, where he attempted to pursue economic and fiscal common sense in a socialist administration committed to nationalisations and reflation. Appointed Commission President in 1985, Delors was quick to generate political momentum to overcome the brooding and stifling atmosphere of Eurosclerosis. Aided by his new Commissioner for Industry, Lord Arthur Cockfield, Delors set out an ambitious programme to implement a single European market with free movement for goods, services, capital and people. In order for it to be taken seriously, the deadline of December 31, 1992 for its accomplishment was publicly set.

In order to prepare the institutional groundwork, an intergovernmental conference was called in February 1986. In a mercifully short amendment ("Single European Act") to the Treaties of Rome, the EU Foreign Ministers threw out the "Luxembourg compromise" and reinstituted qualified majority voting on all internal market matters. Unnoticed by the general public, this "technical provision" was to have far-reaching consequences. Instead of threatening a veto and thereby effortlessly prolonging the stalemate on a given draft regulation under consideration in Council committees, officials and ministers were henceforth forced to work on acceptable compromises in order to minimise the risk of being outvoted. The provisions on the internal market were complemented by new EU competences on environmental protection, safety at work, technology promotion and on funding schemes for disadvantaged regions. They were to become a staple and increasingly expensive sweetener for the "Club Med" member states, but were most effectively used by the Republic of Ireland.

The unqualified success of the internal market was not to be duplicated. The rapid transfer of national competences to the Community level rather stiffened bureaucratic and political resistance. The next Treaty of Maastricht in 1992, which set the ground for monetary union, against Delors' passionate arguments, kept strong inter-governmental elements. They always entailed complex, expensive and utterly untransparent and undemocratic procedures, but allowed heads of governments and their national bureaucrats the illusion of remaining in charge.

Since "Maastricht" the Community consists of a somewhat misconstrued Greek temple. The first pillar, strong, well-developed and sound, consists of the economic and monetary union with the Commission in charge, and the Council, the European Parliament and, ultimately, the European Court of Justice at the controls. Then there are two thin, meagre and under-developed new pillars: the second pillar of a common foreign and security policy, and the third pillar of cooperation in justice and home affairs. The two are inter-governmental, purely bureaucratic inter-ministry affairs with the least public scrutiny or democratic control. Subject to the unanimity principle, it is hardly surprisingly that progress of policy integration has been minimal. Delors, like many, foresaw this and insisted publicly on their integration into Community policies but was overruled.

Clearly, the new elements for the communitarian first pillar provided by Maastricht were much better designed and consequently proved to be effective: foremost, the timing and three-step schedule for monetary union, which was to begin in January 1993 and be accomplished in January 2002 with the physical introduction of the Euro and a fully functional independent European Central Bank. Even the tough stability-oriented convergence criteria were fulfilled by — almost — all EMU participants. Maastricht also provided for Community initiatives on consumer protection and for the setting up of a "cohesion fund" which should help Mediterranean member states to make public investments — notably in transportation networks — to increase their competitiveness while respecting the budgetary discipline imposed by the Maastricht schedule for monetary union. Obviously once monetary union was achieved by 1999 with all Mediterraneans narrowly on board, logically one would have expected the wonderful cohesion fund to be abolished with its mission having been fulfilled so marvellously. This was not to be. Once the lucky recipients became used to "cohesion", they — as usual led by Spain — insisted on having more of it.

Maastricht also provided for more significant co-decision rights for the European Parliament. It also constituted a European citizenship, which allows its proud subjects to sport identical passport and to vote in local and European elections when residing in another EU country. Yet Maastricht clearly fell short of a political union, which, in a federal perspective, is an urgently needed collateral to a successful monetary union. Britain under John Major also continued to object to a joint social charter, which was replete of pious wishes for future action programmes. Denmark, after a negative referendum (50.6%) in June 1992, also secured a series of opt-outs (including from monetary union) to gain acceptance from its sceptical populace. A total of 56.8% then approved the meagre remainder of Maastricht, applicable to Denmark in May 1993.

The ink of the Maastricht ratification was hardly dry when a new inter-governmental conference was called in for 1996. By that time Jacques Delors had retired: the internal market accomplished, the monetary union on its way, and big regional redistribution programmes being administered by his Commission. He could have been proud of his record, but the unfulfilled federal promise still stood out. His successor, Jacques Santer (1935–) was a lawyer from the small Mosel town of Wasserbillig, long-term Prime Minister of Luxembourg, and a Christian Democrat believing in social partnership in a market economy. He shared Delors' federalist convictions, but, being more affable, lacked the intellectual and visionary vigor of his predecessor. "Doing less, but better" was Santer's motto: he felt his predecessor's firework of initiatives had alienated both the EU's national leaders and the general public. In the end he fell in 1999 over a series of improprieties by some of his junior officials and fellow Commissioners — most famously by Mme Edith Cresson, a former French Prime Minister who had hired her dentist friend to do her political work in her home town of Castleraugh at EU taxpayers' expense. Santer was personally blameless, but he failed to fire her in time (a difficult thing to do for a gentle Luxembourger) and to install the controls which had been missing in his predecessor's edifice.

During Santer's tenure, in 1996 the inter-governmental conference was called in Amsterdam, and delivered politically even less than Maastricht. Cynics would argue that heads of government at the European Council wasted too much time on photo opportunities, which in Amsterdam consisted of climbing on Dutch bicycles (Chancellor Kohl for reasons of gravitas declined the occasion).

The European summit in Amsterdam was preceded by year-long preparations. High hopes were entertained. The EU's democratic deficit was to be corrected. The ineffectual second and third pillars of Maastricht were to be integrated into a more accountable and effective Community structure, and the 25 different procedures of co-decision, cooperation and qualified majorities between Commission, Council and Parliament — an arcane act accessible only to a handful of procedural fetishists in each institution — were to be streamlined and simplified so as to accommodate an enlarged union. In short, in Amsterdam federalists hoped for "one pillar" only as the political union that was seen as the necessary collateral to the economic and monetary union created in Maastricht.

All these pious hopes, which both the Dutch Council Presidency and Commission President Santer initially entertained, were to be frustrated. Looking at their opinion polls, heads of government at the summit decided that their subjects worried about jobs, not about a European constitution. In consequence, they decided on a meaningless employment promotion programme, which charged the Commission to produce reports and to finance pilot projects on best practice without creating one single job (except for typists and translators in Brussels). Tony Blair, fresh in power, decided to sign the Social Charter, thus ending the UK's decade-long opt-out, but agreed to little else. There was some fairly inconsequential tinkering with the co-decision procedure, benefiting Parliament, and some operational improvements of the Schengen agreement on the control of travellers from third countries.

As they could agree on little else, the Council's new left-leaning majority gave the Union a new political correctness code to combat "discrimination based on sex, racial or ethnic origin, religion and belief, disability, age or sexual orientation". Heads of government did little to hide their disagreement when they left. Much of the blame was put on the intemperate outbursts of Spain's Prime Minister Aznar. President Santer, initially reminiscent of his own public expectations, called Amsterdam a failure. He later dutifully corrected himself to term it a success. As nothing had been achieved to prepare the Union for enlargement (the negotiations with six Eastern applicant countries were about to start in the spring of 1998), a follow-up summit had to deal with the "leftovers" of this success.

Amsterdam at least posed no difficulty for ratification. Not even the Danes found the Treaty meaningful enough to warrant a referendum. Soon, in the summer of 1999 Santer and his Commission were forced to resign. In came Romano Prodi, who had been a short term centre-left Prime Minister of Italy. As an economics professor in Bologna he had earlier distinguished himself in reforming the IRI holding, one of the giant loss-making state conglomerates, a heritage of Benito Mussolini. As an academic he had written one book, a classic on the Italian ceramic tiles industry. As a Commission President, his views on EU institutional reforms have not been very perceptible, perhaps due to articulation problems: Italians often think that he speaks English, when in fact most Brits at the same time believe that he speaks Italian.

Hence when the French Presidency, led by the quarrelling cohabitation of Messrs Chirac and Jospin, called for yet another summit, at Nice in December 2000, to enforce democracy in the EU and to make it ready for enlargement, the views of the Commission were neither sought nor listened to, and yet another success story was allowed to unfold. Faithfully following the laws of diminishing returns, the summiteers of Nice essentially debated their countries' and the EU applicants' voting strength in the Council, and — to a much lesser extent — their future representation in the Parliament. All eyewitnesses report that the summit offered valuable insights into how not to run a summit and that summitry as an integration method had ultimately outlived its usefulness.

The new allocation of votes in the Council and of seats in Parliament is as follows, after Nice was ratified following a second Irish referendum and after the new member states joined on May 1, 2004:

**Weighting of votes for old and new member states,
as provided by the Treaty of Nice**

Old Member States			New Member States	
		Previously		
Belgium	12	5	(Bulgaria	10)
Denmark	7	3	Cyprus	4
Germany	29	10	Czech Republic	12
Greece	12	5	Estonia	4
Spain	27	8	Hungary	12
France	29	10	Latvia	4
Ireland	7	3	Lithuania	7
Italy	29	10	Malta	3
Luxembourg	4	2	Poland	27
Netherlands	13	5	(Romania	14)
Austria	10	4	Slovakia	7
Portugal	12	5	Slovenia	4
Finland	7	3		
Sweden	10	4		
United Kingdom	29	10		
	237	**87**		**108**

**Allocation of seats in the European Parliament,
as provided by the Treaty of Nice**

Old Member States			New Member States	
		Previously		
Belgium	22	25	(Bulgaria	17)
Denmark	13	16	Cyprus	6
Germany	99	99	Czech Republic	20
Greece	22	25	Estonia	6
Spain	50	64	Hungary	20
France	72	87	Latvia	8
Ireland	12	15	Lithuania	12
Italy	72	87	Malta	5
Luxembourg	6	6	Poland	50
Netherlands	25	31	(Romania	33)
Austria	17	21	Slovakia	13
Portugal	22	25	Slovenia	7
Finland	13	16		
Sweden	18	22		
United Kingdom	72	87		
	545	**626**		**187**

The over-representation of small countries continues, albeit at a reduced level. The changes introduced in Nice were motivated by the fear of the existing member states being out-voted by the multitude of even smaller accession countries.

The fact that Nice had awarded — generously and inexplicably — 27 Council votes to Poland and Spain, which enjoy half the population size of Germany and roughly two thirds of the UK, France and Italy (with 29 votes each), in retrospect triggered feelings of regret and revisionist desires among the summiteers once they had returned home, sobered down, redone their arithmetic and calculated the likely costs of privileging the most aggressive transfer faction. The next IGC was set to correct their mistake, with a nice "constitution" drafted by a "convent" chaired by the venerable Valery Giscard d'Estaing wrapped around it, or so France and Germany thought. Faced with Spanish and Polish intransigence, this request wrecked the IGC of Brussels in December 2003. This episode once again proved a time honoured American proverb to be correct: "It is easier not to give a bone to a dog, than to take away a bone from a dog." EU summit diplomacy unfortunately lacks the sophistication of this insight.

With paralysis looming in a Union with ultimately some 30 members and unanimity ruling still in place, the Council in Nice had expanded qualified majority voting (QMV) to legal cooperation in civil matters and to trade agreements but to little else. In addition, Nice introduced two new QMV elements to be fulfilled, next to (a) the traditional QMV rule of some two thirds of total votes (then at 62/87), (b) the majority of member states, and (c) 62% of the population of the Union. Voting in the Council will now require specially programmed pocket calculators.

The number of Commissioners (under Prodi, 20, including himself as the President) in the next Commission (as from autumn 2004) has been limited to one per country, their total being fixed at 27.

All of these fairly technical provisions could have been inserted in the accession treaties with the candidate countries. After parliamentary ratification they would have become EU primary law. This was done after previous enlargement rounds in the past. Legally there was no need for a summit treaty. On the substantial "leftovers" of Amsterdam, Nice also failed to provide a solution. Hence in May 2004 the Union stumbled, institutionally unprepared, into its largest enlargement adventure.

Are there lessons to be learned from Europe's functionalist integration through a series of treaties? It was successful in the economic areas of integration where functionalist logic appealed to economic common sense and material interest. This applies to the Treaties of Rome (1957), the Single Act (1986) and the Treaty of Maastricht (1993) as far as monetary union is concerned.

The functionalist theory of Ernst Haas assumed that integration in one area would lead to the emergence of a new functional European elite with a corresponding influential European clientele. They would use their experience and influence to achieve integration in adjacent policy fields ("spill over") in which further progress had become a functional need. Thus a customs union, once achieved, required proper competition rules and an operational single internal market. Once a common internal market is realised, a currency union, harmonised macro-economic policies, basic environmental, social and consumer protection standards would need to apply. All this happened over the decades. Its tortuous progress proved functionalism right — up to a limit.

One could argue the same for a fashionable theory of the 1960s and 1970s, the systems theory, which, applied by Leon Lindberg to European integration, assumed that European "outputs" produced by an impartial professional authority like the Commission would be recognised as better outputs than those produced by national politics.

All wonderful theories worked well until they hit high politics stupid. In a "Gaullist reflex" (Heinrich Schneider), most heads of the larger states and governments, as exemplified by Messrs Blair, Aznar and Berlusconi, strongly preferred to be pictured front page on summit pictures with George Bush as partners and subcontractors of the Americans rather than to be relegated to provincial governor status and shown with Jeb Bush on page 17. Equally their foreign ministries did not quite feel the need to merge as a functional elite (a thing into which they had forced their equally disinclined central bankers) and to reduce their ambassadorial career prospects in a functionally merged EU common external diplomatic service by some 95%.

Since economic and monetary union was achieved, the Monnet method of functional incrementalism appears to have reached the limits of its historical usefulness. Skirting around the federalist quantum leap to achieve political integration no longer helps. Maastricht (1993) already was a failure with respect to political union. Maastricht begot Amsterdam (1998). Amsterdam begot Nice (2000). With the ever quicker sequencing of inter-governmental conferences, their preparations became sloppier, more intransparent and self-servingly bureaucratic, with the summit outcomes becoming ever more PR-oriented and unsatisfactory in their substantial results. When solid drafts were prepared, they were invariably watered down or ignored by the presidency and the participants. Nice and the presidency of Jacques Chirac proved too much even for all other participants, who suffered through his performance which focused on the theme "Whose nation values how many votes in the Council?", a theme wonderfully tailor-made to rekindle long forgotten atavisms and unhelpful comparisons. "Never again" was the common *cri de coeur* of those who suffered through the three days and nights.

Hard pressed to identify the progress achieved at Nice, European summiteers were quick to resort to the time honoured method of calling for yet more elaborate preparations for their next session (they had usually felt sovereign enough to ignore precious preparatory work in the past). As mentioned, this time it was a "convent" that prepared the ever more ultimate treaty revision. As a substitute for a constitutional assembly of the unelected, more or less eminent politicians met throughout 2003, with their chairman Giscard finally drafting a "constitution" of sorts.

In a nutshell, it attempts to simplify the unreadable structure of subsequently revised and re-numerated treaties. It also integrates all EU policies into the single "pillar" and significantly streamlines decision-making in the Council. Yet it fails to define properly and systematically the responsibilities between different layers of European, national and regional decision-making. The fairly redundant "charter of fundamental rights", which had been solemnly announced in Nice, but which was left high and dry as regards its applicability, is to be given constitutional rank. Laudable though this appears, most, if not all, of its provisions had already multiple quasi-constitutional quality through Council of Europe and member states' human rights provisions, which are already binding for EU institutions.

In the run up to the Brussels summit of 2003 the age-old dispute between inter-governmentalists and federalists resurfaced. Tony Blair and Jacques Chirac, later seconded by Prime Ministers Aznar and Berlusconi, who jointly share the honour of having wrecked the increasing sequence of failed European summits, insisted on a new five-year presidency of the Council to be held by a senior European statesman (read: possibly Messrs Blair or Aznar after retirement). He would then issue his instructions as the member states' consensus to the European Commission, which would lose its professional independence and its right of initiative and turn into a Council secretariat instead. Inter-governmentalism would triumph: democratic and legal scrutiny would suffer.

Commission President Prodi, in turn publicly supported by Jacques Delors, rather advocated the integration of the second and third pillar activities (except for military intervention) into Community decision-making. There should be a single foreign policy — like the one already existing on trade matters — a common border control police, etc. Strengthened EP competences should make up for abolished Council veto rights. The Commission President (and his Commissioners) should be directly elected by the EP.

With the failure of the IGC in Brussels, the outcome of this debate had been shelved until further notice. Since Maastricht in 1991, European leaders have been aware of the challenge. They knew that agreement among the 12 and later 15 would be easier than among 25. Yet they persistently failed until the Irish Presidency in June 2004 got them to agree on an improved version of the constitution with surprisingly little public ado and dissent.

The New Constitution: A Treaty Too Far?

Reflecting on the poorly designed treaties of Amsterdam and Nice, it finally dawned on the European Council that nights of drinking and shouting matches were a suboptimal way of arriving at yet another treaty addressing the shortcomings of the previous one. Hence a more inclusive convention consisting of member state appointed worthies and a handful of MEPs was dreamt up. As mentioned, its proceedings were chaired by the venerable Giscard d'Estaing, who, two decades earlier, had already modestly declared himself to be a suitable president of Europe.

After 15 months of earnest deliberations the convention came up with a decent draft which true to form the European Council in December 2003 failed to accept, courtesy of the Italian Presidency's particularly inept handling and Polish insistence that its 27 votes (achieved at Nice) were a matter of national honour and survival and hence non-negotiable. Where the Italians (with Signore Berlusconi's confirmed status as an unguided missile) failed, six months later more refined Irish diplomacy succeeded. Bertie Ahern had heads of government agree in advance to a revised draft treaty (without divulging details), and let them mainly debate the *"invocatio Dei"* which the Catholic governments — like the post-Communists of Poland — found sadly missing in the preamble drafted by Giscard.

Empirically there are probably few discernible national policy differences based on whether or not His will is invoked in the constitution. The current version reflects French official agnosticism and refers in earnest dullness to the "inspiration from the cultural, religious and humanist inheritance of Europe".

More seriously the draft represents a good solid treaty — and as such a vast improvement over Amsterdam, Nice and even Maastricht. But, alas, a real constitution establishing a proper federal structure based on a decent division of power and the subsidiarity principle it is not. Although containing constitutional elements, a treaty, and a fairly good one at this, it remains in legal form and substance. Already the first page enumerates all 25 heads of state who agreed on the paper. It does not mention the peoples of Europe who might have written themselves a constitution.

As a treaty consolidating all previous treaty texts from Rome to Nice, the "constitution" contains both old and new provisions. Some is pure rewrapping. The Charter of Fundamental Rights is declared binding — well it already is: by declaration of the European Council and in almost all provisions through national human rights legislation and the Council of Europe's longstanding Human Rights Declaration. There is a statement on the supremacy of EU law over national law — restating long established ECJ doctrine and practice. There is now also an exit clause to leave the EU (perhaps meant as a sales point to sceptics): no novelty value either, since international law allows any country a negotiated departure from any international organisation (witness Greenland's departure from the EU back in 1985, causing a painful 50% territorial loss of a lot of precious arctic ice, useful when it comes to global warming).

What then is new?

Institutionally, the rotating presidency of the Council is replaced by a "President of the European Council", elected by the European Council with QMV for a period of two and a half years, that is, changing only once while the Commission and the EP are in office. Weak, inexperienced or overcharged national presidencies will be a thing of the past. The salutary educational effect of running a presidency, which was helpful in the past, now with 25 members was already very much diluted with the prospect of doing so every 12.5 years only.

There will be a "Foreign Minister of the EU" uniting the functions of the Council's High Representative for the CSFP, who presides over the Council of Foreign Ministers, with the Commission's

Vice President for Foreign Affairs. Constitutionally this may appear as messy, merging executive (Commission) with legislative (Council) functions — but remember that on inter-governmental matters, like the CSFP, the Council has acted both as executive and as legislature already!

As all politics is personal, Javier Solana, the EU's seasoned foreign policy supremo is expected to take over this function once the constitution is approved in 2007, with Benita Ferrero-Waldner, the Austrian Foreign Affairs Commissioner then assuming new responsibilities in the Barroso Commission, perhaps taking over the macroeconomics files left by the then departing Spanish Commissioner.

The new EU Foreign Minister will be in charge of a European diplomatic service consisting of the Commissioner's external relations staff and their budget, augmented by seconded foreign ministry personnel from member states. Hence so far there is little immediate risk that, for instance, the 25 member states' embassies and the EU Delegation in Washington DC (and 170 other capitals) will be merged into one — but the writing, as for erstwhile proud national central bankers, is clearly on the wall.

After each European election, the Commission's President will be elected by the EP based on a European Council proposal established by QMV. EP election campaigns will hence become based on a leadership contest and programmatic alternatives — and not just on the cumulative effect of 25 different national protest votes as last witnessed in June 2004.

As from 2014, there will also be only 18 Commissioners (instead of 25 as at present). The Commission's President will select them based on three proposals from each member state. Instead of having to accept 24 people for 24 jobs, he can scout through 72 resumes for 18 jobs, which will enhance prospects for a better share of the best and the brightest. His Commission team will then be presented to the EP for approval. As not all of the EU's current member states will be represented by Commissioners, it is foreseen that after two terms they will forego one term.

Within the Council, weighted votes (so painfully and weirdly arrived at in Nice) will happily be junked in favour of a new double majority as

QMV mode, 55% of member states (the constitution for unexplained reasons mentions 15 — instead of the mathematically more correct 14), which should at least represent 65% of the EU's population — translating into some 300 million out of 450 million.

QMV will now also cover asylum and integration policies. The old three pillar temple will be demolished. The EP's role is greatly enhanced: it will assure full co-decision rights with the Council on domestic and legal policies (the inter-governmental "third pillar" of old). It will also assume co-responsibility for the EU's entire spending budget — including agriculture! — but still not for funding the EU budget.

On Euro-zone matters, the participating finance ministers' group will be upgraded to monthly meetings and elect their own president (a function currently exercised as "Mr Euro" on a more *ad hoc* basis by Mr Claude Juncker, the able PM of Luxembourg). Price stability and the independence of the ECB will be once more enshrined.

Clearly the constitutional provisions are sensible and level-headed. They squarely address the blatant shortcomings of Nice and Amsterdam — notably the Council's poor functioning and many of the EP's remaining legislative and budgetary deficits in competences.

Yet as Josep Borrell, the EP's new President in 2004 rightly pointed out, too many policies requiring unanimity in the Council remain: taxation, social and labour policies, defense and EU revenues. There is also, courtesy of the nostalgic neutrals (Sweden, Finland, Ireland, Austria) and non-aligneds (Cyprus, Malta), not even a watertight mutual defense guarantee among EU member states!

As stated above, the "constitution" constitutes a good treaty, much better drafted and thought out than the multitude adopted since the Single Act of 1986. The quantum leap to a proper federal constitution has been narrowed, but it still needs to be made, including the devolution of unnecessary competences back to member states and their regions.

How are the constitutional treaty's prospects for adoption? Referenda will be held in Denmark, France, the United Kingdom, Ireland, Luxembourg, Malta, Netherlands, Poland, Portugal, Spain and the

Czech Republic. There may be more and some are not binding. If one or two referenda go negative — which is likely — selective opt-outs for the countries in question can be negotiated — like after the Danish "no" on Maastricht.

But if there are three to four "no"s — there is unfortunately no shortage of candidates, apart from the UK, there are Malta, Poland, the Czech Republic... — the constitution will be a dead duck.

What would happen? Answer: nothing. This is very bad news indeed, since the bad treaties of Amsterdam and Nice would remain in force, with the Council reaching paralysis, the Commission staying oversized and the EP's legislative and controlling deficits becoming intolerable.

The immediate answer would be to try again, perhaps with less pretentious titles ("Constitution", "President", "Foreign Minister"), or in the final instance to go two-tier: a federated Central-Western European continental core, surrounded by an associated periphery of free trading, single market participating countries (the UK, Sweden, Denmark, Poland, Czechs, Malta and ultimately Romania and even Turkey) around it. Surely a constitutionally united Europe with new treaty would be a better — albeit intermediary — answer.

Eurocrats and Euro Institutions

Are European institutions and their staffers important? The Monnet method consisted of almost conspiratorial networking among people in high places to get historical decisions underway. Political memoirs of Commissioners, from Hans von der Groeben to Lord Arthur Cockfield, confirm this view, presumably an inevitable feature in this genre. Glenda M Rosenthal, an American political scientist, in her classic *The Men Behind Decisions*, which covered the origins of the Lomé Agreements, produced a respectable academic theory for the small networks of old boys enlightened in the right places at the right moment. It is probably not difficult to find evidence for similar EU decisions originating at middle or even junior management levels, given the right moment and circumstances. This author's claim to (fairly transitory) historical fame results from producing a documentation and a synoptic table which proved and convinced his British director that Estonia and Slovenia were in fact at least as well, if not better, prepared for EU membership back in 1996 as were the standard front runners at the time: Poland, the Czech Republic and Hungary. My director took my table and convinced our Commissioner, Hans van den Broek, who in turn walked into President Santer's office with my tables. This then became a Commission proposal, which the Council quickly accepted. Like many colleagues, I had also worked through friends in the Danish, German and Austrian permanent representations to prepare some of the ground, if this was needed. The rest is history, but it shows that people *and* institutions are important.

When it is up to the smooth management of established routine operations — from running development projects in Africa to the steel negotiations with the United States, then it is definitely the institutional operations with nameless hardworking qualified staffers that count.

Once a historical decision, like on EU enlargement negotiations, has been taken, one has to accept one's fading away into the background with, hopefully, good grace.

No doubt in Brussels the European Commission, home and hunting ground of the infamous, greedy, corrupt and overpaid Eurocrat, is the most significant and influential institution.

Some 15,000 officials (around a quarter of the number of municipal employees of towns like Paris, Cologne or Vienna) work in some 30 directorate generals and similar half-autonomous units. Until the arrival of Mr Prodi as the Commission's President in 1999, directorate generals used to be numbered from I to XXIV — a sensible system in a multilingual environment. Since Signore Prodi was confused, they were renamed, sometimes sensibly like "Fish" (yes, it's fisheries), "Trade" (right again, it's trade policy), "Comp" for competition, "Agri" for agriculture, "Regio" for regional aid, etc., or, more cryptically, OLAF for anti-fraud, OPOCE for the publication office, TAXUD for taxation, JAI for justice and home affairs, SANCO for health and food hygiene, and so on.

The Commission, as mentioned earlier, was created by the Treaties of Rome as an independent supranational authority, and is headed since 2004 by a President and 24 Commissioners appointed by the member states. These appointments are confirmed by the European Parliament, which has the power to dismiss the Commissioners collectively (something it threatened to do in the summer of 1999; the Santer Commission, however, was quick to resign rather than to face the sack). Governments typically nominate senior politicians as Commissioners, some of which, like most French appointments, have a political future still ahead of them; some, like the Germans, have more of a distinguished past. British Commissioners after their 4–5 years in Brussels have become too tainted by the European bug to be of much use in parochial national politics any longer. Building on the success of the three Delors Commissions (1985–1994), the Santer Commission (1995–1999) had attracted the strongest political calibres so far. About half of them were former prime ministers, ministers of finance, economy and foreign affairs. It proved difficult to accommodate some of these big egos, notably when the field of foreign affairs had to be shared out among four strong-willed gentlemen (Manuel Marin, Sir Leon Brittan, Hans van den Broek and Joao Pinheiro; the latter, however, more frequently visible on golf courses). Since the Prodi Commission we are now partly back to former state secretaries and city councillors, with British tabloids searching in vain for characters big enough to act as suitable hate figures.

The Commission's influence and discretionary powers are mixed. They are most developed in the field of anti-trust, state aid and other competition policies where the Commission can interdict mergers, impose fines and request the reimbursement of state subsidies. In the agricultural field joint management committees, led by senior Commission officials, can undertake quite extensive and expensive public interventions in the food markets. Discretionary powers are also pronounced on spending decisions on about half of the 100 billion Euro annual budget. All of these powers are of course derived from treaties and directives approved by the Council, but often also based on occasionally vague Council instructions and mandates (for instance, on trade negotiations and on the conduct of other external relations). All of the Commission's activities are in principle subject to parliamentary scrutiny, have to be reported back to the Council and can be challenged in the European Court of Justice.

Most — but not all — of the Commission's 4,000 professional (A grade) staff are recruited through French-style open competitions, in which only a handful of the best scoring amongst ten thousands of participants pass. As a result the average Commission officer can be presumed to be intellectually and linguistically better equipped than most of his national counterparts. Dealing with 25 member states on any given issue also should help to broaden horizons.

Still, Commission officials enjoy a uniquely bad press. The term "Eurocrat" has become a scapegoat shorthand with anything gone wrong in "Brussels": be it a British-made meat crisis, an unpopular Council decision, absentee Euro-parliamentarians, paedophile Walloon Socialists or awkward Commission procedures and terminologies.

Admittedly until the advent of Jacques Delors in the mid-1980s, there were quite a few directorate generals, like, for example, those of transport, environment and social affairs with little work and competences. Officials could doodle motorways and express train lines all over the map of Europe or draft feminist social legislation — with no visible consequence. They could equally go for very long lunches or date their secretaries, also hopefully with no consequences. Others spent their work time more productively in learning an impressive array of foreign languages or writing detective novels.

In those days pay was high and morale was low. There was little mobility in the services. Officials were expected to serve in their units as experts for their working life. Often they were the authors of the regulations they were administering and hence disinclined to change. Entire business sectors, be they the sugar industry, the beef fatteners or wood processors, had to live with the likes and dislikes and administrative habits of a single immovable desk officer. Those were the days of glory and of great, or at least memorable, personalities. Now they are all retired or sidelined.

In the meantime, the enormous management tasks taken on by the Delors Commission, the success of the internal market, of the monetary union and the adoption of a multitude of spending programmes — many of which for lack of staffing resources and training had initially been badly mishandled — had taken their toll. The administrative reforms undertaken by Neil Kinnock as the Commission's Vice President (1999–2004) superimposed Anglo-Saxon management jargon and techniques over a resistive French-style administration. Continuous job rotation, benchmarking, streamlining and quarterly redrafts of the organigram became the order of the day from 2000. People in the past complained about inflexible, greying apparatchiks holding sway over their sections. Now they had to get used to ever-changing reassignments. One day a young Spanish lawyer was in charge barking instructions, succeeded three months later by a smooth Italian accountant on a traineeship, followed by a Swedish inspector too depressed by the un-Swedish ways of Brussels to pick up his phone. Indeed within the Commission, for better or for worse, a cultural and generational change took place. Gone is the age of colourful typically Francophone policy makers and European visionaries; in is a curiously expendable conformist breed of Anglophone accountants, lawyers and case handlers. One day they work on telecom standards in Slovenia, the next on resort development in the Alentejo, processing papers with dispassionate disinterest and cool ignorance towards the local realities. Obviously the risk is strong that a depoliticised streamlined institution of this sort will before long turn into a glorified Council secretariat, waiting for instructions.

How does the Commission work? Except for the month of August its officials work a lot, and typically long hours. The boozy business lunches of old have been replaced by sandwiches plus diet coke munched behind PC screens. In contrast to lavishly staffed national authorities with their multitudes of subordinates and regional administrations, the Commission remains desperately short of staff. There is one A grade official in Brussels for 150,000 of his fellow EU citizens in real life. During one year I "managed" some 200 social and health projects with a budget of 80 million Euros in 15 Eastern European countries from Estonia to Albania with the able help of one Finnish assistant. This can only be done with subcontracting, delegation and a willingness to take risks. The Commission's work style is strange to the uninitiated, but follows its own logic. There are thick rule books and "how to" manuals, but they are routinely ignored and only read by the small armies of management consultants hired by VP Kinnock and his failed predecessors. Instead, informal networking between units and inter-service consultations abound. Given the need for consensus and member state acceptance, the value of an official is normally based on his ability to process his draft proposals through the various institutions in a way which ruffles least feathers and generates acceptance. Knowing the right people — not necessarily the top — in the Commission, the Council, the Parliament and organised interest groups is therefore essential.

The Commission's working style is therefore ideally accessible and inclusive. The doors are open and an agreeable informality rules. Different national working styles have to be accommodated. Some nationalities (Germans, Austrians) for unknown reasons start work early, with short lunch breaks and then want to leave in the early afternoon. Others come late, enjoy long lunch breaks as a siesta, but then work late until 8 or 9 pm. A good European compromise then would be to come late, have a lengthy lunch, and leave early. Unfortunately, no longer.

National representation is a problem. Belgians, French and other Mediterraneans are over-represented; Germans, Dutch, Brits and Scandinavians under-represented. Partly this is because working in Brussels and the wage differential are not sufficiently attractive to them; partly they (the Brits) flunk the entry competitions in inordinate numbers. Since 2004 placements also need to be found for a sufficient number of new colleagues from the ten new member states.

Care is taken to avoid national bundling in units. Procurement units should not exclusively be staffed by Italians, Latin American departments by Spaniards, regional aid to Greece by Greeks, accounting and legal affairs by Germans, and strategic decision-making by French officials only — but still many of them manage to be there nonetheless.

Not all senior Commission officials are recruited by the elite track entry competition. In fact, some have risen through the ranks, including one impressive director general who started out as a printing clerk in the Commission's information office in The Hague some 20 years earlier. Many others however have been "parachuted" into senior ranks after service in the Commissioners' personal cabinet offices, through the high level placements after enlargement rounds or after top level interventions by member state governments. Unsurprisingly the record of these non-meritocratic senior managers is fairly mixed.

The future status of the Commission, with its unique role as a policy inducing executive ("right of initiative"), however, crucially depends not only on the charisma and public standing of its chief executive, the President and his fellow Commissioners, but also on the professionalism, vision and political commitment of its senior staff, which now risks being increasingly compromised in the course of half-baked business school reforms.

The Council of Ministers, as the Union's supreme decision-making body, practises permanent conference diplomacy. At its apex the

European Council reigns; it assumed this function in 1972. It meets at least twice per year — in June and in December at the end of each presidency, and at informal summits in the run-up to these formal sessions which are supposed to resolve all of the term's unfinished business in one gigantic and disparate compromise package. Foreign Ministers and Ecofin Ministers meet monthly — if they really show up. Bored by Council routines, they often either send their deputies, or their deputies' deputies, or fly in for lunch and press conference only. Sectoral ministers (for agriculture, environment, interior, social affairs, etc.) take their European business more seriously as they meet more rarely.

A major problem at ministerial councils is the length of speeches, overloaded agendas and a frequently overcharged presidency. Designed for a Community with six members, the Council with 15 ministers worked badly enough. Already the first trial runs in 2001 with the 12 applicant countries in attendance where everybody was relatively polite and business was non-controversial showed the looming disaster. Twelve hours alone were wasted on introductory speeches, which proved again that language means different things to different European tribes. Finns and Estonians say almost nothing and use up little time for this (and are very popular in consequence). The Anglo-Germanic representatives by standards of talkative politicians are still relatively straightforward after polite introductions. Yet the Mediterraneans use language often for poetic purposes and to cheer themselves up for having to speak in a miserably rainy town like Brussels. The French notably use their interventions for a brilliant display of Gallic logic, which they assume will convince *par force majeure* through its sheer brilliance the others around the table. Once so much intellectual capital has been spent, a position once taken clearly cannot be abandoned easily. The search for compromise is then likely to take correspondingly long. The Easterners — especially those from the old nomenclatura which were back in power in most accession countries in the political cycle of 2000/2004 — in long years of state Socialism have internalised the habit of reading out prepared speeches (replacing "XX Party Congress" with "Nice Council", or "Socialist achievements" with "free market economy") in order to avoid mistakes. Not to be outdone, Romania combines the Romanic rhetoric with the Eastern tradition. Under no circumstances will any self-respecting Romanian speech be shorter than two hours — covering philosophy, Romania's place in world history, past and current injustices suffered, followed by any amount of pertinent and non-pertinent detail on the issue under deliberation. All of this is to prove that the orator is a man of substantial education who has given careful thought to the ongoing proceedings. Ministers of course will not put up with this. They walk outside, telephone, smoke, drink coffee or later whisky and leave it up to their underlings to produce lecture notes and to debrief them hours later.

The only institution to suffer through it all is the hapless presidency, which needs to formulate a consensus with which ideally all participants can live. Even with the assistance of an experienced Council secretariat with 15 member states and their different degrees of preparedness and ways of expression (a British "small problem" will become "très très serieux" *en français*), it was intellectually ever more difficult to keep track of the nuances on offer in complex negotiations. With 25, it has become a near impossibility.

The solution is not to fiddle with speaking times and voting rights, but rather to professionalise the Ministerial Council: to delegate, say, the Minister of European Affairs as the national representative to decide all sectoral policy matters under consideration. A single state chamber with its own elected presidency would then replace all the erratic and inconsistent ministerial councils. Every second week such Council meetings could take place in Brussels. They would no longer be a pleasant or annoying side job for hurried national ministers, but a full time occupation for a political professional. Deliberations would inevitably address the point, become specific and result-oriented. No more speeches on philosophy and history to inexistent galleries.

The Council is currently supported by several hundred working groups, some permanent, some *ad hoc*, some half forgotten. Experts from member states ministries cover most of them. Often they meet as a supranational camaraderie in which they agree on regulatory proposals, which individually at home they would never get past their hierarchy and ministers. As a collective European proposal in which an objecting country faces the risk of being outvoted, often the most futurist designs of food hygiene or animal transportation rights thus get passed.

The more serious policy committees are attended by national diplomats stationed at the 25 permanent representations of the member states in Brussels. Their work is crowned by decisions in "Coreper II", where deputy heads of representation meet to decide on more technical issues, or in "Coreper I", where the ambassadors meet every week to deliberate the more august problems of high politics. Discussions are facilitated by the tradition of marking pre-agreed items as A points on the agenda, to be waved through quickly and to focus on the few controversial items, identified as B points, instead.

National influence in Council deliberations depends less on the weighted votes of a country or the length of their speeches, but rather — and obviously — on the quality of the arguments used, on the ability of their diplomats to find allies and to seek mutually acceptable compromises.

As such, Luxembourg is usually more influential than, say, Greece, and Ireland more successful than Italy, for instance. Then it appears that the re-weighting of votes, whose drama overshadowed so much of Nice (courtesy of President Chirac who felt the dignity of France insulted if it had less Council votes than Germany, whose population is larger by 25 million souls), indeed is a fairly theoretical exercise. A decent state chamber in a federal parliament, be it in Switzerland ("Staenderat") or the US Senate uses "one state, one vote" anyway: whether it is huge California or tiny Rhode Island, both have their two senators. Their political influence varies greatly, but it is not because of state size but due to individual differences in political talent and skill.

A lot of ink and intellectual sweat is spent by journalists and academics on perceived alliances and power coalitions in the Council. A mainstay is the Paris-Bonn/Berlin axis. The underlying logic assumes that France insists on a leadership role, with Germany, due to persistent WWII hangovers, willing to follow and to sign the pay cheque. True enough: no great integration project has ever got off the ground without prior German-French understanding. Yet this is more the result by default of the other potential players: Italy well-intentional (until

Berlusconi) but too disorganised; Spain, too obsessed with her positive cash flow, and the UK as an island nation unable for centuries to make lasting alliances or seriously constructive design for the continent. Hence when there were joint proposals by Messrs Blair and Aznar, on what else could they agree than on more inter-governmentalism (whose shaky workings then usually fail when hitting an obsolete rock called Gibraltar)? The unspectacular truth is that France and Germany count for just 58 Council votes out of 421 (and 20 votes out of 87 prior to enlargement) and they need the agreement and the consensus from — well almost — all of the rest. If there were any sinister designs of a duumvirate, this acceptance would not be forthcoming. Decisions by consensus do not make a particularly exciting copy for op-ed pieces or for contributions to "Foreign Affairs". They are, however, the unspectacular reality.

Apart from this, the number of divergent policy interests and different approaches is legion between Paris and Berlin: they range from agricultural policy reform to Eastern EU enlargement, transatlantic relations, trade and competition policy, monetary policy and defense policies. There are no "axes" in the Council, only promiscuous coalitions of interest aiming at the smallest common denominator.

With 12 out of 15 EU countries (all except Ireland, Spain and Luxembourg) ruled by the political left during 1998–2000, for the first time a sort of ideological takeover was attempted by the Council majority. Previously the Community institutions had always taken care not to take ideological sides and ran Europe like a wide church, with all views from centre-right to centre-left having their fair hear and say. In 1999 for the first time, a Commission with a clear Socialist majority was appointed. The results were left-wing policies in social and development policies and attempts to legislate political correctness from gender to sex, race and immigration. This obviously alienated the general public, which voted centre-right parties — starting with a noisily sanctioned Austria in 2000 — back to power in most member states.

In terms of legal substance the Council deals with the ongoing submissions emanating from the Commission on Community ("Pillar I") matters. It needs to approve of regulations (which apply directly to the entire EU), directives (which member states must still "transpose" into national law), and individual binding decisions. It takes note and discusses non-committal recommendations and opinions, which often take the form of "green papers".

In the inter-governmental policy fields, the Common Foreign and Security Policy ("Pillar II") and Justice and Home Affairs ("Pillar III"), the Council has its exclusive and fairly secretive playground. As it still operates with unanimity, mostly very little gets done in real life. There is one notable exception: the appointment of Javier Solana as the Union's "High Representative" of its Foreign and Security Policy in October 1999. With the Union previously torn between pro-Croatian and pro-Serbian camps which had rendered the piously declared foreign policy appearing as a sick joke during the Yugoslav tragedy of 1991–1995, Solana with a small staff has since managed to keep the Union's front (including Greece!) over Bosnia, Kosovo and Macedonia intact.

He was in no small measure helped by the fact that the Milosevic regime had profoundly discredited the Serb cause and that the Americans had appeared forcefully on the scene. Solana's success has now encouraged the inter-governmentalist faction to design plans for a Super-Solana as European President in the Council, while the federalist camp wants Solana and his staff be made honourable members of the European Commission (and thus be made accountable to Parliament as well).

The Council is located in the wonderfully modern Justus Lipsius Building in Brussels, a building reminiscent of the styles of Albert Speer and Benito Mussolini combined, fitfully reducing the handful of ever-present protesters to Legoland size.

The Council is assisted by a staff of 2,300. They draft the minutes, assist the presidencies when they get lost, and do valuable archive, translation and legal work. Being close to the centre of political decision-making and having to suffer on occasion through all night sessions, they regard themselves very highly. Others are tempted to think of overpaid note-takers.

Consisting of men and women of the people who did not pass any concours, but somehow managed to get themselves elected, Parliament is fun. Until 2004 there were 626 members. Their number was to increase to 700 after enlargement according to the Amsterdam Treaty. Nice corrected this generously to 732 (covering all accession countries without Turkey). Originally a fairly perfunctory appointed consultative assembly, since the first direct elections of 1979 the EP has managed to increase its legal powers and actual influence considerably with each new treaty. While it is true that it cannot (like the US Congress in a presidential system) elect a government from amongst its midst or determine taxation like normal parliaments, it has acquired a wide range of powers which are still ignored by most of the media and the voting public:

- to approve the nominations for Commissioner and to dismiss the entire Commission;
- to take the final decision over some 50% of the budget: all those expenditures of a discretionary nature, like social, regional and research funds — but not the "obligatory" spending like the funds for agriculture support;
- to ratify international agreements, including accession treaties;
- to approve in a co-decision procedure most regulations, in which Parliament can also amend or reject a Council position. Ultimately, if both cannot agree, the proposal is rejected.

Visitors to plenary debates held in beautiful Strasbourg in a singularly ugly futuristic building located in a quiet suburb along the river Ill are usually in for a rude shock. The plenary is 98% empty. A handful of MPs linger around until their name is called up. Then they are allowed two minutes of speaking time. Most still manage to run out of time and are cut off in mid-sentence by the Chairman, usually when they have hardly begun to address the issue in question. After their short speech they walk out instantly without waiting for a reply. This is because there is never any reply, as similarly there has hardly ever been any real debate. These short speeches are for the protocol only, which outside parliament nobody ever reads. The only real speeches can be made by the factional chieftains (the centre-right People Party, the Socialists, the Liberals, the Greens, the Communists, the Eurosceptics, etc.), by the Chairmen of the 17 sectoral committees (where the real parliamentary work is done), and by the "rapporteur" who had been in charge of producing an in-depth report on the issue under consideration. There is also the opportunity to question Commissioners and Council representatives in written or oral forms. The latter is an occasion to show intellectual and political sparkle, or to disgrace oneself. As parliament reflects faithfully the electorate at large, it also has its share of the loony fringe. One particularly memorable occasion was President Reagan's address to EP back on May 8, 1985. His teleprompter had collapsed and the old man clearly seemed to be at a loss about where he was, to whom he was talking or what to say. The then Socialist/Communist/Green majority used the commotion for the display of a hooliganism which they may have felt funny at the time, but which now looks quite disgraceful in retrospect.

Voting is similarly arcane and incomprehensible to the uninitiated. MEPs go through long lists of proposed amendments on draft resolutions and regulations, and without further debate vote on them in split seconds one by one electronically. They can do so because their factional leadership has handed them prepared sheets on how to vote on each of the hundreds of amendments. Anybody inattentive or unorganised in this factory-style democracy will get out of step and may easily vote for the opposite of the intended.

The real debates of course took place earlier, in the factions and in the Parliament's working committees, which are normally, however, out of the public's view.

The Parliament's 17 committees cover foreign relations, budgetary control, justice and home affairs, economic and monetary affairs, the internal market, industry, trade, research and industry, social policy, the environment, health and consumer protection, agriculture, fisheries, regional policy and transportation, culture and youth, development aid, constitutional affairs, women's rights, and petitions. Evidently the political importance and depth of the debate of the Committees varies a lot between the budget committee which knocked out the Santer Commission and the sleepy petitions committee. This also applies to the quality of MEPs' contributions. Some grace through regular absence or just write in their names to claim their attendance allowance (they typically walk in late, shake a few hands, check their watch in sudden surprise, and walk out quickly, never to be seen again during the day). Some MEPs use the debate to share their recent foreign travel adventures, relay anecdotes from their constituencies or read out statements unmistakably prepared by lobbyists. Yet in every committee there is inevitably a handful of knowledgeable regulars who master the subject matter. They can grill the Commission briefers. They lead the committee's deliberations, supply the leadership material for its changing chairmanship and act as respected opinion leaders in their political factions.

Attendance and enthusiasm for debate is typically strongest among Greeks (originating not by accident from the mother country of all parliaments), Germans and Austrians , and least visible among the French, the Italians and the Danes.

MEPs are free to speak their minds. Given the national and ideological diversity of the factions, the faction whip is hardly visible (certainly not among the centre-right People's Party). There is some, but not excessive, solidarity with a Commissioner from the same party. Naturally MEPs have constituency and national interests on their mind as well. And it becomes fairly obvious among Spanish MEPs when they have received instructions from national party HQ on how to vote.

MEPs are elected on national or regional lists set up by their party organisation or its leadership. Unfortunately those who proved most hardworking, knowledgeable and influential in the corridors of Brussels and Strasbourg are not always those most popular in their capitals or in their regional party organisation. Turnover of MEPs is high at each election, frequently approaching 50%, with lots of newcomers appearing lost both physically in their buildings and intellectually in their new jobs. For young ambitious MEPs a career and a return to national politics is more attractive as, if successful, it leads to a more pronounced public profile and to ministerial postings. MEP careers do not usually lead to anything in Europe. Only one member of the Prodi Commission (1999–2004) had served in the EP beforehand. Yet the life of an MEP is not bad, provided you get accustomed to the frequency of travel between Brussels, Strasbourg, your capital and your constituency. The pay is fine (best for Italians, least for Brits). There are generous allowances for officers and research staff in Brussels and back home (some have hired wives, girlfriends or other close relations), a respectable public standing, visible political influence if an effort is made, and free food, drink and travel all along the way.

Parliament is supported by a staff of 3,500 in its secretariat general. One third of them are translators, who are skilled to translate even a Finnish joke (should one ever be made) into Portuguese. On top of this factions have their own tax funded staff (some are said to work for national and European party headquarters), and the MEPs their own underpaid assistants and secretaries. All of them make a lively and thirsty supra-partisan and transnational crowd when the campaign for real ale, the producer cooperative for Tuscan fiasci *et allii* distribute their wares in skilful lobbyism well targeted at the nascent European power elite.

Traditionally, that is, from 1979 until 1999, the EP was dominated by the left. At the same time there was always a "grand coalition" groundswell between the large Socialist, Christian Democratic and Liberal factions pursuing a course of enlightened Centrist federalism. The market economy, social partnership and European democracy were and are staples like motherhood and apple pie. The presidency of the EP usually changed every two years, harmoniously shared out between the two major political camps.

In June 1999 due to pronounced electoral swings in Germany and in the UK (in the latter pronounced through her "first past the post" constituency system which was applicable until then), for the first time a centre-right majority emerged in the EP. This majority however is a fairly heterogeneous lot compared to the 200 strong Socialists (organised in the Social Democratic Party of Europe, PSE) who were elected in all member states, and even to the 90 Liberals, who are organised in the Liberal International and currently allied with the People's Party. The 270 strong People Party (PPE) faction comprises a majority of ardent federalists among German, Austrian, Dutch, Belgian and the few surviving Italian Christian Democrats. It also comprises distinctly

Eurosceptic Tories, Forza Italia MEPs, plus a series of other Centrist parties often, like in France, in competition with each other.

There is also a fairly fractious Green faction of 40, a faithful ally of the Socialists, and a troop of 40 Communists, mostly of the unreformed nostalgic Stalinist sort. Thirty-seven opponents to European integration (from Denmark, France, the Netherlands, Poland, the Czech Republic and the UK) have equally federated, as did an oddly combined technical faction of left and right-wingers during 1999–2004 who were exclusively united by the wish to receive the money, personnel and speaking time allocated to factions. On the right, disputes are particularly pronounced, exacerbated, of course, by a hostile press. During the 1989–1994 session, for instance, a right-wing faction composed of Italian fascists (MSI, today as Allianza Nazionale in Berlusconi's government), Le Pen's National Front and the German Republicans fell out over classical nationalist disputes, like who rightly possesses South Tyrol or about autonomy rights for the Alsace. Clearly the wrong people to construct an integrated Europe.

Most of these exciting disputes bypass the European voters. On the back pages of the national quality press there are few reports on what the EP is doing. Partly the Parliament's arcane and intransparent workings are to blame, partly also old stereotypes of a powerless parliament which date back to the 1980s. As a result voter participation (ranging between 90% in Belgium — where voting is compulsory — and 30% in the UK and the Netherlands) is declining from election to election, giving protest and fringe parties possibilities they do not enjoy during national elections. During 1994 the new East European member states have set new negative records: 17% in Slovakia followed by 20% in Poland. With abstention rates at 80% and more, the legitimacy of representative democracy is clearly at risk.

European politics has reacted by giving the EP in many — but certainly not in all and not in the most visible — policy areas powers equivalent to the Council. Yet, to this date, this remains a well guarded secret for most EU voters.

In a federal system like the US, the equivalent of the EP is the House of Representatives. In a pronounced federal order like the US, the Senate as the state chamber is the more powerful institution of the two. Here "one state, one vote" is accepted, as is "one man, one vote" in the popular representation. The EU so far does neither. Post-Nice, 400,000 Luxembourgers elect six MEPs and 81 million Germans 99 MEPs. One Luxembourg deputy represents some 70,000 of his fellow citizens and a German about 800,000. Hence one Luxembourger's vote is worth more than 11 German votes. These discrepancies still need to be addressed if a federalist democracy is to find acceptance and serious implementation in the EU.

There are two consultative assemblies: the venerable European Economic and Social Committee (ESC) founded in 1957, and the more upstart Committee of Regions (COR) set up in 1994. Both are quite useful when deliberating new initiatives in their respective fields of policy expertise, social policy and regional policy respectively, and to secure acceptance from their membership. When they provide often well researched policy input, it is most effective in the early Commission drafting stages. Later when decision time is up, such input is usually disregarded quickly.

The ESC hails from the old post-war tripartite tradition of corporatist social partnership. Its 317 members are composed equally of employers, trade unionists and "third parties" (farmers, consumers, professionals). The ESC's hour of glory came in 1989 when it — including its British members — accepted the Social Charter in defiance of the expressed wishes of the Tory government of the day. In the meantime, more fashionably it claims to represent "civic society". Yet generating little attention nor political excitement its tranquil existence at Rue Ravenstein in Central Brussels would be overlooked if it was not for the odd expense account fiddling scandal — sorry, "financial irregularity". The most prominent of the ESC's staff members was Petra Kelly (placed here by her erstwhile fatherly friend, agriculture Commissioner Sicco Mansholt). She used her time at the ESC productively to found the German Green Party and to campaign against all the evil of this world. When the Greens lost (temporarily as it turned out) in post-unity Germany, she had herself killed in a double suicide in 1992 with another fatherly friend, General Gert Bastian, rather than face a return to the ESC bureaucracy.

The Committee of Regions proves to be a different and more lively kettle of fish. Not that it is more important. It is not. The reason is not that it generates its negative headlines due to alleged nepotism in its recruitment policy (rather than by fiddled travel accounts). None of the above. Most of its 317 members are more flamboyant and (self-) important than the grey suited employers' federation and syndicate chieftains of the ESC. They are the elected prime ministers of the 16 states of Germany (starting with North Rhine Westphalia, population 17 million, and Bavaria, population ten million), the presidents of the regional assemblies of Italy, France, Belgium, Poland and Spain (including those like the Catalans and the Flemmings who see themselves as a de facto independent nation), the elected governors of Austria's nine states, royally appointed Dutch small town mayors and British regional councillors and home ministry officials.

When the regional chieftains descend on Brussels, they are usually less concerned about the COR sub-commission proceedings over which they are supposed to be presiding than about the EU projects they, through direct lobbying, intend to attract to their regions. Most of Europe's regions now have their own more or less abundantly staffed representations in Brussels, which during such high level visitations move into high lobbying and hospitality gear. Back home, more expertly than the local MEP or the ministers in the capital, the elected regional chieftain will tell his folks vividly about the tough talking messages he has delivered in Brussels and which wonderful projects Brussels in response will deliver to their most deserving region. The folks and the papers back home love this act. This performance cannot be done plausibly by basically decent but unimportant Home Office officials or small town mayors, which proves why genuine regionalism performed in the unlikely setting of the COR is good for Europe.

Four Freedoms in a Single Market

Lord Arthur Francis Cockfield (1916–), the creator of the EU's single market, in his professional recollections recalls the background of this unlikely success story. When he was appointed internal market commissioner in the first Delors Commission in 1985, the sense of Eurosclerosis was overwhelming. The previous Thorn Commission (1981–1984) had spent most of its energy and political capital for the solution of the protracted British budget dispute with Mrs Thatcher.

European businessmen and captains of industry became increasingly worried about the continual fall of Europe's world market shares in industrial production and trade. The loss of competitive edge due to fragmented high cost national markets to US and Japanese competitors, followed by a crowd of hungry up-and-going Asian tiger countries, was seen to augur badly for the future of European industries and for Europe's economic and social culture. Hence corporate pressure for reform was strong.

The Commission had already since 1960 entertained plans for an integrated single market. But its harmonisation approach had led to nowhere. After decades it had managed to standardise the norms for tractor seats. But key draft directives, like to harmonise marmalade recipes, remained stalled in the Council and failed unanimous approval even after carrots, out of which the Portuguese seem to make jam, had been reclassified as "fruits". (Ultimately the directive, after 30 years of deliberation, was mercilessly binned in the 1990s, ending a working life of well intended harmonisation attempts.)

Cockfield in a white paper in 1985 then outlined a four-pronged strategy which found the growing support of Jacques Delors:

- to replace the ill-fated harmonisation drive by the mutual recognition principle, provided common minimum standards are established;
- to substitute the unanimity rule by qualified majority voting on internal market matters through a revision of the Treaties;
- to put all ongoing (and mostly blocked) 300 initiatives to liberate the movements of goods, people, services and capital within the EU into one coherent programme;
- to deadline the implementation of the programme for December 31, 1992 and to assure its public acceptance.

This acceptance was helped by a study called "The Costs of Non-Europe" named after a left-wing MEP Paolo Cecchini. The Cecchini Report was based on a "supply shock" theory. The effects of lower production and distribution costs, more economies of scale and more competition would trigger a virtuous economic cycle with increased purchasing power and stronger demand consequently feeding economic growth (+4.5% of GDP on aggregate), thus generating funds for productive investments and new jobs, especially in areas of income elastic demand like services, tourism and housing construction.

The 1992 project was enthusiastically endorsed by big business and their associations who saw an unhindered market of 370 million people as a forceful remedy against national bureaucratic barriers, associated unproductive excess costs and as a means to shed the inertia of Eurosclerosis. Outside the EU the US orchestrated a "Fortress Europe" scare campaign. This was avidly believed in Japan and Korea, who feared that their own mercantilist protectionism would be duplicated. Even though Fortress Europe in the end turned out to be a sandcastle, to the surprise of its authors the effect of the debates and the counter-propaganda was that the 1992 project was being taken seriously by economic actors and political decision-makers alike — something which had not happened to European projects for a long time. This dynamism helped for the smooth passage of the little noticed and obscurely named "Single European Act" through the

Council in 1986. It repealed the "Luxembourg Compromise" with its unanimity principle by QMV on internal market matters. This worked miracles for decision-making in Council sessions. Instead of hiding behind veiled threats of a national veto which encouraged maximum demands (after all, each self-respecting country in the mind of its officials enjoys the world's best standards, towards which everybody else should strive), negotiating officials were now obliged to actively seek workable compromises in order to avoid the most undesirable risk of being outvoted and having to adopt an undesirable compromise worked out by others. Most of the 300 draft regulations and directives proposed by the Commission to implement the internal market were subsequently agreed within the monitored deadlines. Prime Ministers and national ministers regularly instructed their officials not to threaten the project's success which attracted not only domestic but also foreign investment (for Japan and Korea, it was important to be inside Fortress Europe with their "Trojan horses", mostly on the British Isles before it was too late).

Of equally decisive importance was the adoption of the mutual recognition principle. The case law of the European Court of Justice back in 1978 had already shown the way with its celebrated "*Cassis de Dijon*" judgement. *Cassis,* a weakly alcoholic black current syrup (to be mixed with champagne to make ladies' lunches merrier) had been banned from importation into Germany since being neither fish nor flesh it did not fit the solid German customs classification. It was neither a non-alcoholic fruit syrup nor a more serious fruit liquor with an alcohol contents of at least 25%, in which case it could have been imported with no difficulty. The Court ruled that bureaucratic rules based on no seriously compelling reasons (public health, decency, safety) could not be used to ban the importation of this flippant Gallic drink. The Court used the same logic when it threw out the German import ban on foreign beers not brewed according to the 400 year old German purity law. In vain the German government had argued that anything containing other than malt, hops, yeast and water would seriously poison German beer drinkers and thus endanger public health. Unfortunately, it made no scientific effort to prove its case and consequently lost.

The same happened to Italy which argued that foreign pasta imported into Italy was ok, but had to be made from Italian durum wheat only. The list is long, but the result was the same. If basic standards were guaranteed, imports of European products legally and safely in use in other EU countries could not be discriminated against under any pretext.

For citizens the internal market meant the freedom to shop for goods and services, to work and to live anywhere in the European Union. Care was taken for reasons of symbolism and practical doctrine to close down physically all intra-EU customs posts. This was done also for fear once they stayed in operation, reasons would be found to employ its personnel and to find pretexts to reintroduce the border controls which just had been abolished. Once there were no longer any checks on imported private purchases, citizens used the occasion to exploit often significant tax and price differences across the border, notably on fuel, tobacco and liquor. While the suffering retailers in the high tax country (like Belgian car dealers who ran out of business as they were struck with a luxury sales tax of 35%) pressured their fiscal authorities for reductions, the finance ministers saw it differently. Ever since they agitate for the upward "harmonisation" notably of the value added tax (VAT) towards rates between 15–25%, they overlook the fact that indirect tax harmonisation is not needed for an effective internal market. The US, for instance, happily live with competitive tax differentials between their states. A more logical victim were the duty free sales on ferries and flights between EU destinations, which in spite of heavy lobbying by interested retailers and airports, are no longer applicable to intra-EU travel. A lot less liquor is now uselessly flown around in Europe.

When there are restrictions on the importation of goods, they can only be justified if they constitute the least grave means to protect public safety (e.g., firearms), food safety (e.g., BSE infested meat), public morals (like a ban of pornography into the UK), or to protect the historical heritage (e.g., when stolen Etruscan artefacts are exported as souvenirs). Member states remain free to keep their own standards for their own national production (like the German purity standard on beer), even if this discriminates local products against imports when this implies higher production costs compared to EU imports.

In order to permit informed consumer choice, differences in production modes and product composition must be labelled clearly. Consumer protection had to be beefed up and modernised in the laggard member states. The principle of product liability for producers and EU importers was clearly established, including warranty periods, certain rights of return and cancellation of sales contracts. Comprehensive labelling requirements were introduced on components, including colorants and additives (of vital importance to diabetics and those suffering from allergies), sell by/use by dates, clear price indications and the addresses of the producer and/or wholesaler. For pharmaceuticals, a naturally sensitive issue, admission in one member state is usually sufficient for its sale and prescription in the rest of the EU (thus avoiding 24 other costly admission procedures, including often reduplicated tests on animals and humans). For novel high tech medicines, the submission to the new EU Pharmaceutical Agency sited in London is needed.

In general, technical standards and norms were harmonised only where needed in terms of "essential requirements" for human health, safety or the environment. Once these minimum standards were satisfied, for the rest tests and certificates were mutually recognised.

Banks and insurances are permitted since 1995 to operate in the entire EU on the basis of one single license of the home authority responsible for their supervision. In this important aspect, the EU's financial market since then is more integrated than the US with their fragmented state licensing system. A common financial market required the set up of an EU wide deposit insurance (up to 20,000 Euros) and stringent transparency requirements in publishing terms and conditions (especially when operating in a country in which consumers are customarily used to different norms). The effect of more competition in the financial sector are clearly better rates, wider coverage and improved services in both insurance and banking.

Closest to the heart of most EU citizens is their right to work and to reside anywhere in the EU. Even if most don't have any immediate plans to relocate, they like the option of a carefree retirement in the sunny South or the prospect of enhanced study and career mobility for their children.

Within the internal market, any EU citizen is automatically entitled to a residence permit and to his new ID card. Originally this residence permit was limited to working people only. Since the adoption of the so-called "playboy" directive, the self-employed, trainees, students, retirees and people living from capital rents ("playboys") are also entitled. The only caveat: they need to give proof of their health insurance coverage and their sources of income (rents, parental transfers, property, etc.), so as to assure that they don't become welfare burdens in their new host countries from the start. Care is taken that pension rights acquired in different EU countries can be cumulated and that health insurance services are mutually accessible.

A big headache has always been the mutual recognition of professional certificates and diplomas. In Belgium or the UK anybody who can hold a wrench seems to be able to claim to be a professional mechanic, or someone who manages to knock a nail into a tree boast to be a trained carpenter. In Germany and Austria this requires three years of professional traineeship. If someone fails to qualify he cannot practice the trade. In order to become a master mechanic or carpenter, some ten years more of professional training and practice followed by the passage of a tough professional exam before his future peers are needed. The qualitative differences between the two different approaches to professional training clearly show! Yet the right to work abroad implies that Belgian and British mechanics and carpenters, whatever their training, should also be allowed to practice their trade in Germany and Austria. The European compromise regulation allows them to do this after having given proof of five years of professional experience in their trade. This gentle ruling however does not apply to German or Austrian nationals who want to shirk or who have flunked their countries' tough professional exams!

Similar problems apply to the tertiary level, that is university training. British and Irish graduates enter the graduate job market on average at age 22, Germans and Danes at the mature age of 28. Some might not want to cross a bridge which a 23-year-old British civil engineer from a polytechnic had constructed. Others could argue that over-aged German graduates have spent most of their university days in student politics, on existentialist trips to India or organising rock concerts. The European compromise: equivalency is assumed with at least three years of tertiary education, followed by five years of related professional practice. Only in rare justified cases supplementary examinations may be required. If, for instance, a trained Finnish elementary teacher wants to work in a Portuguese school, she or he may rightly be asked to show proof of sufficient knowledge of the Portuguese language, history and civic structure, but not be re-examined on how to teach basic writing or computing skills. The only taboo areas not available to EU citizens of foreign nationalities for reasons of national security are positions in the military, the police, the judiciary and as elected senior officials, starting at the level of mayors.

Another touchy area is real estate. Nobody (except the profit-seeking seller) likes sacred national land being bought up by rich foreigners (only worse if it is stolen by conquering poor foreigners). In principle EU internal market law interdicts all discrimination when trading in real estate: it could be a capital investment, a residential home near his place of work, a location for doing business (an office, farm, factory, etc.).

Within the European Union income levels and the propensity to save and to invest into real estate vary greatly. By coincidence it is the Germans who still have good salaries, save a lot and love real estate as an investment, including secondary homes at their favourite vacation sites abroad. Brits follow with sizeable investments in vacation and retirement homes in France, Spain and Italy.

Fears are strong (and vastly exaggerated) that rich EU foreigners (read: Germans) would buy up scarce housing in sought-after inner-city areas from Salzburg/Austria to Florence/Italy. Or that these foreigners would buy up wonderful estates near lakes or the sea coasts, build monstrous concrete castles and block public access to these sea sites.

There is however nothing in EU law which prevents local and regional authorities to enact proper land use and preservation laws which would prevent anybody, be they domestic or foreign developers, to ruin landscapes or access to the sea. But such laws should be non-discriminatory as regards the nationality of the EU investors. The same applies to urban housing and conservation ordinances.

There is only one permissible exemption enshrined in EU primary law which allows discrimination on grounds of nationality. An annex to the Treaty of Maastricht perpetuates an originally temporary exception which Denmark had negotiated for in her accession treaty in 1987. Hence the vacation cottage industry, wooden shacks over which the Danebrog is flying proudly, mostly in rain and storm, remains exclusively in the hands of Danish nationals (quite a few of whom in Northern Slesvig are German in ethnic origin). This is the one and only (and fairly minor) piece of original sin which the EU's laws of non-discrimination permit as regards capital investment in the single market. The accession of Malta in 2004, a sunny attractive island rich in rocks but short of land, triggered a repeat of this original sin of permanent discriminatory exception.

Without having a similar dispensation, Greece tried the same in declaring unilaterally all of her islands and large chunks of her Northern mountains — almost half of Greece's territory — as military zones. And for security reasons, foreigners of any sort cannot acquire real estate in military zones, you understand. This fairly blatant attempt at discrimination did not hold water and, like similar attempts elsewhere, was quickly thrown out when challenged by the European Court of Justice.

The gist of most of the excitement surrounding foreign investment in real estate is quite simple: most people (who is to blame them?) find their place to be the best in the world (or at least in Europe) and naturally expect that most of their fellow EU citizens would want to live and invest there. In fact, these also like their own places best and usually stay home. Yet even in the most attractive sites in the Balearics, the Cote d'Azur, the Tuscan mountains and the Carinthian lakelands, there is no disfiguring development which could not have been prevented in a non-discriminatory fashion by proper regional planning laws or tough local zoning codes.

What has happened since 1993? Internal border posts with their long waiting queues are a thing of the past. EU producers and traders enjoy larger economies of scale and reduced procurement and distribution costs. Capital could find its best rates of return. There is less paperwork and transportation time. There are overall simplified standards and type approval certification for a market much larger than the US. The internal market has stimulated the reinvigoration of Europe's economy and reversed its seemingly irresistible stagnation in the 1990s. Job and welfare gains are equally undeniable.

Yet there were shortcomings: until April 2000 some 1,500 internal market regulations had to be enacted to alleviate them. Legislative obstacles were (and are) notably persistent in postal services with their delivery monopolies for letters, in transportation (airport slots notably), in energy distribution, in the artisanal trades and in indirect taxation.

Member states were found deficient in implementation. Best scored member states with efficient public administrations like Denmark and the UK, worst Italy (passionate in her declarations of European faith, but much less so when the implementation costs lira and Euros). Also, cumbersome federal countries like Germany, Belgium and Austria don't score well, as additional layers of regional governments spell additional layers of resistance. The deficiencies apply in particular to costly veterinary law, transportation, food legislation and environmental norms.

It is the Commission's statutory duty to watch over implementation, to warn off infringements and ultimately to take miscreant governments to court. It is the foremost recipient of complaints from member states, business associations and individual citizens upon which it has to act. In 1998/1999 alone the Commission received 680 formal infringement complaints, out of which only 280 could be resolved amicably during that period. Often extensive training schemes for national officials and customs officers help to alleviate misconceptions over the internal market and its rules of mutual recognition. Ultimately the Commission is entitled to fine member state governments (a very effective tool!) if other means of recourse are exhausted.

In the meantime, with the upturn of pan-European trade and transportation, physical bottlenecks became painfully visible at the border linkages of Europe's transportation networks, which in the past were conceived almost exclusively for national needs. The demands for EU funding of such Trans-European Networks (TEN) was strongest amongst those member states who found themselves at the periphery of the new Europe and felt that it was the Central regions: the South of England, Benelux, Central and Northern France, West Germany, Austria, Northern Italy and Northeast Spain which would benefit most. The resulting requests for redistribution through social and regional "cohesion" via the Commission contributed a lot to economies based on permanent subsidisation and probably undid a fair amount of the internal market's undisputed political and economic success.

The Euro:
From Funny Money to Serious Cash

The coins, with their different national backsides, have become an unlikely collector's item. The sport is to collect all eight coins starting from one cent to two Euros from all 12 Euro countries, but also the much rarer mints from the Vatican, San Marino and Andorra, where the Euro has been in circulation since January 2002.

More important: it is real money, buys real stuff, has been accepted by the people (with often mixed feelings) and within only a few weeks in early 2002 has replaced century-old national currencies like the Deutsche and Finnish mark, the Dutch florin, the Austrian shilling, the French, Belgian and Luxembourg franc, the Italian lira, the Spanish peseta, the Portuguese escudo, the Greek drachma and the Irish pound without a trace.

Thirteen billions of notes and 66 billions of coins were exchanged, all without a hitch, without hundreds of little old ladies being hit over the head while carrying their life savings to the bank, or counterfeiters producing billions of fakes of the unknown bills on their colour photocopiers. It was popular among some businessmen — and quite a few public authorities — to round their prices upward during the changeover period. But most have come down (or gone out of business) since, as sensitised customers stayed away. In the low inflation countries (except for Ireland), inflation statistics have hardly shown a blip. In the traditional high inflation countries of the South, inflation has further gone down.

When the Community was set up in the good old days of fixed exchange rates, the need for a common currency was not seen. It was only in 1968 when serious monetary turmoil hit Europe, with the

Deutsche mark being revalued and the French franc devalued (it made good economic sense, but was seen as a public humiliation by Parisian officialdom). Long-established profitable trading links and investments suddenly turned into loss makers and the carefully prepared common agricultural policy with its common commodity prices set in a European Currency Unit (ECU) basket, saw the returns for French farmers drastically increased, with those for their German colleagues equally diminished. This turmoil called for an orderly European response.

In 1970 Pierre Werner, Prime Minister of Luxembourg, wrote his "Werner Report" setting out how by 1980 a European Monetary Union (EMU) could be set up based on fixed exchange rates to the US dollar.

Just one year later this report landed in the archives. Burdened by military expenditures in Vietnam, Richard Nixon in 1971 allowed the dollar to float, which blew the Werner Report and Europe's fragile monetary cooperation to pieces. In 1972, picking up these pieces, a system was set up in which the participating EU central banks would intervene to limit their exchange rate fluctuations within narrow perimeters ("snake in the tunnel"). When the oil crisis of 1974/1975 knocked out the weaker European currencies, the "snake in the tunnel" was effectively reduced to a DM zone (comprising the DM, the Dutch florin, the Danish crown, and the Austrian schilling). Once monetary eruptions had calmed, in 1979 a new attempt was made in the hope of a central-bank-supported European Monetary System (EMS), which allowed margins of fluctuations up to +/−2.25% from a fixed central rate, with the lira being granted a cavalier +/−6.00% margin. The EMS arrangement worked well for more than one decade, until ironically the days of the Maastricht summit. Then in October 1992 monetary turmoil threw the lira and pound sterling out and forced a widening of the fluctuation bands to +/−15%.

The economic costs of these events contributed equally forcefully to the codification of monetary union at Maastricht, as did the experience of 12 years of successful joint exchange rate management. For all economic actors it was clear to see that the single market about to be achieved in late 1992 would remain very theoretical as long as different currencies, whose fluctuations regularly disrupted trade and investment flows, made economic life unpredictable beyond national borders and encouraged nationally differentiated pricing and marketing strategies.

Contrary to popular myth, which persistently claims that European monetary union had been the "price" paid by Germany in order to gain French (obviously not British) acceptance of reunification in 1990, Chancellor Kohl and President Mitterrand had already in 1988 (long before the implosion of the Eastern bloc had become evident, except to a handful of dissidents and anti-Communist visionaries) given a mandate to Commission President Delors to design a time-table for monetary union after the liberalisation of capital movements which was to be implemented by 1990.

The Delors plan foresaw three steps:

- Starting July 1990 close coordination would make economic and monetary policies of member states more convergent;
- In January 1994 a European Monetary Institute (EMI) was to be set up as predecessor to a European Central Bank (ECB);
- In January 1999 the transfer of foreign exchange control and other monetary policy competences to the EMI would be completed. It would then become the ECB functioning within a European System of Central Banks (ESCB). Conversion rates between participating currencies and the Euro are then fixed. The Euro would start its existence as a virtual currency basket. Public bonds are issued in Euro. Economic and Monetary Union (EMU) would start irrevocably.

Remarkably the Delors plan which was then enshrined in the Maastricht Treaty of 1993 was kept to the letter. The Maastricht Treaty famously defined four further fairly tough "objective" criteria, which a participating currency had to fulfil in order to keep the future coherence and stability of the merged new currency. These are:

- price stability: with an inflation rate of at most 1.5% above the average of the three most stable countries;
- sound public finances: a current budget deficit of at most 3% of GDP, and a cumulative total public debt of at most 60% of GDP;

- stable exchange rates: two years of participation in the EMS currency system without major exchange rate fluctuations;
- economic convergence: long term interest rates of at most 2% above the average of the two most stable countries.

Then, back in 1993, most EU member states were far from reaching notably the first two criteria. Average EU inflation stood at 4.3%. With inflation rates above 3% it was too high in Luxembourg, Italy, Germany, Spain, Portugal and Greece (16%). The current budget deficit was in excess of 3% of GDP in the Netherlands, France, Spain, Portugal, the UK, Germany, Belgium, Italy (11%) and Greece (13%). Cumulative public debts were above the limit of 60% of GDP in Portugal, Denmark, the Netherlands, Ireland, Greece, Italy (both at 107%), and Belgium (an astronomical 132%, touching contemporary Japanese dimensions). Even the long-term interest rates (the limit then stood at 8.9%) were too high in Italy, Spain, Portugal (13.6%) and Greece (18.3%).

Given the magnitude of the adjustment efforts required, most observers assumed either monetary union was a long way off or, if it was to happen, it would be an enlarged DM zone North of the Alps.

Both expectations were proved wrong and not even for the reason that standards were (slightly) watered down.

In 1998 heads of government then decided who was to be in: among those willing it was all, except Greece. The UK and Denmark used their legal opt out provisions. Sweden, which had secured none in her accession treaty of 1994, used a minor aberration of her crown's exchange rate to stay out. Member states had made enormous strides to consolidate their budgets (all current deficits were below 3% p.a. in 1998). Belgium and Italy made great efforts to reduce their overall indebtedness levels. Privatisations of lethargic state conglomerates were undertaken by both left and right wing governments all over the Union, thus reducing debt and revitalising the economy. With all countries consolidating, only Germany, the inventor of the convergence criteria, continued to indulge in deficit spending. Her overall public debts crossed the 60% threshold in 1998 at 61.3%. In the summer of 2000 Greece was admitted as the twelfth Euro country. Premier Simitis had made dramatic progress towards rectifying the profligate spendthrift and reflationary ways of his predecessor Papandreou, although both were from the same Socialist PASOK party.

It was an open secret that some countries had reached their stability miracles with the help of creative accounting. The debts of public companies, the uncovered obligations of social security systems and of state guarantees were usually not consolidated. Italy asked her citizens to pay a one off "Euro contribution" (which reduced the budget deficit) and promised to reimburse them once Italy joined. If this was to happen (unlikely though it is that a fisc ever honoured its promises), the deficit would promptly increase. The German Bundestag rightly discovered that Maastricht set tough conditions for entry, but none for those who made it. It did not buy the Commission's wonderful propaganda line, once a country had made the painful adjustment effort and discovered the virtues of monetary stability it would henceforth never stray off this path ever again. The Bundestag insisted as a pre-condition to its acceptance of the Maastricht Treaty that a stability pact would need to be concluded between all participating countries. It defined excessive budget deficits as the prime reason for inflation (many economists doubt this strongly — but who cares about academic economists?) and requested participants to commit themselves to keeping these deficits permanently below 3% of GDP with the objective of balancing the budget or even arriving at surplus in the medium term.

A sinning country was to be warned off by the Commission and if unrepentant and not correcting its ways could ultimately be sanctioned by the Council of Economic and Finance Ministers (Ecofin) in a QMV decision. Ecofin could, based on a Commission report, tell the country how to run her economy and set dates for compliance. If this did not work, it could go nuclear: strike off all EU regional aid and impose a fine amounting to between 0.2% to 0.5% of GDP. All Euro countries have signed this pact. The first test case of a candidate to face the music was Portugal in 2002, followed by France, interestingly Germany and Italy in 2003 and 2004. Many of these countries had conservative governments about to clean up their Socialist predecessors' creative accounting. Portugal in 2001 obtained a grace period of one year. Yet in 2002 her budget deficit stood obstinately at 4.1%, with Germany,

France and Italy also set to cross the 3% threshold. All of them had become lax in fiscal consolidation since 2000 in introducing tax cuts without corresponding savings in expenditure. Economic stagnation worsened the revenue shortfall.

The jury is out as to whether political arm twisting from Germany, France and Italy would save Portugal and thus wreck the stability pact and further damage the fragile public confidence in the Euro. The poor external value of the Euro until 2003 was certainly welcomed by struggling exporters, and given the size of the Euro-zone, hurt consumers much less than a similar devaluation of their erstwhile national currency would have done. Nonetheless international confidence continued to lack sorely, until the Bush administration's war in Iraq and its profligate spending in 2003 and 2004 weakened the US dollar even more.

In 2001 Ireland received a Commission warning for allowing her economy to overheat and thus fuel inflation. According to the laws of Euroland, this was a misdemeanour not to be sanctioned with any fines.

In the meantime, the European Council had attended to serious business. Back in 1995 it had renamed the European Currency Unit (ECU), also the name of a French medieval coin, to the more nondescript Euro. After lengthy horse trading Frankfurt was confirmed as the permanent seat of the European Central Bank (ECB). Against violent French opposition the designated first ECB president, Wim Duisenberg, an experienced Dutch central banker was appointed President in 1998. His illegible signature now graces all Euro bills. Chirac however forced him to promise to resign for reasons of old age and health in the middle of his legally fixed eight-year term, to make way for his new French deputy, Jean Claude Trichet. At the best of health Duisenberg then resigned in November 2003 to make way for Trichet, who had just survived the Credit Lyonais scandal. These widely publicised antics discredited the loudly proclaimed independence of the ECB and of its senior management.

The ECB is quite obviously modelled after the Bundesbank. It is led by a directorate composed of six members, including its president Duisenberg and his deputy Trichet. It decides on monetary and exchange rate policies together with the presidents of the 12 participating central banks with simple majority. Here, where economic weight really counts, for once heads of government had decided absurdly: one country, one vote! If uncorrected this could mean after the Eastern enlargement of the Euro-zone — which the new members could join after 2006 (Estonia, Lithuania and Slovenia are strong first candidates) fulfilling more or less the Maastricht criteria — that a majority of relatively small states at the periphery of the economic power houses of Western Europe could dominate European monetary policy, decide on its foreign exchange rate operations and manage the foreign reserves of Euroland. As already visible in the case of Ireland, in a currency zone so wide and with three prosperous core EU members missing, the risk of asymmetrical economic cycles is still high. In response, with good reasons one country might want to reflate while others want to curtail inflation.

The disappearance of national management of the exchange rate mechanism implies the loss of an essential instrument of balancing differences between heterogeneous economies. If France, the UK and the Mediterranean member states in the past experienced the loss of international competitiveness, for a temporary respite they could resort to devaluations. With the Euro in place they must address their structural problems squarely, even at the cost of increased unemployment. In case of crisis, demands for more transfer payments from smaller and poorer member states are likely. There are however limits to the financial solidarity which members of a loose confederation can expect. The larger countries, like France and Germany in 2003 and 2004, are more likely to resort to more deficit spending.

A currency union also requires common or at least closely synchronised macroeconomic, fiscal and social policies — which in turn determine largely successful monetary policies. Monthly Ecofin councils with their guidelines on macroeconomic indicators are no substitute for genuine common policies.

The Swiss franc and the US dollar were also the results of monetary unions. But their success stories are based on well-organised popularly accepted federal states (give and take one or two civil wars). History knows of no currency union which survived for long without a common state. This does not mean that the Euro must fail in the short to medium term; far from it. But in the long run (meaning ten years plus), it could well find itself reduced or split into economically more compatible and inter-linked zones, one of them a resurrected DM zone, if a political union does not happen.

If well managed, like the velvet divorce of the Czechoslovak crown in 1991 (Czech President Vaclav Klaus has already publicly offered his consultancy services to the ECB), a monetary divorce can be done at minimal trouble and costs. If done as a hostile divorce with all participants reflating for temporary gain, it can end as an economic catastrophe as in the case of the Yugoslav dinar and the Soviet rouble.

Admittedly, the risk of such a doomsday is happily remote. But a reminder of the nefarious consequences of irresponsibility can be useful on occasion. So far the Euro in its three years of theoretical and three years of real life existence has been a success. It has helped to reduce inflation and fiscal deficits, disciplined economic policies and helped policy reforms to reduce the unproductive state sector and often to reduce fiscal and para-fiscal burdens as well. It helped to make the internal market a visible and psychological reality for all consumers and businessmen. It significantly contributed to reduced transaction costs for foreign travel and money transfers. Banks, companies and private households could reduce their foreign cash holdings which are essentially unproductive and risky liquidity.

The Euro still is a young toddler needing continuous attention and care in order to prosper. Currently, it seems to be growing up in a hippy commune where nobody feels responsible. It is still too young to notice. But in order to make it into a stable, balanced and productive adulthood, it needs to be adopted into a proper family environment of a decent and well organised federal state.

The Wondrous CAP: Of Cash-Eating Cows, Multiplying Olive Trees, Happy Chickens and Unhappy Farmers

There is a case to be made for agricultural protectionism, and it runs as follows: agriculture is different from all other sectors. There are millions of small-scale producers producing fairly standard commodities, like cereals, milk, sugar, fruit and meat. But, courtesy of the weather and the good Lord, they have little influence over the actual quality and quantity of their output, or over their sales prices which are, if left unattended, being determined in large measure by a handful of computerised commodity brokers on the world market. Food products are different also from other goods as demand is fairly inelastic. We can live with shortages of toilet paper, shaving cream and newsprint, but we cannot go without food for more than a fortnight.

When the CAP was enshrined in the Treaties of Rome in 1957, the famines and food rationing of both world wars and their aftermath were still recent memories for all concerned. The absence of "food security" had helped to lend credence to the propaganda on the need for more living space (*lebensraum*) in Eastern Europe or in colonies in order to advance self-sufficiency. One of the successes of the CAP was surely to have done away with this sort of reasoning once and for all quite thoroughly. In the mid-1950s, however, this was far from clear.

With the repeal of the Corn Laws, since the mid-19th century the UK had sent its surplus farmers either into coal mines and shipyards or dispatched them to New Zealand, Australia, Canada, South Africa and Rhodesia. Food security for the British Isles was henceforth synonymous with a strong navy. Continental Europe did not have this option. Most of its colonies were either already well settled or semi-arid and tropical and unsuitable for temperate zone commodities. Setting up strong tariff protection seemed cheaper and more advisable than building up naval power and provoking the British Empire, as William II had to learn at his expense.

The UK and Sweden apart, there seems to be a universal law on the old Eurasian continent — applicable not only to the EU but also from Norway and Switzerland to Japan, Korea and Taiwan: after the initial discrimination and exploitation of the rural economy during the early industrialisation, the farm sector is being assisted in growing measure now that urbanisation and industralisation have reduced it to a marginal economic status. This is done for a series of reasons, foremost political ones: the centre-right parties which had usually been pushing industrialisation realised that in consequence there was often industrial and political unrest exploited by the left. Supporting the more conservative rural population helped to preserve their hold on power. Also in terms of social planning, making life in the countryside a more viable alternative helped to reduce migratory moves to the cities, which during their rapid growth suffered from serious strains on the infrastructure, creating housing shortages, and ever more cramped, polluted and unhealthy living conditions. Compared to the stressful and socially disintegrating metropolitan existence, life in the countryside in conservative ideology appeared idyllic: God-fearing fathers raising many healthy children with rustic virtues, obedient to authorities and loyal to the fatherland. Farm support had the added virtue of having been made possible by increased tax revenues from successful industrialisation, gradually higher disposable urban incomes and the fact that the beneficiary farming population had rapidly become minoritarian. By the time the Treaties of Rome were signed even in Italy and France, "only" 37% and 26% of the working population were still labouring on farms (much like in Romania and Poland today).

Reasons of equity and of a more balanced regional development also spoke for farming support as the sector's income had fallen significantly behind those of urban households. The same applied to average income levels of rural regions compared to their urbanised counterparts. An economic case could be made for small producers with little capital base facing vagaries of income and price fluctuations, which due to weather and market conditions were beyond their control.

Taking these arguments and factors together, they explain why six European countries with booming post-war industries in the Treaties of Rome of 1957 agreed to embark on what turned out to be seriously protectionist agricultural policies. More than one trillion Euro would be spent on the sector during 1962–2004 with no real visible and clear-cut policy achievement in consequence, neither on desired farm structures, food qualities, the genetic pool of farm animals, the rural environment nor village life, etc., which mostly deteriorated regardless of the protection accorded.

Yet it is always important to remember that initially there were good reasons for the CAP, which in its heydays of the mid-1980s reached the summit of absurd protectionism — almost as good as East Germany's 5-year plans at the time — even though these honestly good reasons turned out to be wrong.

Reflecting the consensus of the six founding members, which had all embarked on protectionist farm policies of their own at the time (and not just rural France wanting industrial Germany, as popular belief has it, pay for market access in France and Italy), the Treaties of Rome postulated the following main common agricultural policy objectives:

- increase productivity;
- permit an adequate standard of living for the farmers;
- stabilise markets (from price cycles);
- safeguard food security.

Already in 1958, at a conference in Stresa, these fairly precise treaty objectives had been translated into a concrete policy design for a common agricultural policy. The new EEC members agreed on a common "organisation" of agricultural markets, a single price policy for farm products and joint Community funds for financing the necessary expenditure. They also agreed on the structural objective of viable modernised family farms, that is, neither part-timers nor agro-industry.

With clockwork-like precision starting in 1962, common market organisations were set up product by product. For most commodities (cereals, milk, beef and sugar), ingenuous "market organisations" were established based on external protection, internal price guarantees and export subsidies.

The core element of the internal market support is the intervention price. Should the internal market price fall below the intervention price, farmers will have to sell their crop to an EU-funded public intervention board as a guaranteed outlet. In order to remain undisturbed by imports, not a fixed tariff, but a variable levy is slapped on them which drives the import price to a predetermined target price level, far in excess of existing market prices. Imports subjected to the variable levy then have only very theoretical possibilities on the market. In turn agricultural exports are subsidised with the help of export refunds. An exporter can claim these refunds as the difference between the EU's domestic market price (at which he bought) and the usually much lower world market price prevalent in his export area. With the right amount of export refund, then exporting surplus stocks to the Soviet Union, the Arab world and other importing regions did not prove too difficult (except when facing over-subsidised US competition). About 70% worth of EU farm products are covered by these comprehensive market organisations.

The rest was subjected to lighter regimes: storage aids for pork, some fruits, vegetable and table wine; external protection only in the shape of an over-high importation price (ingeniously called "sluicegate price") for eggs, poultry, fruit, vegetables and quality wine; aids given to processors of domestic rape, sunflower seeds, soy, other protein plants (since these plants did not enjoy import protection, as they were mostly used as animal feed) and tobacco; lump sum support for hops, flax, hemp (the fibre-producing plant only!), plant seeds and for silk worms; and finally processing aids for commodities in structural surplus, like for table wine distillation into industrial alcohol, sugar to be used in the chemical industry, starch production, etc.

Such was the complex edifice of an "organised market". With the prices set at "political levels" by the farm ministers for their clientele and all costs borne by the EU budget, incentives to set prices far above market levels were strong, particularly so during the first decade of the CAP's existence until the late 1970s when self-sufficiency rates hardly exceeded 100% and wasteful expenditure for storage, disposal and export refunds was still limited. The obsession with self-sufficiency hailed from the French "planification" of the post-war years, when Jean Monnet was the first Commissaire du Plan. It was still spooking around when I joined the Commission's directorate general for agriculture back in 1984.

Whenever then an official was asked to produce a briefing on a given commodity, be it honey, hazelnuts or bananas, he would invariably design an import/export/domestic consumption chart and draw interventionist conclusions if the self-sufficiency levels were below 100% (or for good measure of food security 105%). It was heresy to mention the fuel or feed import dependencies of Europe's farmers, let alone the fact that an affluent continent in times of peace can always import foodstuff in case of regional or so far historically unknown global shortages.

Termed politely, the CAP became a victim of its own success. Massive mechanisation, abundant fertilisers, improved seed and breeds, better training and extension services, and last but not least, relatively stable high prices modernised this traditionally backward sector and, good year, bad year, productivity increased relentlessly by 2% p.a. This output growth was matched only inadequately by a growth of consumption by only +0.5% p.a. Not unlike the sorcerer's apprentice, by the mid 1970s, self-sufficiency was permanently attained by the major assisted commodities. Ever increasing amounts of export refunds had since to be paid to subsidise the import bill of those countries in North and Central Africa, the Middle East and the Communist world, whose agricultural policies had failed to provide incentives for improved productivity (which the EU, the US and Japan provided in abundance).

For over-produced commodities, like say milk, the Union paid in many ways: separated in its fat (butter) and non-fat segments (skim milk powder) to be made durable, it was bought into intervention from the dairies at intervention price levels. Then they were kept in cold storage for 1–2 years in the vain hope of shortages which never occurred. By mid 1985 also one million tonnes of beef were in storage — much of it on cooling ships since build-up facilities were overflowing, as were 25 million tonnes of cereals, some 200,000 tonnes of butter, five million litres of alcohol distilled from undrinkable table wines, as well as unknown quantities of olive oil and tobacco, all of the poorest qualities. In cold storage one thing is certain: in difference to cognac or whisky in oak barrels, quality unfortunately does not improve over time.

Hence it had to be sold. One very expensive way to make people happy was a free butter giveaway at Christmas time to pensioners and other deserving people (which however mostly displaced butter sales at commercial prices). It was slightly less costly to sell it in keen competition with equally subsidised US exports to the Soviets, who could thus fatten its military and could prove to their otherwise starving population the superiority of the Socialist system.

In order to deal with the Soviets, the EU had to go through an intermediary called Jean Claude Doumeng. Doumeng, in the process of effortless mediation, quickly became a multi-millionaire, with stables of race horses and a fleet of personally owned airplanes. Through his firm Interagra he was also the main financier of the French Communist Party. With billions available for surplus disposal there were many Doumeng characters around. Sometimes they were decent commodity traders and rural cooperatives, but often they were not. In Italy the men in black were called the Mafia. They were dealing not in dairy, beef and wheat but in Mediterranean products like tobacco, olive oil, durum wheat and table wine, and it was very advisable for EU inspectors not to poke their noses too deeply into caves which were declared to contain high quality surplus olive oil. More and more money went into the pockets of processors, storage operators and traders (both of good repute and of less), and correspondingly less into those of the farmers as the originally intended beneficiaries. Clearly a thorough CAP reform was called for.

The CAP in many ways has subsequently become a sort of Bolshevism in reverse. While Communist planners tried to force their reluctant collectivised worker-farmers to increase output in spite of non-remunerative prices and wages, the CAP in various reform attempts now tried to induce farmers to produce less in spite of relatively high producer prices. The first agricultural Commissioner who seriously contemplated CAP reforms was Dutchman Frans Andriessen.

The Commission realised — with the delay worthy of a thoroughly thinking bureaucracy — that agricultural budgets exploded, with less and less money going to support the struggling farm families, that surplus production since 1975 was no longer cyclical but structural, and that the gains of the CAP were distributed very unevenly. As a support price system that rewards the quantities produced, large farmers and agro businesses benefited most. In fact, 80% of the CAP intervention budget went to the output of the 20% largest and most productive farms. These were typically 200-hectare sited cereal farms in the Ile de France, in Norfolk, and in Southern Sweden, large latifundias in the plains of the Ebro and the Po, the cooperative successors of the formerly collectivised state farms in East Germany, and industrial cattle holdings in the Netherlands. Typically specialist farms with a monocultural orientation, their contribution to a diversified environment or a pleasant landscape is usually negative. One elderly but still very active farm woman turned out to be by far the largest recipient of CAP largesse. It is her Britannic Majesty Elizabeth II. To continue to justify CAP expenditure with God-fearing starving mountain farmers appeared more and more ludicrous. Public criticism became increasingly vocal. As the CAP in the mid-1980s was clearly the most visible achievement of European integration, its legitimacy began to suffer from the apparent absurdities of the CAP.

Afraid of violent farmers' demonstrations, which was an annual event in early summer — in the boring off-season between sowing and harvesting French farmers burnt their local prefectural offices and trucks with foreign produce (a habit which Polish farmers have taken up with gusto since) —, Commissioner Andriessen in 1985 chose a rather piecemeal approach to reforms.

Already in 1984 a quota system had been introduced as a transitional measure in the dairy sector: support prices would be left high. But farmers who overproduced faced steep price cuts for their excess quantities of milk. These quotas were made transferable, which meant that they were capitalised and sold as a licence to milk. This system, similar to an earlier quota system in the sugar sector, proved to be popular with farmers, which explains why this transitional measure still exists two decades later. Andriessen introduced a series of non-spectacular, seemingly technical modifications, like freezing support prices, introducing "co-responsibility levies" to share the costs of surplus disposal (in effect a producer tax on surplus commodities). Intervention guarantees were relaxed by insisting on certain qualities for the products bought, and by limiting purchasing seasons and quantities. Automatic price cuts were introduced as "stabilisers" for the following year if certain quantities were over-produced in the current crop year. These technical reforms were unsuitable to trigger public passions, even though their intended effect was clearly to reduce prices through the back door. For two to three years these tinkering reforms worked. Then the old surpluses were back. There were also special aids for scrapping low quality vineyards, for the early retirement of farmers and other measures to extensify farm production. As these schemes were voluntary there was little acceptance.

Andriessen was succeeded in 1990 by Ray MacSharry. MacSharry was a tough self-made businessman from West of the Shannon who had entered Irish politics after having worked his way up in the rural road haulage and livestock industry. As a no-nonsense budget cutter he well earned his nickname "Mac the Knife" as Irish Minister of Finance. As Commissioner of Agriculture for the first time probably farm lobbyists were more afraid of him than the other way around. The thrust of his reforms in 1992 was to move from price support gradually to income support, which was paid as an acreage premium for each hectar of farmland and as a headage payment for cattle. MacSharry cut intervention prices for cereals by 29% during 1992/1996. It was hoped that cheaper EU feed grains would then become competitive with imported feeds like tapioca, soy and corn gluten. Direct aids for acreage were only paid, if 5–15% of the land was taken out of production as "set-asides". Prices for oil seeds were cut by 23–37% to world market levels. Producers were compensated by acreage payments. The new prices reduced the feed costs for livestock farmers. Beef prices then in turn were cut by 15% in the hope of increasing consumption. Cattle farms were compensated by a premium for up to 90 cows per farm, provided it had a minimum grazing area. MacSharry hoped that his reform would entail budgetary savings: with extensive production there would be less purchases into intervention. With reduced prices and quantities there would be less need for export refunds. With intervention returning to its intended role as outlet of the last resort, he expected farmers to intensify their efforts at quality improvements which would allow them to charge premium prices above the reduced market rates.

MacSharry's reforms worked well for a few years, until relentless productivity gains caught up with them.

His reforms also required plenty of new controls and paper work. In order to qualify for acreage payments cadaster extracts had to be supplied, as there was the risk that in a certain Southern member state her farmland would double overnight. (Her fruit-bearing olive trees had in fact doubled as a biological wonder when back in the early 1980s olive oil support was introduced. In real life a tree reaches maturity only after 14 years.) With the introduction of headage payments, this country's cattle herd also very quickly overshot the one million mark. The farm minister had then to admit that the country had cheated on her dairy quotas since their inception. The reader will have guessed it by now: yes, it is bella Italia, the inventor of the one-eared cows. Once an EU culling premium was introduced for elderly dairy cows, one ear was asked for by the skeptical Eurocrats as proof of their untimely demise. Most Italian farmers, humanists at heart, took mercy with their animals, cut off one ear, took the premium and left the beast alive until old age when it was ripe for bisteca Fiorentina (to be served to tourists with healthy teeth from Brussels). Fraud in the agricultural sector is clearly a problem of most member states and is certainly not limited to Italy. The only countries not known to have defrauded the CAP budget are the Scandinavians, possibly because they lack the imagination to do so. One one-eared cow on a Swedish pasture would invite scientific, NGO, press, fiscal and police inquiries. In Italy there were tens of thousands around with no silly questions asked about the obvious.

In the meantime, after seven arduous years the GATT Uruguay Round was concluded in 1993, with its results entering into force in 1995. This GATT agreement for the first time ever included a discipline on permissible agricultural protection, covering both types of support: those granted by consumers (price support) and those given by tax-payers (budget support). The GATT agreement which was to improve the prospects of freer trade, judged and restrained subsidies depending on their trade distortive character. For the EU the agreement meant that until 2001 the output-oriented budgetary support was to be cut by 20%. All import restrictions, including the ingenious variable levies, were to be tariffed and cut by 36%. About 5% of the domestic market was to be accessible for imports. The budget for export refunds was to be cut by 36% and the subsidised export volumes to be reduced by 21%.

In contrast, income support for environmental protection and other extensifying income support ("green box" measures) were permissible, as was food aid and regional and social support. Equally acceptable remained acreage and headage premia, and deficiency payments (which cover the difference between the actual market price and a target price) as long as they did not distort competition.

The logic behind the GATT agreement was based on an extensive, valuable OECD study which demonstrated if all major subsidising countries (EU, EFTA, US, Canada, Japan, Korea, etc.) brought down their public support simultaneously and ended their misallocations of capital and labour to the farm sector, producer prices would initially fall and consumer demand could pick up. With the end of over-production producer prices would eventually recover, thus rendering the "sacrifice" of the farmer much more theoretical than real.

This message was not lost on Franz Fischler, who took over the Commission's farm and fisheries brief with Austria's accession in 1995 until 2004.

Fischler, an academically trained dairyman from Tyrol who was previously a reform-oriented farm minister in Austria, saw his future policies squeezed into a triple straitjacket of budget limitations, the next WTO round following up on GATT's Uruguay Round, and the EU's forthcoming Eastern enlargement with candidate countries replete of unfulfilled agricultural potential.

Fischler defined as his objectives a structure of family-based farm enterprises with a sound economic basis which would produce high quality healthy foodstuffs in an environment-friendly fashion and maintain a pleasantly diversified rural landscape. A more ecological orientation required a strengthening of MacSharry's line of income rather than price support. It also made a re-orientation of the EU's structural agricultural policies imperative which since their inception in the mid-1970s had always been an undernourished stepbrother of the tenfold more expensive farm product policies.

So far they had mainly served to modernise farm structures and the processing and marketing of its produce. Now the emphasis had to go towards a social component (basic farm incomes, early retirement), to support an ecological re-orientation (to safeguard soil and ground water purity, the diversity of species and of landscapes), and to promote rural development in generating alternative employment in local food and wood processing, rural tourism, etc., in order to counteract the paralysing impact of gradual rural depopulation and ageing. Austria had always been vocal in promoting the fate of "handicapped mountain farmers", by which they meant, as I found out later, not a physical or mental handicap — the gentlemen usually had a good main income as skiing instructors or directors of local savings banks — but the steepness of the pastures which their dairy cattle had to climb.

At the Berlin summit of March 1999 which should have prepared the CAP for Eastern enlargement and the doubling of its farmers, the resistance of Jacques Chirac, who is wont to see global and EU events rather through the eyes of his rustic voters in his home district of Correze, watered down Fischler's more radical, far-sighted proposals. Yet the following remained: the prices for cereals were cut by 15% (and compensated by higher acreage payments); the support for oil seeds was reduced to the levels of cereals, with an obligatory set aside of 10%; the BSE-damaged beef prices were cut by 20%; and those of milk products by 15%, but only during 2003/2006.

Since 1999 tough new rules have applied. One is called "cross-compliance": direct payments are only made if certain environmental standards are kept. The second rule of brave new Fischlerland is called "modulation": a member state can decide to cut direct payments to farms if these are deemed too small, too big, or receiving too much subsidised cash already. The cash saved by the member state may then be used for its own structural or environmental measures.

At his second reform attempt, termed "mid-term review" in 2002, Commissioner Fischler in view of enlargement and the start of the Doha Round of the WTO proposed direct payments to be decoupled from current production altogether but rather to be based on the output of the past three years. The maximal allowable limit of public support should be fixed at 300,000 Euros per farm. The monies freed from product support (which still count for 90% of the 44 billion Euros CAP budget) through "cross-compliance" (i.e., farms which did not comply with ecological animal welfare and food quality conditions) and "modulation" would be used for rural development.

Fischler's far-reaching proposals faced rough going in the Council, the resistance being publicly led by President Chirac, joined by the other net recipient countries like Spain, Greece, Portugal and Ireland. Again the reform was watered down and delayed.

Yet a real reform decoupling agricultural income support from output is imperative if Eastern enlargement is to remain manageable financially once the farmers from the new member states insist on parity of support — in 2006 at the latest. The alternative would be to dismantle the CAP entirely, "renationalise" the support components; that is, to leave member states to manage their own subsidy schemes (if any), provided that they do not distort inter-EU competition. Apart from safeguarding competition rules, the Commission's role could then be restricted to enforcing basic food hygiene, animal protection and agro-environmental rules as well as handling international trade negotiations. This would free half of the EU's budget, a lot of its management time and be a practical step towards the virtue of subsidiarity. Agriculture employing less than 5% of the workforce and producing 2% of the EU's GDP after all is no longer a strategic sector for integration.

The CAP could go with nobody, except for the farm lobby, shedding any more tears, than for the demise of the European Coal and Steel Community (which ended on December 2002).

At least some 1 trillion Euros have been spent on the CAP in the four decades of her existence. A similar amount in addition was contributed by EU consumers in terms of higher food prices. These are staggering amounts. Had they been invested in education, R&D or, say, in modern railway infrastructure, Europe's competitive situation would have been greatly improved.

It is not even clear whether the CAP has accelerated or slowed down structural change in the country side. In any event, this happened regardless of heavy subsidisation. In 1960 there were 25 million farmers in the EU 15. Four decades later a mere seven million were left. The same about the environment: high output prices helped to industrialise agriculture and to create mono-cultures. Left to market forces this would have happened equally. No doubt Irish and Spanish farm villages now look more prosperous than twenty years ago; but so do all other parts of both countries.

Extensification and ecologically friendly farming and help for mountain farmers would have found national and regional public support anyway. This was amply demonstrated by Austria and Finland prior to joining the EU in 1995.

In sum the CAP then appears as a fairly expendable commodity ready for sacrifice on the altar of effective EU subsidiarity.

CHAPTER 8

Too Few Fish, Too Many Fishermen: The Common Fisheries Policy

The EU's fisheries policy has always been considered the smaller step-brother of the mighty CAP. Although the original policy objectives were similar (increase productivity and producer incomes, modernise the sector), the policy similarities are deceiving. The basis of the business ethic and the public control needs are fundamentally different.

Fishing, in difference to agriculture even in its high-tech variants (if we disregard fish farming), belongs to the earlier human condition of hunting and gathering. The products harvested are not sown or raised; they are hunted and caught. And in difference to hunting on land (if we disregard the slaughter of migratory birds), there is normally very little direct co-relation between the fisherman's personal predatory behaviour and future stocks available to him. This means that whether or not he hunts responsibly will affect his future catches only marginally, but the aggregate behaviour of his and all his fishing colleagues will be decisive not only to their own livelihood but also the EU's and the world's future supply of marine protein. Hence intrinsically sensible policy intervention is called for.

EU policy intervention was quick on the spot, following and substituting maritime member states' similar policies. Unfortunately the resulting common fisheries policies (CFP) was not always sensible. According to the UN up to 600 million Euros of CFP funds were ploughed annually into a modernised shipping fleet, thus contributing to global over-capacities and over-exploitation — the most flagrant sinners being Asian and former Comecon operators. As a result of global over-fishing, the world catch has been falling ever since 1989.

The increasing use of sonar and radar technologies for searching and finding the last hiding grounds, of detailed fishing maps and of overlong nylon drift nets, could only delay the day of reckoning and make its consequences all the more severe. Globally 3.5 million trawlers, of which 90,000 sail under EU flags, are ploughing the seas, a fleet at least 50% too large. In particular deep sea fish are at risk due to their slow growth and rates of renewal, and so are blue fin tuna (a staple for sushi and sashimi), free salmon, flatfish, mackerel, herring, etc. Already in the first two post-war decades, modernised fishing fleets have led to a tripling of total catches. As signs of over-fishing were ominous, one of the CFP's first measures has extended the EU's fishing zone by 200 miles in the North Sea and the North Atlantic for the free access and common use for the fleet of all EU member states.

Coastal zones of up to 12 miles, also in the Mediterranean Sea, remained in national management. In the common EU waters, in line with resource management, catch quotas were established, fishing stocks surpervised and control systems manned by EU inspectors set up. There are minimum sizes of net mashes, so as to allow undersize young fish to escape, limits to "side catches" and "industrial fish" and seasonal or total interdictions for catches in breeding grounds. Since 2002 the use of drift nets ("walls of death") for tuna is also prohibited.

In order to protect the livelihood of the EU's 300,000 fishermen and to shore up the economies of coastal areas and islands dependent on fishing, following the role model of the CAP, "market organisations" were set up. They aimed at "stabilising" politically-set high prices and fishermen's incomes. Premia were paid for storage. With public money caught fish were "withdrawn" from the market, as the usual CAP/CFP euphemism goes (mostly to process fish fit for human consumption into feedstuff). Producer associations and cooperatives were sponsored for processing and marketing. More significant was the structural policy of the CFP which aimed at the "rationalisation" of the fleets. It involved steep subsidies for both modernised ships, including enhanced deepwater fishing capacities, and for capacity cuts with money going for scrapping old boats.

As already amply evident in the CAP, political bargaining in the Council seriously exacerbated the distortions of a policy induced anti-market "market organisation". In the case of the CFP, matters were made worse by the lack of public interest and public scrutiny for a seemingly marginal and technically complicated sectoral economic policy, and by the ultimate finality of the resources "harvested" in a high tech fashion with pre-modern hunting instincts.

In line with the short-termism of their clientele, against the Commission's advice ministers typically set total allowable catches (TAC), which are in effect quotas set for each species and hunting season for each member state, too high. They also resisted capacity cuts for their own fleets and insisted on generous sweeteners for "modernisation".

One, though increasingly expensive, way around was to catch other people's fish. Over the years some 26 fisheries agreements were concluded. First with the US to get access to the under-fished waters of this carnivorous nation, then in the Southern Seas, the coastal states of West Africa, Morocco being of foremost importance, but also with Argentina and Mauritius. In 1997 alone, 300 million Euros were paid for access to these waters. The Southern agreements mainly benefit the Spanish fleet operating from the Canary Islands, Andalusia, Galicia and the Basque country, where they have considerable importance for the local economy in terms of processing and for specialised shipyards. With the Spaniards (and to a lesser extent Portuguese and French) catching valuable tuna, shrimp and octopus along the sunny African coast, it is mainly the Danes (often based on Bornholm) who operate in rough Northern waters where they typically harvest "industrial fish" to be processed into fish meal and fish oil in large quantities. The Northern agreements with Greenland, Iceland, the Faroe Islands and Norway are mostly based on mutual reciprocity of access and thus come relatively cheap. Ecologically, however, the masses of small "industrial fish" are also missing in the maritime food chain which comes at the price of aggravating global over-fishing. Year by year the Council fudged the real issue of over-capacities by compromising with modernisation programmes and insufficient TACs, which in the following years regularly proved to have worsened the situation of fish and fishermen on aggregate.

Hence one more last Commission attempt to rescue the CFP from ultimate disintegration in 2002. Commissioner Fischler, in spite of his name a Tyrolean mountain farmer and unlikely fisheries expert, proposed to reduce TACs by up to 60%, to wreck 10% of the EU's fishing fleet of 90,000 (representing 18% of its tonnage), to reduce by up to 60% the "fishing effort", i.e., the permissible time spent on sea, for the remainder, to finally end all subsidies for new ships and fleet modernisation, and to move from annual TACs set by the Council towards more appropriate conservationist pluri-annual resource management. These radical and sensible proposals were greeted with a predictable outcry by the usual suspects (Spain and France) citing the usually mistaken evidence of resource recovery here and there for continuing the CFPs habitual misery.

What then are alternatives should Fischler's reforms fail? Eamon Gallagher, a former director general of fisheries at the Commission, recognicant of the fact that conservation efforts in the coastal areas in the absence of restrictions can only induce distant neighbours to raid them, argued for the regional management of coastal fishery resources. This would mean, e.g., Basque waters for Basque fishermen, and so forth.

It would acknowledge the reality of failed national, let alone EU, policies of joint responsible resource management. Given the gravity of the situation — after all 15 to 20% of healthy human protein supply via fish is under terminal threat — perhaps it is time to abandon ideology in the name of more effective practical subsidiarity. The CFP judging by the number of violent and often deadly disputes in the Bay of Biscay, around the Channel Islands and elsewhere, does not appear to be a particularly peace-inducing policy anyway. The European policy dimension could sensibly be limited to the coordination of regional conservation efforts, to handling standards and quality policy, to international matters and funding of coastal development for alternatives like well-managed aquaculture and tourism.

The Beauty of Sustainable Poverty: Europe's Regions and Regional Funding

Normally host countries show their best sides and shiniest sites to visiting dignitaries. When Bruce Millan, then the EU Commissioner for Regional Development, visited the East Austrian province of Burgenland back in 1993, he was treated to a rare spectacle. His convoy travelled the bumpiest country road imaginable. He was invited to witness a folk dance performance of the local Croat minority in a creaky old barn. Later rustic lunch was served in a historic farmhouse which also served as a makeshift barracks for young soldiers patrolling Austria's Eastern border. This was followed with a briefing by the regional governor, Karl Stix, a former school teacher who explained to his patiently listening guest, a fellow socialist, the tales of historical woes which had befallen his home state: originally part of German-speaking West Hungary, the Hungarian military had occupied the area's larger towns in 1919 when the borders were to be redrawn. During a plebiscite this prevented the German cities to vote in favour of accession to Austria, which was joined consequently only by their rural hinterland, renamed Burgenland.

Impoverished and crisis ridden Austria could do little to help its poor new cousin in the inter-war years. Unemployment and migration — especially to the US — was high. During the last months of the war Burgenland was conquered and plundered by the Red Army which stayed until 1955. Then the small state remained cut off in the shadow of the iron curtain, which stretched from Slovakia along the Hungarian border down to the Slovene part of Yugoslavia. Now Burgenland faced new low cost competitors in the liberated East and had to prepare for a borderless future in an enlarged EU.

Bruce Millan was a sober Scottish accountant. As a former occupation officer in South East Austria he was no doubt familiar with local history and the natives' skills in negotiating drama. Whether the visit, Austria's generous global financial offers during the EU membership talks, or Governor Stix's carefully engineered poverty status carried the day will never be known. In any event, when Austria joined the EU on January 1, 1995, Burgenland secured the coveted "Objective 1" status, which meant EU funds for development had to be matched by only 25% of regional or national funds. Two years later, Bruce Millan's successor, a German former trade union leader, Monika Wulf-Matthies, was flown into Burgenland as well. She was spared the jeep ride and the Croat barn, but rather flown by military helicopter to a series of cattle pastures where exited local officials unveiled visions of future industrial riches. Wulf-Matthies in short speeches replied that these would only materialise if they also built proper waste water facilities, trained the local women and hired handicapped minority members. The locals inevitably looked slightly baffled as to why these no doubt worthy but rather peripheral factors would be so decisive, but nonetheless dutifully assured the Commissioner that they would do their utmost, while her entourage, including this author, helped themselves to the schnapps (which forms an integral part of Burgenland hospitality).

Burgenland had always been very close to crossing the 75% EU average income level above which "Objective 1" status was no longer possible. Back in 1995 it expected to be sponsored only for the period ending 2000. However, they managed to spend their EU funds almost exclusively on largely unused industrial parks, subsequently bankrupted the state budget due to co-financing requirements in the process and drove the largest public Burgenland Bank into insolvency. Properly impoverished Burgenland was thus successful in retaining its "Objective 1" status even after the "Agenda 2000" pruning exercise was able to earmark a large chunk of previous aid recipients (including such prominent areas like South and East Ireland, Corsica and Greater Lisbon) for the gradual withdrawal from the cosy world of regional funding. The Burgenland story in a nutshell hence raises a couple of interesting questions, starting with the role of the regions in an integrated Europe and ending with the sense and nonsense of regional subsidisation.

As Europe is not meant to be a melting pot, regional structures and traditions remain strong and alive, economic and cultural globalisation notwithstanding. This is not only true in federal EU states like Belgium, Germany and Austria, but also in famously staunch Centrist states like Spain (17 regions with varying degrees of autonomy, including Catalonia, Galicia, the Basque country, the Balearics, etc.), Italy (seven autonomous regions, including South Tyrol-Trient, Fiuli, the Aosta Valley, Sicily, Sardinia, etc.), France (which has set up 22 regions), and even the UK (which has permitted local self-government in London and a Scottish assembly in Edinburgh).

Regions predate the nation state, and strong opponents of the latter among postwar European federalists have even proposed a European federation of the 252 regions which can be identified in the EU 15. Yet the fate of contemporary Africa and a bit of historical research shows that societies organised along tribal lines are not by necessity more peaceful than those with effective nation states, which after all represent a higher level of political and cultural development.

While the "Europe of Regions" deserves to remain a pipe dream, there is a fair case to be made for stronger regional competences in the name of subsidiarity. As enshrined in Maastricht, this principle implies that, wherever possible and sensible, political decisions should be taken at the level closest to the people concerned, where expertise on local conditions and chances of participatory democracy are highest.

A high degree of self-determination — of taxation and spending decisions — is helpful at regional level to encourage rational fund use and to prevent the usual "cultures of dependency" in which "foreign" funds are typically wasted: a stronger regional role is also beneficial for the protection of autochthonous minorities, which typically reside in peripheral regions or in formerly disputed border areas. Effective linguistic and cultural rights and political representation, which is usually more relevant at the regional than at the national level, has proven to diffuse potentially disruptive ethnic disputes which have bedeviled the relations of Europe's nation states for so long. This healthy lesson still needs to be learned in some parts of Eastern Europe and perhaps in Greece as well.

It is generally accepted that in the absence of any corrective redistribution, two large central areas would be the main beneficiaries of the EU's huge integrated internal market. Economic geographers have invented these regions. The first is the "trapeze of growth", the prosperous area between London, Paris, Stuttgart, Munich and Copenhagen, on the one hand, and a second even more exotic area termed "Golden Banana", a sort of Alpine sunbelt, stretching from Barcelona via the Cote d'Azur, Lombardy (generously including Switzerland) into Bavaria and Austria. These are the central regions where income and education levels are highest, cultural activities and the quality of life often considered most attractive and where public services and the physical infrastructure are best developed. While labour costs may be higher, costs for transportation and communication are less. In the absence of policy intervention, these privileged regions would attract a strong inflow of investment with concomitant job opportunities and a massive transfer of internal (and external) migrants, thus over-burdening public services, the environment and the infrastructure, leading to social strain, disorganisation and housing shortages. Correspondingly, the European periphery, the countryside and certain declining urban areas within the larger growth regions would suffer from depopulation, the out-migration of their best educated, youngest and most dynamic people, witness the unraveling of the economic and social infrastructure and see social alienation and economic stagnation and decline. This disparate regional development hence is undesirable for both sides and sensible instruments of redistributive equity are called for. In a process of trial and error and of political arm twisting, the EU has developed such instruments.

After decades of policy induced expansions of the support area — in 1999 some 50% of EU territory and population benefited from a warm, thin and ineffectual summer rain of EU regional subsidies — in the end, Monika Wulf-Matthies, the tough trade union lady turned Commissioner, managed to consolidate the unwieldy range of overlapping target areas ("objectives") into three, and cut the messy proliferation of alphabet soup type Community initiatives down to four. These reforms were part of the Commission's "Agenda 2000" proposals which were accepted at the Berlin summit in July 1999.

The previous "Objective 1" remained in prioritising support for regions which lagged behind in their economic development, as indicated by a GDP per capita of less than 75% of EU average. The importance of the reform was the recognition of the perceptible improvement of the incomes of formerly deprived regions. Large chunks of Ireland — the East, the North, the South — whose income after two decades of successfully catching up had reached 90% of the EU average in 1995 (1983: 64%), were finally allowed to "graduate", and so was the greater Lisbon area, Hainaut in Belgium, Flevoland in the Netherlands, Corsica, the Highlands and Isles, Asturias in Spain and the Abbruzi in Italy. Their departure from intensive subsidisation was to be sweetened with a gradual "phasing out" support as a withdrawal programme to quit the regional subsidy addiction. Those who managed to continually mismanage their regional economy, like most parts of Spain, the remainder of Portugal, Southern Italy, Greece, East Germany, the Burgenland, and chunks of Wales and Cornwall remained, as did France's very European overseas territories of Guyana, Guadeloupe, Martinique and Reunion (for whatever sense it may make that these relaxed colonial leftovers reach any EU average). For good measure the "arctic lands" of Northern Sweden and Finland (formerly "Objective 6") were added, not because they are poor, but to compensate them for long distances and cold dark winters.

For the period 2000–2006, 136 billion Euros are earmarked for "Objective 1" territories, home to 22% of the EU's population. They represent 68% of all EU regional funds. If well managed, these funds, aimed foremost at infrastructure modernisation, are bound to make a difference. National and regional co-funding requirements remain at 25% only.

The new "Objective 2" covers smaller regions, industrial areas in decline and pockets of rural and coastal stagnation. These are parts of North England, of the Midlands, Wales, of Brittany, Normandy, the Ardennes, Lorraine, the Massif Central, large parts of Southern

France and North East Spain, Central Italy, of the Alps, the German and Austrian border areas to the Czech Republic, Friesland, Schleswig, some Danish islands, Gotland, parts of Central Sweden and Finland, and Western Karelia. Again the main achievement of the reform was re-focusing. Previously depressed urban and rural areas, which managed their transition successfully — like the East of Scotland, Northern Jutland, the Ruhr area, most parts of Bavaria, the Palatinate, Central Austria and Tuscany, were made to "graduate", once again benefiting from transitional aids to wean them off the subsidy habit. The remaining "Objective 2" regions in crisis are inhabited by 15% of the EU's population. They receive 22.5 billion Euros (or 11.5%) of total EU regional funding. For them the co-financing requirement stands at 50%, which should encourage more sensible projects.

Finally there is as a horizontal theme "Objective 3", covering all of the EU except for "Objective 1" regions: these are European Social Fund monies for education, training and employment promotion. With 24 billion Euros, "Objective 3" is funded with 12% of all structural funds available during 2000–2006.

Still there are the Community initiatives: there used to be a proliferation of a mouth-watering alphabet soup of up to 11 special interest support schemes (each self-respecting Commission regional officer seemed to have designed his own pet scheme). They were called Konver (transforming armament and garrison towns), Retex (transforming textile towns), Resider (transforming steel towns), Recite (promoting inter-local cooperation), Regis (promoting socio-economic integration), Regen (creating diversified regional energy networks and sources), etc. These worthy, if somewhat confusingly administered and ultimately under-funded causes, were consolidated in four new Community initiatives.

The four surviving Community initiatives are: "Leader" for rural areas, "Urban" for run down metropolitan areas, "Interreg" for regional cross-border cooperation, probably the Union's most effective and best run programme ever, and "Equal", which is to sponsor political and gender correctness wherever for whatever it is worth.

The programming and approval procedures are in principle relatively straightforward. Regions work out development schemes. These wish lists to Santa Claus are then pruned out by the national government, and coordinated multi-annual development plans with regional and national priorities are submitted to the European Commission. This procedure makes sense: let regional and national authorities weed out fashionable duplication and predictable failures. When I was Head of the Commission's Office in Vienna, there was a relentless stream of well intentioned visitors who wished their ancestral castles, abandoned after they were looted and burned by the Red Army back in 1945/1946, could be turned into European convention centres once they were restored with the kind help of EU funds. If a village in the Waldviertel dreamt up a golf course as the key for its future development, within a fortnight all of its neighbours came up with the same idea. The same happened with thermal spas in Upper Styria or ski lifts in Tyrol. Early weeding out helps to reduce future inevitable frustration, be it the rejection by the Brussels Eurocrats, or worse, eventual business failure once the funds have been misspent.

In the second stage, Community funds are negotiated and agreed between the member state and the Commission in a framework agreement. In the third stage the multi-annual operative programmes are consecutively implemented and jointly funded.

As a simplification, development and financing plans comprising own funds, EIB credits and EU funds are jointly elaborated and submitted.

The *prima facie* evidence of regional schemes is not negative. Travelling across Europe you find EU funded motorways on the arid Canary Islands and Andalusia where they could not have created much environmental damage except for flattening a few scorpions. In Germany and Austria you witness plenty of possibly redundant niceties: like bicycle ferries across Friesian channels, educational trails in Thyringian mountain swamps. Nothing wrong with them, but should Germany need to pay 2 Euros into the EU budget to get 1 Euro back after a lot of paperwork for swamp hiking trails?

Unlikely though this seems, the EU regional development programmes with their requirement of sophisticated planning and cost/benefit assessments have led to a new professionalism in the field, in vivid contrast to old style political lobbyism — a regional chieftain pushing his more or less unsound pet projects at the national level. When they have reached and survived the European level most, but surely not all, evident insanity will be weeded out (mostly by pre-screening procedures).

The political importance of regional development is getting more pronounced, notably in the rural field as the CAP's classical product price support schemes appear as increasingly more failed. The main purpose of rural development is to encourage non-agricultural employment in the countryside and to diversify the rural economy. It could well include thermal spas, golf courses and castle restorations, if they made sense in an integrated rural planning document (and hopefully in reality).

The following are favourites for rural development support. Thematic product marketing for regional wines, spirits, beer, cheese, meat, herbs, spices and bio-products. For urban renewal, village restoration, the renovation of local castles, churches, monasteries and other historical landmarks. In the context of soft tourism, the designation of national parks, vacation on farms, water sports, heritage trails, paths for bicycles and horse riding, long distance skiing, walking and hiking are promoted. For investments in industry and services, high tech parks with full infrastructural access and the set-up of new businesses is supported. In the rural economy the processing of food, wood and fibres, rural tourism, electronics and environmental technologies are evergreens in EU promotional schemes, as are waste disposal and waste water treatment as well as the old classics of irrigation and soil melioration (while paying other land to be put out of production), reforestation and rural roads.

In the EU's mountain areas such as the Alps, the Pyrenees, the Massif Central, the Apenines, the Sierra Nevada, the Highlands, etc., some 30 million people face often fairly isolating and tough climatic conditions. EU involvement is called for since most mountain areas are typically underdeveloped ("Objective 1"), otherwise stagnating ("Objective 2"), or disadvantaged ("Leader"). High mountain ranges, like big rivers, have often constituted ethnic and national frontiers in Europe in the past. Economic and infrastructural development then also stopped there.

EU intervention is to overcome these barriers and modernise the local economies (confounded by the natural conservatism of the montagnards). The challenge is hence to square the dilemma to try to preserve traditional lifestyles and the old countryside while attempting to modernise it with public money. In concrete terms this aims to stop the depopulation which threatens to unravel the social fabric, including the abandonment of valleys settled for centuries. But it also needs to take proper care of a fragile Alpine environment which should neither become a museum nor a Disneyland. In the mountains the Commission then supports schemes like lavender farming and marketing in France, hiking trails in the Highlands, drinking water on Madeira, local handicraft centers in Portugal and North Sweden, eco-house constructions in Carinthia, etc.

Ecological subsidies are given to compensate eco-farmers for their income losses. Thus the UK, France, Spain and German states pay premia for extensive grazing, especially in mountain areas, to maintain traditional crop rotation, to preserve rare utility animal races, to keep hedges, waterways, natural habitats and to reduce the input of fertilisers, pesticides and herbicides. In large measure these subsidies are reimbursed by EU funds.

The regional support story is similar for islands and remote coastal areas. They strongly depend on agriculture and fisheries, which are dead-end for most. The challenge is to develop tourism and shipping where people had not yet had this smart idea. The EU's heart seems to bleed with particular intensity for the French overseas departments (Guadeloupe, Martinique, Guyana, Reunion), which unfortunately forgot to declare independence in time, and now — like the equally disfavoured Canary Islands, Azores and Madeira — suffer from extensive sunshine and long distance from the EU mainland, and from high cost production in their low labour cost Carribean or Indian Ocean environment. The proud amount of 7 billion Euros has been spent on these territories during the decade 1989–1999 without of course being able to make much of a difference to their "natural" handicap.

For the European island and coastal economies, most of which enjoy either "Objective 1" or "Objective 2" status, EU support means to support port economies — the classical tasks of stevedoring, transport, distribution, storage and processing —, to promote seaside tourism, not only on the shores of the Mediterranean; and to preserve the fragile coastal ecosystems, which as vital links between land and sea are essential for bio-diversity.

In consequence, the EU funded fishing and shipping museums in Bremerhafen, Urk (Netherlands), and St Nazaire, fleet and port modernisation in Peniche (Portgual), riverside development in Belfast, aquaculture in Greece, a second road bridge between the two main islands of Guadeloupe, modernised ports in Italy, Portugal, Ireland and on Martinique, extended airports in Ajaccio (Corsica) and Lanzarote (Azores), a local train on Ruegen, a Russian transit cargo port in Kokkola (Finland), etc.

Europe's civilisation is inseparably connected with her urban culture, the freedom of the cities and their hard-fought self-governing rights. Well explained by Max Weber, this distinguishes European urban development from the Asian pattern, let alone from American or African agglomerations. Yet with poorly controlled immigration of low skilled masses of people from non-European cultures, many of which are either unable or unwilling to integrate, depending on the state of town planning either parts of inner cities (in Brussels, Marseilles, Liverpool, Berlin) or entire previously working class suburbs (London, Paris, Lyon, Hamburg) risk turning into lawless slums.

The EU's urban programme is poorly placed to combat the root causes of urban degradation which lie in uncontrolled immigration, lacking repatriation, poor urban education and industrial decline, but like in similarly affected US cities it attempts to fight urban blight, stem the flight of the middle classes, the concomitant decline in the tax base and in public services with the usual well intentioned and equally ineffectual revitalisation programmes.

The EU's probably most successful Community initiatives are the successive Interreg programmes. They benefit border regions which in the past suffered from truncated infrastructure and economic development that ended at national borders (some member states purposefully had discriminated against these foreign influenced regions in their national development). Typically affected border regions have set up spontaneous "Euro-regions" to overcome these externally imposed barriers to development. Examples of such Euregios are the Maas/Lower Rhine between Maastricht, Aachen, Limburg and Liege, the Upper Rhine with Bale, Mulhouse and Freiburg which even set up a joint airport, the reunited Tyrol area, other adjacent areas of the Alps and the Pyrenees. Along the Isonzo, where Austria and Italy fought 14 bloody battles during WWI (which inspired a seriously wounded Ernest Hemingway to write his *Farewell to Arms* there), a Euro region now inspires neighbouring Italy and Slovenia to a less poetic joint river clear up scheme. Typical Euro-region activities are regional tourism promotion, cross-border public transport, environmental protection, energy supply and waste water treatment (which in the past was usually sent downstream across the border untreated).

The EU's regional support programmes have grown from 60 billion Euros (1989/1993) to 140 billion Euros (1994/1999) and to 275 billion Euros (2000/2006), including 21 billion Euros of infrastructure bound cohesion funds, and 47 billion Euros of aid for the Eastern accession countries.

Quite naturally the beneficiaries have remained silent while critics were vocal. It is in particular German policy research institutes which claimed the following regarding EU regional funds:

- they created cultures of dependency and destroyed incentives for self-help;
- for "Objective 1" projects, EU contributions at 75% of costs were too high to optimise project selection;
- areas of EU regional support were too large (since 2000 reduced from 50% of the EU's population to 40%);
- support allocations were intransparent and inconsistent;

- administrative efforts with three levels of administration (regional, national, European) were too cumbersome;
- with the economic crisis and budgetary cut backs in the North, co-financing requirement in the "rich" areas were too high;
- the EU's pilot and networking projects served mainly to exchange frustrations at Community procedures and about the Commission's administration.

Some of the criticism has been taken into account in the EU's "Agenda 2000" (i.e., by cutting down the irritatingly wild under-growth of "Community initiatives").

An alternative idea is to distribute EU funds according to a pre-agreed key of regional solidarity, and to leave regions to use the funds allocated to them freely according to their own best knowledge and responsibility. This worked wonderfully (more or less) in the German West. It patently did not work in East Germany. It would have worked in Ireland, which since the 1970s seriously pursued consistently solid macro-economic policies and over decades pushed human resource development. It would have also worked wonders in Wales, Scotland and the Merseyside where the Regional Development Boards are exceptionally competent. In Greece however, where on a per capita basis most EU aid is spent, the decade-long PASOK government of left-populist Premier Andreas Papandreou managed to expand the public service massively with his political retainers and left the financing of public infrastructure to the unloved EU. The only major constraint on fund disbursement in Greece was the incompetence of her administration to draft proper development plans and to fill out the proper claims form in time. With the advent of Costas Simitis as the Greek Prime Minister (1996–2004), administrative professionalism, macro-economic solidity and the effectiveness of regional aid have increased considerably.

The experience of EU pre-accession funds in Eastern European accession countries has shown that many of them appear all too similar to Papandreou-era managers, eager to "absorb" EU funds as quickly and maximally as possible, with everything else, including the ratio-nale of development, treated as merely annoying formalities. It may well be that without proper macro-economic policies and professional administrative structures, structural funds won't work, but we will see more of them in the new member states regardless. It will remain important to resist politically-favoured white elephants and the expansion of unproductive armies of civil servants.

Yet, in spite of all odds, the EU undeniably has its fair share of regional success stories — from Southern Ireland to Eastern Finland — which the new Eastern European members should follow in their own interest. As a temporary support for self-help, EU regional support has its legitimate place. As a permanent cash cow for Spanish, East German and Polish politicians, it will be doomed.

Smoking Chimneys and Shining High Tech: The Trials and Errors of Industrial Policies

Industrial policies have been part and parcel of Europe's economic development since the days of mercantilism with benevolent monarchs promoting local manufacturing and foreign exchange earnings. The sophistication of instruments probably increased, but the principle of public intervention in the market mechanism remained.

The success of Japan's industrial policies in the postwar era lent a new lease of life to Europe's industrial policies in the late 1970s and early 1980s. Then the Belgian banker and industrialist Etienne Viscomte Davignon as a Vice President (1977–1984) was the Commission's influential Commissioner for Industry. Europe's old industries were in deep trouble as the result of the oil crisis of 1974 and 1979 and in view of the onslaught of increasingly competitive, narrowly focused Japanese and other Asian exports. A series of protectionist measures, "voluntary" import restraints, anti-dumping duties, minimum import prices, and public subsidies for gentle restructuring was provided for Europe's sunset industries, ranging from coal and steel to shipbuilding and textiles. The outcome of these policies was predictable. In spite of high costs to consumers and tax-payers the inevitable "adjustment" — restructuring, downsizing and closures — could only be delayed.

"Picking winners", the fashionable past-time during that last summer of industrial policies, did not fare much better, regardless of whether it was undertaken at the European or at the national level. Germany, for instance, spent most of her public R&D funds on space and on nuclear technologies. However, Germany (like some other EU countries) for reasons of her own has since opted out of nuclear energy and is not known as a major outer space operator either.

The failure of protectionist industrial policies was gradually recognised, a reality check aided in no small measure by the lengthy reign of Mrs Thatcher. Her government, after a delay of a few years, actually began to practise the liberal beliefs, which all British government profess loudly and relentlessly ever since.

In coincidence, the interventionist camp traditionally located in the Romanic South turned silent, since also in Paris, the retired cheerleader of protectionism, "*ultraliberalisme*" and economic modernity became *le dernier cri* of the political class. When the liberal Martin Bangemann, a mercurial former Economics Minister of Germany, became Commissioner for Industry in 1989, the Commission finally also formally phased out its old style industrial policies. The new focus was to improve the overall business environment "horizontally" across the board.

In a celebrated report on competitiveness in 1997, Bangemann took a long hard look at the reasons of lower productivity, job creation, profitability and innovation of Europe's industry which then lagged far behind the US and Japan. Rates for R&D were lower. Costs for services, like communication, transport and financing, as well as for utilities (energy, water) were higher. In addition, the taxation of labour, already high enough, increased relentlessly. Since the creation of the internal market, the structural changes of the world economy had accelerated. Within a decade, for many sectors such as cars, chemicals, pharmaceuticals, telecom, banking, etc., the decisive scene had moved from the "internal" EU market to the global market place. Globalisation meant ever faster and more intensive flows of worldwide trade, capital and information. Since 1950 world trade had grown by 6.3% annually while production had only increased by 4% per year. Investment followed trade. In 1985 total foreign direct investment flows stood at US$50 billion per annum. By 1997 they had multiplied to US$382 billion p.a. Services were similarly globalised. International payments for fees and royalties grew from US$10 billion (1983) to US$50 billion (1997) in hardly more than one decade.

With ever-quickening changes in ownership, economic focus and regional orientation of the major companies, it has become difficult to measure regional or national competitiveness.

Yet it remains obvious that Europe's specific competitiveness lies in high value added products. They are either traditional products using technical know-how, cultural wealth and workers' well trained competence to produce top quality textiles, apparel, furnishings, processed quality foods and drinks, sports goods, crafts as well as cultural tourism, or they are technically sophisticated R&D intensive products like machine tools, specialist machinery, cars, airplanes, pharmaceuticals, special chemicals, etc. Europe remains relatively weak in the information technologies and electronics industries (and thus escaped relatively unscathed once the dot-com and telecom bubbles burst in 2001).

On average, EU firms invested less in equipment and infrastructure, including ICT, than US or Japanese companies. Courtesy of Pentagon and NASA contracts, US R&D investment is far higher. US universities and federal research institutes naturally cooperate with industry to achieve practical research implementation. The Japanese government as an explicit industrial policy encourages high tech consortia between industrial competitors and research institutes. In the EU, however, national procurement is done with little encouragement of R&D. As a result, the US share in world patents — aided by swift and cheap patent facilities in the US — as well as income from royalties and related intellectual property fees is growing quickly. Even in the cultural sector, in which audiovisual products on the EU market thanks to relentless French lobbying enjoyed protection due to their "cultural specificity", the global EU market share on audio visual products went down from 19% (1988) to 10% one decade later, while the US share grew correspondingly even stronger from 56% to 78%.

All in all the diagnosis points to a lack of entrepreneurial spirit in the EU. Venture capital is available at the same order of magnitude like in the US (US$10 billion), but little is invested in high tech sectors like IT or biotechnology.

Recognisant of the fact that by far most employment in Europe is generated and maintained by small and medium-sized enterprises

(SMEs), the Commission has since long been fond of declaring her special love and attention to this sector of business which, in difference to the captains of big industry and finance, has always been poorly represented in Brussels. In 2001 the Commission announced its new SME and enterprise policy. While laudably doing away with past ineffectual subsidisation schemes, the main trust now is to go for "education for entrepreneurial risk taking" from early schooling to university, employing media campaigns and award giving (it is always particularly touching to see politicians and bureaucrats with safe monthly salaries to exhort the virtues of uncertain returns). Through public guarantee schemes, access to seed capital should be facilitated for budding entrepreneurs. Equal access to R&D is to be improved: through cooperation between universities and SME research centres, a more affordable EU-wide patent protection (which should trigger reforms in the operations of the European Patent Office in Munich) and a more practical orientation of EU funded research. The report does not fail to note vast differences in attitudes towards research spending — both public and private — among EU member states. Notably in Sweden and Finland more than 3% of GDP are spent on R&D. If all EU member states did similarly, the EU would not face problems in high tech competitiveness. But notably the rest spends much less, especially along the sunny shores of the Mediterranean where less than 1% of GDP are invested in R&D. Finally the Commission asks for a better quality of public administration and more business friendly support services, like, for instance, comprehensive "one stop shops" located at chambers of commerce, and for simplified company registrations. For some decades already the Commission is supporting the set-up and operations of some 270 Euro Info Centres (EIC) at host institutions, located in chambers of commerce and in regional investment and public business advisory societies. Annual support for each EIC stands at 25,000 Euros p.a. only. These worthy institutions handle inquiries regarding internal market legislation, public procurement tenders and business opportunities in Eastern Europe notably for the benefit of SMEs, as larger businesses are usually better equipped to source such information in-house.

Other *desiderata* of a more effective horizontal EU industrial policy are enumerated as initiatives for life-long learning for human capital development, effective European standardisation (perhaps starting with electrical plugs), a European company statute, harmonised national tax systems (even though one could fairly argue that downward competition in corporate and labour taxation could be quite healthy for business revival) and liberalised utilities — notably for the supply of electricity, gas, telecom and public transport — which is well on its way in most member states, even in France. Finally, EU initiatives to establish multilateral vigilance as regards R&D subsidies by external trading partners is called for, in order to develop a new WTO discipline in competition law and to assure an international level playing field for EU operators.

All in all, these down-scaled industrial policies appear by and large as reasonable, business and employment oriented and in line with the subsidiarity principle — as implementation is largely left to member states and their regional public and statutory authorities. The Union has clearly learnt its lessons of costly interventionist industrial policies in the past. Unfortunately the same cannot be said about some member states that continue to protect national champions, be they Fiat, Air Iberia, the Electricité de France (EDF), or the German savings and *landesbanks*, at high economic costs.

The Rise and Fall of the Commission's Competition Ayatollahs

Fair competition — or "level playing field" in US parlance — is clearly essential in any free trade arrangement, customs union and even more so in a common internal market. Already the Treaties of Rome, with wise foresight, prohibited any abuse of monopolistic positions and cartels, subjected public enterprises to competition rules, and permitted public subsidies only if they had been notified to the Commission and approved as not distorting competition. The objective was to permit the smooth operation of markets, to enhance consumer choice and to reduce prices. After 17 years of Council deliberations, in 1990 merger control provisions were also added to the arsenal of the EU's trust busters. In 2002, however, a series of defeats in the European Court of Justice (ECJ), which threw out several of the Commission's anti-merger decisions on account of their sloppy economics, made a reform of the system and its procedures imperative.

Controversy is not new to the Commission's competition policy. National and regional politicians eager to sponsor national champions and to subsidise all sorts of funny industries suitably defined as "strategic", ranging from road haulage to coal mining, from car manufacture to pig fattening, are regularly and publicly annoyed when the Commission refuses their wasteful and distorted disbursement of taxpayers' money. The motherland of competition law, Germany, whose Commissioner Hans von der Groeben had set the EU's competition policy on track in the 1960s, is by far the worst and unrepentant subsidisation sinner.

When looking after cartel and other corporate arrangements, the Commission needs to distinguish between (prohibited) horizontal deals between competitors and (legitimate) vertical contracts upstream and downstream, that is, with suppliers or distributing agents. Illegal horizontal provisions are arrangement regarding prices, rebates, on production decisions, market sharing, the discrimination of business partners and boycotts. Common purchasing arrangements are permissible among small operators, which may organise themselves as cooperatives. In general a *de minimis* rule applies: the Commission does not bother about companies with less than 5% market share or with a turnover of less than 200 million Euros.

Often the cartel busters operate with James Bond-like methods, rely on denunciations by competitors and promise immunity to collaborating enterprises who expose the deals cooked up on Swiss golf courses or on Mediterranean yachts. Things were easier in a celebrated case where eight Austrian banks, during 1994/1996, met as the "Lombard Club" in the exclusive Hotel Bristol in Vienna. In some 300 meetings they openly fixed, in time-honoured fashion, interest rates and commissions until they were publicly exposed by a competition-minded politician called Jörg Haider. In 2002 the banks of the Lombard Club were fined 124 million Euros by the Commission.

German car manufacturers were fined in 1998 in a similar case of abuse. They were found to have instructed their Italian traders during 1993/1995 not to sell cars to German and Austrian customers, as car retail prices were higher in Germany and Austria than in Italy. This author had his five minutes of fame when, to his surprise, speaking in Vienna at a press conference on Eurobarometer survey results, he was suddenly asked whether he thought this practice was compatible with EU law. He declared that it appeared to him that it was not and called on those concerned to come forward with evidence of discrimination suffered to be forwarded to and examined by the Commission's competition authorities. This appeal was aired in the ORF national television's evening news. Soon a basketful of testimonials, including photographs of written signs in South Tyrolian shop windows stating "We don't sell to Austrians and Germans" (for fear of losing their exclusive dealer's license) were received and duly forwarded. Volkswagen alone was fined 102 million Euros, which in view of this author justifies his moderate salary for the rest of his professional life.

The abuse of market dominance is similarly prohibited. Note that is not market domination *per se* which is illegal, but its misuse in charging overly high prices, in controlling suppliers or distributors, and forcing them to accept unusual conditions, or to limit production, distribution or technical development to the detriment of consumers. In a typical case the Commission in 2002 threatened Deutsche Post with a 570 million Euros fine as it had illegally (and fairly flagrantly) used its mail monopoly to overcharge consumers to subsidise its commercial parcel division against private competitors. In general it is assumed that a market share of 40% and above can enable these practices.

Since 1990, cross-national mergers or the acquisition of a controlling influence in a competing enterprise are also being investigated. The threshold to warrant an examination on the two involved companies stands at a combined turnover of at least 250 million Euros within the EU, or globally at 5 billion Euros. The Commission must make its decision public within a tight deadline of one month after notification. In 90% of cases, they are cleared as unproblematic. Less than 1% (i.e., 18 out of 2000 cases examined during the period 1990–2002) are prohibited, resulting in the annulment of the merger. The rest was accepted under certain conditions (like disinvesting from some business lines or national markets in which monopoly situations could arise). In the early 1990s the Commission had to examine some 50 cases per year, but in the merger mania of the late 1990s the caseload increased sevenfold until 2001. Only since 2002 with the growing — probably only temporary — realisation among business leaders that most cross-border mergers result in failures did the workload begin to recede.

Then in the summer of 2002 the unthinkable happened. The Court of First Instance (CFI) of the European Court of Justice smashed the Commission's 100% victory series in competition cases and spectacularly threw out three of the Commission's anti-merger decisions. First the CFI declared the merger prohibition between the British tour operations, Air Tours and First Choice, of 1999 to be null and void. The judges noted factual errors and the lack of economic logic in the Commission's reasoning. It had based its ban on the theoretical assumption that the major UK operators as a result of the merger would exercise "collective dominance" (i.e., an oligopoly) in the UK tour travel economy. In the Court's view, however, there must be concrete evidence of collusion and the prevention of new market entrants, not just the existence of an oligopolistic structure.

A few months later the ECJ threw out the Commission's merger prohibition of the two large French electrical manufacturers, Schneider Electric and Legrand, again citing mistakes, gaps and contradictions in the Commission's economic analysis of the likely effects of the resulting 15 billion Euros electronics giant. Later the blocked merger between Tetra Laval, a packaging product and Sidel, a machinery maker, was similarly allowed. Other victims of blocked mergers, like General Electric's intended takeover of Honeywell, have lined up their complaints with the Court in Luxembourg.

Equally, its mandatory controls of public subsidies regularly bring the Commission into political hot water. Member states are obliged to notify all their public subsidies paid out to economic operators, be they farmers, fishermen, coal miners, high tech boys, the shipping industry or the railways.

Admissible is public sector support for specific social, regional and common interest purposes as well as rehabilitation from natural disasters. In crisis sectors support for capacity cuts and restructuring is considered legitimate. Not permissible are subsidies for ongoing operations without restructuring. The Commission has to examine whether the notified subsidy primarily serves the declared laudable purposes or whether in reality it rather distorts competition or restricts trade. In the latter case the support is declared illegal, and the company, most famously Volkswagen in the case of its new (capacity increasing) car plant in Saxony, had to reimburse the public subsidy to the (curiously) angry public authorities which thus felt their favourite economic policy tool endangered. In the summer of 2002 again an unholy alliance of member states emerged which united against the Commission's competition people to push for senseless tax breaks for truck fuel (Netherlands, France, Italy), subsidies for loss-making airlines

(Greece: Olympic) or the coal industry (Germany). The Commission's undiplomatic toughness (the author has witnessed an anti-subsidy investigation into a dying bus maker in the beautiful, but crisis-hit town of Steyr in Upper Austria back in 1994, and did not like it at all), however brought member states' corporate subsidisation down from 104 billion Euros (1996) to 80 billion Euros in 1999. These necessarily unpopular policy reduces the waste of taxpayers' money, of unfair competition and national rivalries which such public prop-ups inevitably entail among other concerned member states. Hence they are and remain a clear must.

Competition commissioners like Peter Sutherland, Sir Leon Brittan, Karel Van Miert, and Mario Monti have typically been flamboyant and well regarded characters who enjoyed the intellectual rigour and economic power of their brief. Given the Commission's case handler method, some of their underlings have since appeared as poorly supervised and arrogant, typically known in the trade as ayatollahs with their indigestible mixture of hybris and little controlled discretionary powers.

Since their beginnings in 1962, with hundreds of Commission and ECJ decisions, a consistent and detailed legal and procedural framework has developed. Sometimes praised for its speed, efficiency and simplicity, at the same time the Commission being prosecutor, judge and jury for the same case is seen as arbitrary and intransparent. Upon hearing of a complaint (typically by a competitor) or being notified officially, the Commission then organises a hearing with the parties concerned and decides on its own, while, for instance, in the US the anti-trust authorities must seek a court injunction to block a merger. UNICE, the EU's industry lobby, has criticised this decisive difference as lack of due process and of insufficient checks and balances, for instance, in the field of merger controls. In response, Commissioner Mario Monti announced improved merger control assessments, including an internal peer review of the case handlers' findings and conclusions and the recruitment of an eminent "chief economist" to brush up his staff's knowledge of contemporary industrial economics. These reforms, however, remain a far cry from a straightforward judicial review *ab initio*. The fact that the Commission's decisions have to be approved by the college of all Commissioners also opens it to the charge of undue political influence in decision-making. A neater solution would be an independent European competition authority which submits its recommendation for action to a proper and open court procedure for a legal decision.

Liberalisation policies are not the unique preserve of the Commission's competition directorate general. The telecom sector offers an instructive example. The telecom industry, formerly a stagnant overpriced public monopoly, was liberalised step-by-step during 1988–1998:

- first, the supply of terminal equipment;
- second, value added services and data communications;
- third, satellite sources and equipment;
- fourth, cable TV and other networks, mobile phones;
- fifth, all infrastructure and voice telephone services.

All networks were made open to all users and all service providers. At the same time the principle of "universal service" applies: every operator has to guarantee that every user has access to high quality basic service at an affordable price. The frequent notion of long distance callers subsidising local calls is a thing of the past. A monitoring agency which is independent from the public operator and the Ministry of Posts and Telecommunications has to be set up in each member state.

EU-wide deregulation has clearly given a boost to the telecom industries, even in a post bubble perspective. It helped to maximise consumer choice: people can choose freely the provider who best suits their requirements in terms of charges and the range of services offered. This has helped Europe to keep up with the ongoing IT revolution: it made teleworking, long distance learning, IT health networks, database consultation and mass Internet use and e-mail correspondence possible within less than a decade.

Telecoms, postal and financial services are surely success stories of EU-wide liberalisation which brought lower prices, increased productivity and a better quality of service (and hence higher demand and more jobs). Yet a few important difficulties remain. A "Community patent", essential for more effective intellectual property protection, is still blocked in the Council due to arguments over languages. Simplified rules on public procurement (which account for 15% of GDP) remain in limbo. On utilities, France insists on public control of gas and electricity supplies, notably of the Electricite de France (EDF), which had happily used other member states' liberalisation to buy itself, with well protected and cheap nuclear profits, into their systems.

On the Road, at Sea and in the Air: The Common Transport Policy

It was the European Court of Justice which, back in 1985, put the common transport policy on track. Already the Treaties of Rome had postulated a common policy, but for the next 28 years nothing happened. Member states and their bureaucrats happily tended their highly protected over-regulated national patches and at Council meetings cheerfully agreed to disagree. The Court, reacting to a complaint brought by the EP, found inaction not good enough and condemned the Council to remove all national discrimination of operators. The judgement came in good time for the internal market. Transportation after all is an essential factor of production. The more cost effectively it performs, the better for an EU-wide division of labour within well organised economies of scale.

The Court's wake-up call worked. Right in time for the single market, by 1993 all quantitative restrictions were abolished for EU operators. Prior to that, only the River Rhine as Europe's most important international inland waterway had been the continent's unrestricted transport channel. Now "cabotage" was made possible: operators can pick up freight on return trips from anywhere within the EU, thus reducing the useless and costly empty return trips of the past. The rapid increase of EU transport licences, for the award of which only professional reliability and qualification counts, equally contributes to a better load factor. For fair competition in a functioning liberalised internal market in the traditionally heavily regulated transport sector, a series of complicated conditions had to be fulfilled: technical standards as regards weight (like the 40 ton truck), safety, noise and toxic emission levels, and their control had been made compatible or harmonised.

Sometimes this proved physically impossible. Most British road bridges are too weak for heavy lorry weights. The working hours of drivers operating across the continent had to be properly regulated and effectively controlled, given the security implications of tired drivers in this rough and highly competitive sector. Finally, widely differing national taxes on vehicles, diesel fuel and road use had to be gradually brought into line. Fuel duties in low tax Spain, Luxembourg and Greece were subsequently raised to non-distortive minima.

Common vehicle standards are to follow environmental imperatives, given the increase of car use and its inevitable nefarious environmental consequences. The reduction of toxic emissions and waste generated per car is hoped to mitigate somewhat the overall effect. With EU regulations currently in force, between 2000 and 2005 the emissions of nitrogen oxides (NO_x), benzene, carbon monoxide and sulphur will gradually be reduced by up to 40% per car. CO_2 emission reductions are subject to a fairly inconsequential "voluntary agreement" with the car industry, covering their entire output as a vehicle fleet: easy for small car makers like Fiat to reach, very difficult for gas guzzling luxury and off road car makers (who then might add a tiny "smart" car to their range to reach the objective statistically).

Car recycling is a similarly thorny issue. So far only 75% of the metal used is actually recycled. In some member states, notably in the sunny South, up to 7% of old vehicles are simply dumped to embellish the landscape in varying states of decay (Spaniards and Greeks seem to relish such sights, as do most Eastern Europeans for unfathomable reasons). The elimination of heavy metals and hazardous materials is of particular importance. A Commission draft had provided for its costs to be borne by manufacturers, and had set recycling objectives of 80% by 2005 and 85% by 2015. This draft was shamelessly vetoed by the "Green" German Minister of the Environment, Jürgen Trittin, a former Trotskyte, after heavy industry lobbying with Chancellor Schröder.

There is no doubt that railways are indefinitely more environmental-friendly: they consume less space, use less energy and provide less emissions and more safety per unit travelled. During the period 1970–1990, the EU share of rail cargo had halved from 30% to 16%. Road transport increased from 55% to 74%. Yet the railways' "modal split", their market share compared to road transport of goods and people, continues to worsen further.

In 1991 the EU decided to modernise the organisation of the railways. Rolling stock operations and rail infrastructure were to be separated with their own management structures. Their financial situation was improved by clearing out old debt mountains (suitably left with public railways as conveniently half-hidden public sector debt). Railway nets were to be opened to other EU operators. To enhance their commercial orientation, railway societies were freed to set their own pricing policies, with welfare services being made explicit by the specific contractual allocation of public subsidies (e.g., for school children, youngsters, old folks, etc.). Increasingly, standards for rolling stock (locomotives and carriages), signalling, track width and train safety are made compatible EU-wide, so as to enable urgently needed inter-operability. Combined road/rail transport — rail would cover long distances, and road the short distance delivery at each end — is particularly promoted by financing rolling stock and EU-wide rail/road terminals for the transfer of containers.

This is in response to changed realities of the transportation business. Manufacturing is increasingly done on green sites, outside towns, inaccessible to rail networks. Production methods have shifted away from the bulk production of heavy industry towards smaller and more urgent batches. For personal transport the emerging service economy implied more business travel. Higher disposable incomes translated into more car ownership, more leisure travel and more dispersed housing, all bad news for mass transportation systems.

On world shipping the EU also subscribes to a liberal WTO-oriented approach. Within the EU national cabotage has been possible since 1999 (for the Greek islands, this happens for other EU operators in 2004). EU waters are open to all flags, except for those countries which limit access to their markets (safeguards then apply). Given the toughness of global, often substandard competition, in order to facilitate fair trade anti-dumping rules ("corrective measures"), EU guidelines on state aid apply against the flagging out to flags of convenience, which limit granting certain national tax incentives, training support and social payment relief to shipping companies.

There was an unending series of maritime disasters involving substandard oil tankers — most notorious until 2002 was the "Erika" which in December 1999 was stranded in the Bay of Biscay and polluted 400 km of coastline with horrendous consequences for the environment, wildlife and the fishing and tourism sectors. The rust bowl was found to have an Italian owner, sailed under the Maltese flag, carried French oil, was of obsolete Japanese design and had an overcharged Indian captain. In November 2002 the 26 year old, single hull "Prestige" sank with 70,000 tons of heavy oil off the Atlantic coast, polluting the Spanish shoreline. It was registered in the Bahamas by a Liberian company headquartered in Athens. Its cargo was owned by a Russian company registered in Switzerland. According to Commission Vice President Loyola de Palacio (1999–2004), the EU needs more effective controls of the sea-worthiness of ships, and stricter port controls for high risk ships in particular. Like in the US, single hull oil carriers should be prohibited from travelling to EU harbours. On top of this, liabilities for oil pollution should be increased, safe unloading of bulk carriers improved and waste reception areas in harbours created or expanded. These public wishes now need to be translated into legislative action.

In the aviation sector, the Commission's approach similarly envisages a liberalised market and improved safety and reduced noise and emissions, which in the air are particularly noxious to the ozone layer and contributing to the greenhouse effect. On the ground the waste of de-icing chemicals and oil spills are problematic.

The Commission published a celebrated white paper on "sustainable mobility" in 1992. If nothing was done, it predicted an increase in road cargo transport by 42% (during 1990–2010), of rail cargo by +33%, of individual car use by +45%, and of air traffic by +74%. Responsible were increased commuter traffic, more complex industrial processes with Japanese style "just-in-time" (*Kanban*) deliveries and more personal affluence. Paradoxically the improved mobility, if unchecked, would then threaten sustainable mobility through bottlenecks in the infrastructure, incompatible national networks, reduced urban and environmental quality of life and increased safety risks. Every year 60,000 people get killed on EU roads (the equivalent of total US losses in the Vietnam War) and 1.5 million people are injured.

Road transport accounts for 75% of all EU travel. Yet it is responsible for 90% of accidents, congestion, air and noise pollution. Road transport also consumes 30% of all EU primary energy. About 84% of energy use for transport goes for car and truck use and 11% for aviation. A total of 1.3% of the EU's total surface is already paved for car use (roads and parking lots), only 0.03% is used for railways. The white paper logically recommends the transfer of these external costs to the users through higher road tolls, fuel duties, vehicle taxes and emission fees, depending on emission levels per car type. Amongst positive incentives for more sustainable transport, the paper lists improved public transport systems, combined transport (with door to door delivery), improved regional and urban planning, car free zones, tougher safety standards notably for transports of dangerous goods, and the promotion of research for cleaner cars and fuels (the Commission programmes "Save", "Joule" and "Thermie"). Some of the proposed policy measures have since been adopted, like toughened emission standards for all vehicle types, the introduction of cabotage and the reorganisation of railway operations.

Policy *desiderata* like improved mass transportation systems and urban planning, however, remain clearly in the realm of local and regional authorities (which is where they rightly belong).

In order to link national networks (and to close the persistent gaps and bottlenecks between them), and to create genuine European transcontinental transport corridors also reaching the peripheries, the Commission since 1990 has developed its Trans-European Networks (TEN) initiative. It was enshrined as a Community competence in the Treaty of Maastricht (1993) and covered not only transport networks but also telecom, electricity and gas grids. The objective was to create the physical infrastructure to allow all regions, including those in the periphery, to participate fully in the blossoming single internal market.

Funds allocated for transportation networks were to be split roughly 50:50 between road (notably for motorways to the periphery) and rail (mostly for high speed trains and rail cargo traffic, e.g., across the Alps). The high speed Northern axis of London-Paris-Brussels-Cologne has already been realised. *Inter alia*, it shortened the important psychological distance between London and Paris to less than three hours. A Southern axis of Seville-Madrid-Barcelona-Turin-Venice is being constructed. Ultimately a dense network of a dozen corridors criss-crossing the whole of Europe up to Moscow, St Petersburg, Kiev and Ankara is being planned, allowing effective and safer competition to road and air traffic. The role of the Commission is typically limited to issuing guidelines, to defining projects as of European interest, to financing feasibility studies and, in complementarity to member states, providing credit guarantees and interest rate subsidies. The main finance as a rule must come from national public or private sources (given the volumes involved and long term nature of the investments most suitably in conjunction).

The Commission has only seed money to spend in the North. But it has considerably more leverage in the Southern cohesion countries and in Ireland, where generous cohesion fund money can be tapped, and in Eastern Europe where the EU's pre-accession regional funds (ISPA) are used, supplemented by EIB and EBRD credits. Friends of the Earth criticised that this often happened with horrifying consequences for important wildlife areas as motorways were bulldozed through Mediterranean natural parks, forests and wetlands. In the meantime, the same is happening in Eastern Europe with, e.g., the Via Baltica motorway cutting through primeval Masurian forests and wetlands in North East Poland.

The universal contradiction between motorised transportation and environmental protection has not been resolved at the European level either. One is hence well advised not to confuse declarations of environmental intent with the road building reality.

Dwindling Resources and Mounting Policies: The Energy Policy

Energy as a subject of EU policy suffers the fate of human primary needs: once satisfied people gladly lose interest, all the more so if their object of erstwhile concern turns out to be overly complicated and subject to an inordinate amount of misinformation.

With conservationist objectives energy should constitute a classic case for a European policy competence, and so it had been (partially) foreseen by the founding fathers, who in their profound (but unfortunately only partial) foresight set out from the beginning two sources, coal and nuclear, as objects for common European policies.

For coal, the ECSC Treaty of 1952 established non-discriminatory access to resources for the next 50 years until 2002 (when no one cared any longer about these uncompetitive resources). The venerable treaty, which was allowed to lapse upon expiry, also imposed a discipline on coal subsidies. Although dear to the heart of the German government, which wished to support the employment of the mostly Turkish miners in the Ruhr area by forcing German power plants to buy overpriced coal, finally in 1998 a gradual phasing out of this most un-economical, un-environmental and un-conservationist of all useless subsidies was agreed upon.

The Euratom Treaty of 1957 was based on the then fashionable development of a seemingly limitless and safe new source of energy. It provided for common European research initiatives on nuclear safety and a supply agency to negotiate uranium and plutonium deliveries from third countries.

In spite of this promising start, for the next 50 years EU energy policies remained a curious patchwork of policy elements derived from these two treaties and from internal market, competition, transport, environment and research policies. Distinct national energy interests and political passions proved too strong.

Italy, Ireland and Denmark have no national energy resources whatsoever. The UK and the Netherlands, in contrast, are self-sufficient, courtesy of Yorkshire coal and North Sea oil, and of Groningen Gas (discovered in 1959) respectively. For everybody else there remains a strong import dependency.

The oil crises of 1974 and 1979 caught EU member states with their pants pretty much down and scrambling for supplies. In consequence, a series of energy saving programmes ("Thermie", "Save") were launched by the Commission, which aimed at breaking the link between economic growth and increased demand for energy, notably for fossil fuels.

North Sea oil production will decline after 2010 and be entirely exhausted by 2025 (by that time Norway will be likely to join the EU). Then the Dutch gas fields are likely to run dry as well. The EU has 200 years of solid fuel supply (coal). But it is often of mixed quality and increasingly difficult to extract. Compared to open strip mining in North America, Australia and South Africa, EU coal remains uncompetitive. Portugal, Belgium and France will cease production by 2005. Germany and Spain will continue their gradual decline. The same also applies to Polish and Czech coal mining. Serious efforts to become competitive are only undertaken in the UK. For the others, the sad objective of continued mining is just to maintain minimum operations in order to preserve equipment and the technology of clean coal mining for future generations. While consumption keeps growing, nuclear and coal being phased out, and North Sea oil and Dutch gas nearing exhaustion, the EU's long term energy future looks pretty bleak. The share of renewables is impressive in only a few member states, like Sweden (29%), Austria (23%) and Finland (22%). But being mostly hydro-electrical, due to limits of nature and geography, an expansion is only marginally possible. EU programmes ("Altener") to support R&D on wind turbines, bio-mass, solar, hydro and wave energy have not yielded any significant breakthrough.

A Commission white paper on energy security published in 2000 rightly starts from the premise that the EU will not be able to reduce her energy dependency. EU industry has realised significant savings, but households (with more appliances and using larger units), services and the transport sector continue to increase consumption. From 1985 to 1998 the number of passenger cars has grown from 132 million to 189 million in the EU. Air traffic grew exponentially until September 11, 2001. As policies to control consumption had failed, it was more imperative to reduce the risks of dependence. By 2025 the EU energy import dependency would increase from 50% (2000) to 70%. Already in 1999, a year of moderate oil prices, the EU faced an import bill of 240 billion Euros (representing 1.2% of GDP), 40% of which went to natural gas from Russia, and 45% to oil from the Middle East. The needs of households and transportation (as well as electricity producers) depend especially on imported sources.

EU energy sources

	2000	2030
Oil	41%	38%
Gas	22%	29%
Coal	16%	19%
Nuclear	15%	6%
Renewables	6%	8%

Hence the diversification of sources of supply — by products and by areas of origin — is essential to minimise risks. Oil stocks are proposed to be increased from 90 days of consumption to 120 days, and new gas stocks in underground facilities to be created, and, like the US strategic reserve, managed jointly by the Union so as to permit more effective negotiations with OPEC.

With due caution the Commission also advocates a "reflection" on nuclear energy (as most member states facing popular pressure are about to opt out), which in France still produces 80%, in

Belgium 55%, in Sweden 40%, and in the UK, Spain, Germany and Finland up to 30% of electricity. Most of Euratom research funds continue to go into nuclear safety and protection from radiation. The accession of the new East European members with their Soviet designed nuclear power stations raised new fears. Medium term closures were negotiated with Lithuania (Ignalina), Bulgaria (Kosludj) and Slovakia (Bohunice). But other plants in the Czech Republic (Temelin), Hungary (Pecs) and Slovakia (Krsko) also pose potential risks. EBRD funds were made available to modernise and upgrade the security of these reactors (a fact which triggered public hysteria in nuclear free Austria which happens to be surrounded by these plants).

The Commission in 2002 hence proposed to enact a Community-wide concept for reactor safety and reliable nuclear waste disposal in time for Eastern accession. This would make common rules on nuclear safety compulsory for all member states. They are compatible with the rules of the UN's International Atomic Energy Agency (IAEA), covering rules for regular inspection, compliance and eventual closure (including common funds for this purpose). Equally, member states will be compelled to provide sufficient underground storage for radioactive wastes by 2008. Currently much is still kept in unsafe temporary storage above ground.

In the meantime the EU tried to improve the operations of the Union's originally very disparate energy market, in which most national operators were structured as fairly costly public monopolies.

In order to enhance competition and market access, energy suppliers were forced to "unbundle", meaning to create separate societies for production, transportation and distribution. Pricing was made transparent to consumers. Third parties were given access to energy grids and pipelines, thus allowing large industrial customers to select their own suppliers (in Denmark and Sweden, this is also possible for individual households). As part of the Trans-European Network (TEN) initiative the interconnection of hitherto isolated national electricity networks was funded — like between Italy and Greece (1997) and between the UK and Ireland (1998). National gas pipelines were connected, and new links created, e.g., running from mainland Italy to Sardinia and Corsica.

Internationally the Energy Charter Treaty, to which 50 countries plus the European Commission had signed up in 1990, was supportive. They all pledged to liberalise energy markets, to free transit for energy products and materials, and to work together for safer supplies and increased efficiency of production, use and transportation, and to encourage investments in the energy sector.

Environmental NGO criticism was not far away: they felt that a more competitive energy market would result in fewer incentives for energy savings, as privatised utilities would wish to increase sales and energy volumes. Already in response to the international conventions on climatic change (Rio and Kyoto), the Commission had proposed the introduction of taxes on energy use, including on hitherto tax-exempt aviation fuel, and to cut taxation of labour correspondingly. So far only four (Denmark, Finland, Sweden and the Netherlands) out of then 15 member states have declared themselves in favour. The eco-friendly PR noises of the rest have obviously not been worth the recycled paper they were printed on.

It may be recalled that the Rio conference of 1992 had asked for CO_2 emissions, which cause 60% of greenhouse problems, to be stabilised at 1990 levels by 2000. The Kyoto convention of 1997 called for the output of the six greenhouse gases [CO_2, methane (CH_4), halocarbons and nitrous oxide (N_2O)] to be cut by 2008/2012 by −8% below their 1990 levels. With 6% of the world population and causing 15% of world energy consumption, the EU's responsibility in using effective policy and taxation instruments is clearly called for.

Closer to home, environmental impact assessments since 1988 have to be undertaken by developers of large energy facilities (refineries, thermal and nuclear power stations, waste deposits, large dams, pipelines, wind farms, deep drillings, open cast mines, etc.) and be submitted to public authorities prior to permit approval.

In view of the subsidiarity principle, it seems clear that the Union should be in effective charge of overall strategy, including deregulation and taxation given the long term convergence of energy interest among member states. Urgently needed R&D and vast savings potentials leave sufficient room for member states and their regions to improve their competitiveness with cost savings and sustainable energy development in a wonderfully compatible European division of labour.

Blue Skies and Yellow Rivers: The Environmental Policies

The protection of Europe's environment aptly illustrates the case for multiple and complementary interventions by different levels of actors. In many problem areas of cross border pollution and risks, EU policies play a significant role: they concern emissions into the air (affecting forests up to the ozone layer), emissions affecting water quality (both ground water and surface waters — rivers and then oceans), solid waste, noise and radiation risks. The preservation of natural habitats and the protection of endangered indigenous species similarly have a continental European dimension.

At the same time, there is sufficient room for local initiative (e.g., for emission reduction, better public transportation, noise reduction or habitat preservation), national measures (for stricter measures or thorough implementation) and for agreements at global level (like the CITES restrictions on trade in endangered species, and the Rio and Kyoto protocols at CO_2 and greenhouse gas reductions).

A series of valid arguments can be made for effective environmental policies: the ethical argument (nature has intrinsic value and should be protected), which had led to the EU's habitat directive and the directive to protect migratory birds (not to be eaten by Italians and the Maltese); the welfare argument (public health is endangered through bad air, polluted food and water, and future generations — "intergenerational equity" — are hurt through a damaged ozone layer, depleted or poisoned ground water), and economic arguments (internalisation of costs: polluter pays principle; prevention at source which is more effective than later clean ups; level playing field for all operators: no free rides; interest to sell environmental technologies, etc.).

Already, in Maastricht (1992), sustainable development had been declared an objective of the Union. In Amsterdam (1997), QMV was introduced in a complicated co-decision procedure with the EP. This helped to overcome the regular opposition by the UK and Spain. The European Parliament in any event has a strong environmental-friendly record (except of course when MEPs travel by air).

Next to sector specific regulations (water, air, noise, waste management, habitat) and to general ("horizontal") environmental rules, the objective is to integrate environmental policies into all other EU policies (agriculture, regional development, fisheries, energy, transportation, development aid), with contradictions which are not always easy to reconcile.

In some EU-funded programmes the environmental benefits are fairly clear-cut: the Northern shores of the Mediterranean (and visiting tourists) have benefited visibly and orifactorily from waste water treatment plants constructed, expanded and modernised all along the coast. The EU-funded environmental schemes in the accession countries will have the same effect on the Baltic Sea, which as a relatively flat and low current "interior" sea is highly at risk due to effluents carried by rivers through Poland, Russia and the Baltics. In research, there is a strong focus on renewable energy sources, like photovoltaic cells and wind energy.

Yet in the EU environmental policy record there is clearly light and shadow. Among ODA schemes plenty of ecological projects are listed, but also the construction of motorways across primeval jungle (across Gabon, for instance). Once a road is built across a jungle, as any school child and even the World Bank by now knows, settlers will follow with slash and burn methods and the jungle and its bio-diversity gone in less than a decade. Within the EU, attempts with the "Natura 2000" scheme are made to expand and link the 10,000 existing nature parks as much as possible. Yet at the same time, this does not prevent EU from funding nationally planned motorways to cut through bird sanctuaries in the Pyrenees or through primeval Masurian wetlands. The dilemmas and contradictions between development and the environment are more frequent and real than admitted in the tons of glossy "green" PR brochures.

The CAP used to be a notorious environmental sinner. High support prices encouraged intensified production, higher mechanisation, higher fertiliser use, larger feed-fed animal holdings producing more manure, with the EU landscape moving towards mono-cultures of US-style agro-industries and the Ile de France beginning to look undistinguishable from Iowa. Since the late 1980's extensification policies with their direct payments largely decoupled from output have removed the incentives to maximise yields. Rather farms have an interest to reduce costs by economising on purchases of feed and fertilisers. Paid set-asides, farm land left fallow, and premia for grazing land, for reforestation, and for keeping and expanding hedges, ponds and national habitats support the return of bio-diversity and an esthetically more pleasing landscape (which may convince urban tax-payers and consumers of some purpose in environmentally oriented farm subsidies). Gradually, against strong resistance of vested interests, conditions for animal holdings, transport and slaughter were made more "humane". Implementation and supervision by certain member states, less the EU regulatory aspects, are now the problem. Since 1998 also the use of animal tests for the use of cosmetics, toiletries and other frivolous applications have been banned. The mutual recognition of test results between member states and between the EU and other industrialised countries (the US, Japan, etc.), which adhere to the OECD's code of good laboratory practice, has significantly reduced the number of uselessly duplicated animal tests and untold suffering.

A Commission white paper on transportation and the environment published back in 1993 clearly shows the externalised costs of modern individualised mobility. It lists CO_2 emissions as contributing to global warming, increasing surface ozone levels, acid rain, waste of non-renewable energy (30% of which is burnt for transportation in the EU), damage to nature, and noise and vibration hurting buildings and the quality of life.

Some of the policy responses are in the EU's realm: the policies on cabotage, railway privatisation, the rules on the transport of dangerous goods and tighter emission controls (including lead-free petrol) are in line with the conclusions of the white book on sustainable mobility.

The extensive role of road construction in regional development and their large share in the TEN are hardly in line with the notions of sustainability. Other sensible recommendations like shifting the tax burden from labour to fossil energy use has not, to any perceptible extent, been followed up by member states. On the good advice to improve public mass transport and to set up large car-free inner cities, the municipal/metropolitan response in the member states is mixed at best.

Classical environmental policy protects directly the elements. In the air the EU's main task is to reduce pollution, especially across borders. Since 1980 emissions of sulphur dioxide, nitrogen dioxide, lead and black smoke particles have been limited. This mainly applies to stationary sources like power stations and heavy industry.

For mobile sources, like cars, there are limitations on sulfur contents and a ban on lead in fuels. Already in 1995 the production of fluorocarbons (CFCs), identified as the ozone killer, was banned.

On surface and sea waters EU directives interdict the emission of dangerous substances. There are limits placed on the disposal of nitrates (which usually end up in ground water). Member states have been under obligation to clear their waste water mechanically and biologically for decades. Towns with a maritime tradition and the inland town of Brussels seem to have persistent difficulties in compliance. Seafood fed on their recycled waste seems to have a particular appeal. The quality of drinking water and of "bathing" (meaning: beach) water is regularly controlled by directives. The "bathing water" survey has turned out to be quite popular among the media and the tourism industry: it allows them to compare the environmental and health quality of coastal resorts. Obviously high class resorts have a strong incentive to get off the black list.

Noise does not generate lasting damage to nature, but it still hurts human health. Both at the work place and in traffic the EU has established upper decibel levels for technical equipment. As machinery, including motor cycles and lawn movers, are traded freely in Europe, the higher noise tolerance levels of Southern Europeans is being reigned in to avoid murders of noisy lawn-mowing neighbours being committed in quiet Northern suburbs.

Every year some 2,000 new patented chemicals are being sold by the trade. Following the 1982 Soweso dioxin disaster, all potentially hazardous and new chemicals need to be notified and classified according to their risks, with readable labeling on proper safety and disposal handling.

Waste may be an unsavoury subject, but it rightly is a priority for European environmental protection. As almost all industrial production sooner or later turns into waste, space in deposits gets scarcer and recycling facilities cannot keep up with the growing volumes of trash (2.2 billion tons in 1995, out of which 30 million tons were toxic). Without proper regulations and controls a lucrative new trade would develop: the cross-border tourism of garbage — particularly of toxic wastes expensive to dispose — into the countries of least control and risk awareness. After German unity, for instance, the German tax payer has had the privilege of clearing up East German toxic dumps into which the cash-strapped Communist regime had dropped West European waste in exchange for hard currency. Already in 1975 an EU directive had addressed waste management which UK tabloids later denounced as uncivilised: "Eurocrats Want Us to Sort Our Rubbish", titled a disgusted *Daily Mail* on July 16, 1992. The objectives were to reduce waste (to encourage more durable products and cleaner modes of production), to recycle more waste and save raw materials, to increase member states' facilities for proper waste management, to control operators in the rough and tough waste business more effectively, and to dispose of toxic wastes with a minimum of risk to humans and to the environment. The policy priority is to recycle and reuse the materials; safe thermic disposal comes second. If there are to be deposits, they should be safe without risks to ground water, the soil and the habitat or degrading the landscape or the site's neighbourhood. Member states should handle their own rubbish as much as possible (for once autarchy is advocated), minimise dubious and dangerous exports and to dispose of it closest to source. The polluter should pay: he is either the (previous) owner or the producer of the good turned trash.

Detailed directives regulate the disposal of such problematic waste as waste oil, sewage sludge, communal waste water, PCB/PCT and wastes generated in titanium dioxide production, all subject to controlled disposal by licensed specialists only. In July 2002 the Commission threatened non-compliance suits against nine member states, i.e., against Germany (for insufficient handling of old batteries), Italy, Greece and the UK (for sloppy disposal site management), and against Belgium, Greece and the UK (for violating the waste oil directive).

Migratory wild animals as a rule pay only scant attention to international borders: birds, fish and mammals, on land and in the sea, all require cross-border protection. This has started with the directive to protect migratory birds and their habitat back in 1979, which collided with the Italian and French hunting tradition (dating back to the French revolution of 1789) to be allowed to shoot in any state of intoxication at anything which moves at any given time (including of course at fellow hunters and their pick-up trucks who at a certain point all look like rabbits). Understandably this evil Eurocratic intervention restraining the free gun use of the drunken proletariat has been resisted by successive well thinking French and Italian administrations for decades now, while the Commission insisted on shortened hunting seasons and the prohibition of glue nets.

A similarly demented scourge are global souvenir hunters and apparel wearers of species close to extinction. The CITES ban enacted by the Washington Agreement, to which the EU was a leading party, bans whaling products, ivory, sea turtle shells, the skins and paws of rare animals, etc. It thus reduces the incentives for poachers. Within Europe the habitat policy seeks to expand nature parks and to establish new biotops for locally endangered species. In the third world, EU development funds are earmarked to preserve some chunks of the tropical rain forests, which together with their species and genetic heritage are threatened by extinction in a decade from now.

Global concerns dealing with the ozone layer, the climatic system, bio-diversity and marine life in the oceans, are dealt with at EU level both with joint initiatives for local action and problem resolution and for a coordinated European input at international negotiations. At the Rio summit the resolution arrived at a CO_2 freeze. In Kyoto, a summit wrecked by the US and the Texan oil lobby, the EU committed herself to reduce greenhouse emissions by 20% by 2020. Following the Montreal protocol, chlorofluorocarbon (CFC) gases were banned from production and use. To their global ends the EU favours multilateral environmental agreements (MEA) and an effective dispute settlement mechanism in the WTO, which should help to alleviate LDCs fears that they would be used as a convenient pretext for protectionist policies.

The EU also pursues environmental policies of a more general ("horizontal") nature. They require environmental impact assessments prior to large scale infrastructure projects, allow public access to environmental information (important for NGOs), civil liability for environmental damage, procedures for voluntary environmental audits for companies, eco-labelling (not very successful as they compete with a multitude of national eco-labels), and CO_2 tax plans which since 1992 await adoption.

There is little doubt that most of the EU's environmental legislation passes the subsidiarity test. Rather the problem is one of toothlessness: voluntary codes with industry (e.g., on car emissions) or decade-long cavalier disregard of member states violating the "*acquis*" (ranging from bird protection to nitrate emissions in farming and inexistant waste water facilities in places like Brussels, Milan and Marseille). It is only very recently that the Commission with its energetic Swedish environmental Commissioner, Margot Wallstroem, (1999–) has acted toughly in suing recalcitrant member states in the ECJ.

On occasion there are flaws in the design of the policies: environmental assessments can be done by the investors themselves and their predictable study results handed to the evaluating public authorities (who often commissioned the development scheme in the first place). Don't expect surprises then. The "polluter pays" principle is not always kept: on many occasions costs to rectify environmental degradation are externalised to society (witness public environmental rehabilitation budgets). There is also no shortage of past and current contradictions in the Commission's own policies, notably in the big spending programmes of agriculture, fisheries, regional and development policies.

Judging by its own publicly announced yardsticks ("benchmarks"), by the year 2000 the EU had not reached its planned target reductions for CO_2, NO_x, waste, noise, pesticides and nitrate emissions in the groundwater. It was on target only with respect to CFCs (which were banned) and SO_2 (due to closures and upgrading investments in thermal power stations).

In summary, environmental policy remains clearly a case of too little rather than too much European policy competence and enforcement.

The Bleeding Heart of Europe: The Social Policies

Critics of the lack of an EU social policy had, for a long time, a fair point. The Treaties of Rome ignored social policy reflecting the neo-liberal belief that economic growth would automatically generate welfare. In the rebellious 1960s, the Community then acquired an image of being a capitalist stooge only of benefit to the fat cats, an image which stuck for a long time.

Only after Willy Brandt became the first Social Democratic Chancellor of Germany, did the EU at her 1972 Paris summit announce "vigorous action in the social field". However, this vigour had to wait. By the early 1980s a few harmonised rules on the physical safety of work places and on equal treatment had been set up, but very little else. The social affairs council met rarely. But when they met, the Social Ministers [notably the German Social Minister Norbert Blüm who occupied this post during the 16 long years (1982–1998) of Helmut Kohl's reign] cheerfully agreed that social policy should remain a member state prerogative.

This line of reasoning remained acceptable until the single market was about to arrive in 1992. Quickly a "social dimension" had to be packaged as part of the desired "cohesion" to generate acceptance by European trade union leaders, who entertained the distinct suspicion that their clientele was about to shoulder the flip side of market integration (adjustment costs and employment dislocation) exclusively. Hence the Commission under Jacques Delors designed a Social Charter, replete with pious common places, which soon found the blessings of the EU's venerable Economic and Social Committee, including the EU's "social partners", the European bodies of labour representatives

(ETUC) and of employers (UNICE, the employers federation, and CEEP, the public enterprises). Attached to the lofty Charter principles was however an "action programme", which was to acquire significant operational meaning.

The 12-point Social Charter was to gain particular fame in the UK, which under Tory rule was adamantly set against it. As the British Isles cultivated their new image as a substandard off-shore sweat shop to attract like-minded Japanese, Korean and Taiwanese investments, John Major memorably explained to his subjects "they (meaning: the continentals) may have the Charter, but we get the jobs" (*The European*, March 4, 1993). True enough, from 1989, the Charter only applied to 11 (out of 12) member states then, and the wonderful action programmes remained stymied, as even in Maastricht, the UK continued to block the introduction of qualified majority voting (QMV) on social matters and insisted on unanimity. Even politically hyper-correct and actually also sensible Commission drafts to protect the rights of part-time workers (mostly women) and of handicapped people in the labour market, were met by a dogmatic British *nyet*, which under the unanimity rule applicable to the subject area was a straightforward kill. As the policy theme of "safety at work" was the only social policy area subject to QMV, the Commission over years tried valiantly to sell every piece of social legislation as a "safety at work" theme (which explains some of the convoluted twisted technical reasoning of many directives of that era).

In 1997 the Amsterdam Treaty conference was held. The conference was all about grand constitutional deliberation (but achieved little, as we know by now) and cared little in reality about social exclusion and employment creation. Yet as freshly elected Tony Blair signed the Social Charter, which was now applicable in all of the EU empire, and as the participants (including the new British prime minister) could agree on little else, in the last rescue attempts for the summit, declamatory social objectives were inserted into the Treaty (and promptly helped to sell the whole thing as a success of sorts): one of the Union's objectives was now to achieve "a high degree of employment and of social protection, equality between men and women...". This grand declaration also helped to address popular fears that monetary union with its imperative to balance budgets would trigger an erosion of social protection. While heads of governments made forceful statements on the European social model as one of the strongest safety nets on the globe, in reality they made sure to keep their national competences in social policy. Most member states would just agree to certain minimum standards in order to avoid hospital tourism and social services shopping across the borders.

In consequence, then, EU legislation remains fairly extensive in the area of safety at work: the protection of workers from toxic materials, radiation or overlong work hours (for instance in road transport), to improve safety in mines and at construction sites (the work environment with the highest risks of deadly accidents), or to protect pregnant or recent mothers at work (including job protection). Understandably an integrated market should not entail a downward competition on safety standards.

Typically, the minimum standards of EU labour law are rules entitling employees to a work contract which stipulates pay, leave entitlements and the period of notice; granting them a rest period of at least 11 hours between two working days; banning youngsters from working until they are 15 (a rule safely disregarded in the informal sector of newspaper boys and babysitters), and no overtime being permissible until 18.

Since its early days (witness the creation of the Economic and Social Committee back in 1957), the Community has cherished the notion of "social dialogue" over class warfare and ultra-liberalism. Not only did the "social partners" (in the earnest European sense of the word — in America it means having more fun together) at EU level agree on the Social Charter, but they also negotiated between themselves schemes on parental leave (with the right to return to the same or an equivalent job afterwards), on part-time work and on fixed term employment. This helped greatly to have them adopted as EU Council directives later on.

The tradition of neo-corporatism is evident in the European Work Council directive. These work councils have to be set up in each company that employs at least 1,000 people in all of the EU, of which at least 100 people are in each of two EU member states. Some 600 work councils exist already. They are composed of up to 30 worker representatives elected by their national branch councillors. The Work Council is to be informed and consulted about corporate strategies affecting the work force, new investment plans, the introduction of new technologies and about corporate restructuring which affect national subsidiaries. In countries like Germany and the Netherlands, where the organised work force has more far-reaching participation rights, these remain untouched. They are however now well complemented at the European level. Companies are free, of course, to grant their work force more significant co-determination rights than the con-committal consultations foreseen in the EU regulations. The European Work Council seems harmless enough, but with its obligation to basic civic intercourse, already seems to have had a major civilising effect on labour relations in countries suffering traditionally from labour militancy and management arrogance. During trans-Atlantic mergers, US unions are also willing and eager participants (like the UAW after the Daimler-Chrysler takeover).

At the European level, the EU always insisted on having one single interlocutor from each camp among its "social partners". In countries with a pragmatic unitary trade union movement, like Germany, Sweden or the UK, this was relatively easy. For those countries with strong ideological splits in their trade union movements, ranging from Communists to Christian Democrats (Italy, France, Spain, Belgium, including the EU institutions' own staff unions), this proved a more difficult learning experience. With good reason since Maastricht, the EU has clearly renounced any claim to decide or settle wage policies (which are up to the respective national "social partners" to settle) or to deal with concrete issues of the right of association, collective bargaining and of settling labour disputes. All this remains to be handled exclusively at the national, regional or corporate level. Although labour markets integrate increasingly — most strongly so in those professions offering trans-border services (transport, telecommunications or mobile labour for construction) — collective bargaining at the European level between the union federation (ETUC) and the employers (UNICE — private, and CEEP — public) does not yet exist. Unions in the richer and better paying countries have argued for years for Europe-wide wage settlements in order to narrow the wage differentials by upgrading the pay of the less productive performers. Predictably there is little enthusiasm on the employers' side. Equally, the organisational strength of the unions' side at the European level is not particularly pronounced. Its nominal member strength with 50 million paying adherents is impressive only on paper. In reality unionisation rates are continuously declining in most member states. For better or worse there are no prospects for EU-wide walkouts and strikes (although the truckers' fuel tax protests of summer 2000 came dangerously close). As social rights historically had always to be fought for, with no fights at EU level, social regulation remains a patchwork of incoherent legislative pieces (held together only skimpily by tons of unreadable ideological verbiage put out by the Commission's word re-processing machines). The real actions and competences for labour relations and social protection remain at the national level until further notice.

Productivity and wage levels already remained too disparate in the EU 15 (roughly 4:1, between high value added, highly capitalised, well educated and equipped, reasonably managed and motivated work forces of Scandinavia, the Netherlands, West Germany, urban France, etc. and, say, those of the more relaxed and traditional rural regions of the sunny South). It took decades to recognise this reality in having the so-called "dispatch directive" approved by the Council: wherever workers work in other EU countries the wage and welfare legislation of their host country applies regardless of the contractual situation into which they entered in their country of origin. This was necessary to prevent work gangs recruited abroad (originally in Scotland, now in Portugal, as the Scots' productivity turned out to be rather minimal on Mondays) working at construction sites in high cost Germany at rates just marginally above those back home, thus justifying fears of social dumping and downward competition in the integrated market for labour.

Other problems emanating from increased worker mobility, like the mutual recognition of diplomas and professional qualifications, as well as the accumulation of pension rights acquired in different EU countries, were gradually resolved in decade-long technical deliberations.

Starting from the "equal pay for equal work" principle enshrined in the Treaties of Rome (1957) — implemented in the member states only in 1975 — the Commission has long been active on the gender front.

In 1976 a directive on equal treatment in access to employment, training, promotion and working conditions was enacted, and in 1992 equal treatment in social security, rights to maternity leave and safety rules for expecting and nursing mothers became law in EU land. During the tenure of Pat Flynn (1993–1999), the most unlikely and implausible convert to feminism in the Commission's social affairs portfolio, the Commission also produced an avalanche of recommendations on best practice of positive action in the fields of vocational training (with girls turning inevitably into coal miners and car mechanics), child care, equal opportunities, and suppressing unwanted sexual advances at work (no doubt disregarding the Commission's own fair share of hushed-up cases in this unsavoury field).

The Amsterdam Treaty of 1997, which, as we know, failed to achieve its primary task, namely political union, instead attempted to rescue its public relations glory by setting norms of political and societal correctness. Thus, without any public debate, the Treaty decreed as the EU's task to eliminate inequality and discriminatory obstacles to the advancement of women, covering recruitment and employment, new organisations of work, health protection and promotion prospects. Scandinavian realities, where gainful employment rates of women aged 20 to 59 stand at 85%, were set as the norm for the rest of the EU whose overall average then stood at 59% (with Greece, Italy and Ireland at the bottom with around 50%). There is certainly nothing wrong with female employment and career advancement, including, if necessary, a reasonable measure of "positive discrimination" (in Orwellian correct speak now: "positive action", meaning negative action for men), but it remains a mystery why normative decisions affecting personal and societal choices of this magnitude should be taken at a poorly legitimised EU level.

In consequence, now the European Court of Justice has decreed that women should serve in combat roles, a doctrinal decision taken by people who have never experienced combat except in Western movies and on CNN. The Commission has equally taken the normative hint and declared itself to be pursuing gender mainstreaming in all aspects of society, family life, work, schooling, education and politics. If this was for real, it would be a scary tale of Big Sister is Watching You. In reality however most of this verbiage is inconsequential nonsense. Female professional careers (and the miserable demographic situation of most member states) would greatly be enhanced if proper day care and day schooling centres (like in Belgium, France and Scandinavia) were universally available in the EU. Predictably, however, not a cent of EU funds goes into such schemes. Rather, women-specific EU programmes fund the pet schemes of childless feminist lobbyists like safe houses against violence ("Daphne") and women's counselling and information centres ("Now").

The European Parliament maintains a Committee on Women's Rights whose deliberations are so predictable that even its most passionate members are sufficiently bored to generate the second worst attendance record (surpassed only by the exciting Petitions Committee). Already in 1984 the lady MEPs had demanded that henceforth equal opportunity prescriptions should be inserted in each and every EU social and structural grant or vocational training scheme.

The EU's employment policies similarly reflect more political opportunism than economic effectiveness. For more than a decade now on average one in ten workers (20 million in total) in the old EU15 is out of job. On top of this, the EU's employment rate remains at 60%, which is 10% lower than in the US or in Japan. The problem is not new. Already during 1970–1990 the US created 29 million new jobs, Japan 11 million, and the much larger EU only 8.8 million. It is almost a commonplace by now, that the low employment and the high unemployment rates are structural, not cyclical, in nature, as European policy makers have chosen to continue to tax the use of labour inordinately (50% of total fiscal revenue), while cementing the rigidities of the labour market and happily topping them up with mainstreaming and other anti-discrimination provisions.

Instead of dealing with structural issues (like reducing taxes on labour, making unemployment benefits conditional on requalification, to modernise vocational training, to improve conditions for part-time jobs and work at odd hours, etc.), the EU and its member states indulge in predictably useless and expensive employment programmes, job pacts and other publicly financed straw fires. The reason: polls reveal that the public wants Europe to "do something" about unemployment (like doing something about third world hunger, cruelty against animals and children, war in Yugoslavia, violence against women and whales). The absurdity of it all is not lost on the primary movers and shakers. I once had the privilege of participating in a "working breakfast" (that uncivilised US invention) between an EU Prime Minister and a Commission President (both are in political retirement now, which permits these state secrets to be revealed) in the run up to Amsterdam. The Prime Minister (Chancellor) asked for an EU employment initiative. The Commission President replied that such initiatives were useless; besides, they would sidetrack the summit from its real business, which was political union. The Prime Minister agreed that employment pacts would not employ anyone, "but this is what people want". Two months later the Commission President publicly called for a European employment initiative, and (unlike political union) it was promptly delivered in Amsterdam.

The EU employment strategy (developed back in 1995 when it was announced that the monitoring exercise would cut the unemployment rate by half by 2000) now requires the Commission to produce a multi-causal employment report (covering issues like the quality of the workforce, sectoral employment growth, direct and indirect wage costs, specific groups in the labour market, etc.) to the Council. The Council (of Social Ministers) then decides on annual guidelines for employment targets to be met. Member states, after consulting with social partners, regional and local authorities, then draw up national action plans. Commission and Council examine the plan and issue recommendations for improvement in the light of best practice in other member states. The number of perceptive white papers on employment creation in the meantime fills small libraries as graveyards of good intentions. As unions don't concede on labour flexibility and most fiscal authorities do not move from conveniently taxing labour, the results are pious pleas but no jobs.

As a hard-working administration the Commission nonetheless has created a firework of well funded labour enhancing initiatives which the European Social Funds ("Objective 3") sponsors through national employment offices. They cover those who are out of work, those who are at risk and those who, while remaining employed, are in need of retraining. Training schemes are usually geared at the usual suspects: women, youngsters, the elderly, the handicapped, those living in the countryside, in the disadvantaged periphery and those in the disadvantaged inner cities, young and old businessmen, the long term unemployed and the under-educated, then again those who are over-educated and in need of some post-doc requalification (perhaps a cabbie licence). In short, the target priority ESF groups, if we go through the lists of working programmes and initiatives, cover training, employment and retraining schemes for some 80–90% of the EU's adult population.

There is no doubt that the human resource promotion which forms a sizeable component also of other EU initiatives (regional, rural, research, infrastructure) is helpful in many instances. At the same time as most member states failed to address the structural root causes of unemployment, on aggregate they had to fail, and so they did. It is usually claimed that the EU's social spending programmes complement member states' initiatives. Usually they just help to co-finance them. Typically, existing national programmes are re-labelled to suit the Commission's "new" focused objectives, which can be trusted to be never so new or so focused anyway. Hence, in sum, they fail the test of subsidiarity.

Happy Oxen and Their Happy Eaters: Consumer Protection, Food Safety and Public Health

Directly related to the functioning of the internal market is consumer protection. With some justification consumers have come to expect the same level of protection when purchasing in other EU countries as back home. This is of particular relevance when unscrupulous traders sell their unsuspecting victims overpriced and essentially unwanted products and services while preying on their carefree holiday mood or their ignorance of local laws. The purchase of time-share property in Spanish resorts is a classical case. The single market triggered a regulatory need and the Community institutions reacted timely and comprehensively.

With its established principles of product safety, producer liability and fair competition, EU law for the protection of consumers is fairly wide ranging. Apart from these general principles it covers a series of specific provisions. In field of product safety there are, for instance, provisions covering cosmetics, pharmaceuticals, toys and the wide range of food hygiene and safety. On product information, EU rules require transparent price indications (this also applies to consumer credit terms) and precise labelling of the contents for foodstuffs and for textiles.

In advertisements, EU regulations specify restrictions on comparative or potentially misleading pronouncements, e.g., in case of pharmaceuticals. There are specific provisions to protect consumers in sales off premises, be it in door-to-door sales, at a distance by mail order, or through the Internet or by television. More recent regulations allow the protection of consumers on problems related to mass tourism, like package tours and the mentioned time-share property, allowing the hapless victim to cancel overpriced deals within a period of quiet reflection and sober calculation.

There are also EU rules governing producer warranties and repair services for durable consumer goods.

The Commission works hard to improve access to justice on consumer issues, particularly in cases of compensation for producer liability.

The biggest crisis of consumer confidence the EU has ever faced was the prolonged BSE drama of 1986–1999. The prime culprits were surely the singular incompetence of the livestock feed industry, the veterinary services and the agricultural ministry of a certain island country. But the Commission services had also shown themselves to be too credulous and unable and unwilling to verify the false assertions emanating from the said capital and its ill-fated Prime Minister, thus allowing the disease to spread to the continent and into third markets.

Food safety has always been a touchy issue in affluent societies, with consumer worries particularly strong about life-stock products, whipped up by sensationalist reporting easily displaying all signs of public hysteria for a few months (until superseded by a new issue), during which time producers have suffered enormous damage due to a collapse in demand.

This repeated experience of listeria in French cheese, dioxin in Belgian poultry, salmonella in eggs (mostly in careless domestic fridges) and other periodic delights, led to a strong focus on food quality and food safety in the reformed CAP over the last decade. Abandoning the old mainstay of reworking support prices for a purely quantitative output, the new emphasis on food quality has to be pursued with more diverse instruments.

In rural development local processing is encouraged and support given to improve local facilities and marketing. Organic farming practices, which now cover 2.2 million hectares (3%) of the EU's arable land, critically is supported (at the range of 900 Euros per hectare) for losses incurred by farmers during the switch-over period from conventional agriculture. It takes about two years to regain residue free soil. Checks on food safety have been vastly improved. Member states' food safety authorities remain in charge to assure freedom from harmful substances, like microbes, chemicals and production residues (stemming from veterinary medicines, pesticides, feed additives). Permissible additives (like vitamins, mineral salts, flavourings, etc.) must be properly labelled for consumer information. The Dublin based European Food and Veterinary Office (FVO) then checks the national authorities' works, including thorough spot checks.

The FVO's task is also to monitor infectious animal diseases, like foot and mouth, and to ban movements of animals and animal products if necessary. According to lessons learnt from the BSE crisis, systems of rapid alert and of quick access to independent expert advice have been set up, as no doubt the next food health crisis (not always limited to livestock products: even coke, mineral water and pasta have recently been affected) will surely come at an unsuspecting moment in an unlikely place.

EU food law does not proscribe proper good tastes (as some venerable national food codes do, like the Codex Alimentarius Austriacus), but differences to reasonable consumer expectations must be clearly labelled. Consumers on the continent expect chocolate to contain and to taste of real cocoa contents, whilst in the UK a product called chocolate mainly contains palm oil extract. This stuff is not particularly unhealthy (although on occasion it tastes like sweetened cardboard), but the contents must be labelled legibly in order to avoid misleading consumers who expect the real thing.

Part of the quality drive is the protection of traditional production and origin names, like Rocquefort cheese and Serrano ham, against imitation products. In an integrated food market like the EU, food safety clearly needs regulation and control of the controllers. The lessons of BSE could not have been more painfully straightforward.

BSE tragically killed a few dozen people during the last decade. They surely constituted a miniscule fraction of nutrition-related premature deaths in the EU. Unhealthy fatty and sugary eating habits, smoking and drinking killed a million-fold multiple through strokes, cancer and heart attacks during the same period. Should public health not be a subject of EU concern, then?

Looking at comparative statistics of mortality and disease patterns, the differences are striking in terms of avoidable suffering, pain and premature death. The difference is made by changes in ways of life, ranging from nutrition to drug abuse, precaution at the work place, in traffic, at home and in sex life. Effective information campaigns and large-scale regular check-ups could help for a start. But there is also the question of affordable and timely access to best possible medical help.

Medical education and training, efficient hospital management, and the use of updated equipment and medication at reasonable costs in an ever-ageing society are the primary tasks of contemporary health policy.

The European Council so far has found fit to leave most of the glory and blame of health policy in national competence, and to have health initiatives undertaken at EU level only in case of internal market or trans-border specific problems. As a result, they consist of a patchwork of largely complementary policy measures, which, though not unimportant *per se*, in sum hardly justify the name "public health".

As mentioned, in the field of preventive medicine, they cover health and safety regulations in the workplace, safety standards for tradeable commodities like food, pharmaceuticals and toys, safety provisions for motor vehicles, action plans against drug abuse, and extensive pan European research into endemic diseases like cancer, cardio-vascular diseases, diabetes and AIDS, and related preventive information programmes.

The EU's tobacco policy is a wonderful case of apparent policy contradictions. Following the fervent wish of Health Commissioner David Byrne (1999–2004), Commission and Parliament want to see tobacco advertisements banned and ever shriller health warnings, if possible with skulls and crossbones, put on cigarette packs. At the same time, tobacco growing (cheap EU table wine is not exactly a health tonic either) is subsidised from CAP funds with 900 million Euros annually.

Yet, as Agricultural Commissioner Franz Fischler (1995–2004) correctly pointed out, without these subsidies Europeans would not smoke less. They smoke imported American Virginia tobacco, not the subsidised Greek ("Turkish") blends, most of which are in fact exported to

Russia and Bulgaria where they compete with *machorka*. The waste of these funds is hence a CAP problem, and one for Russian public health.

There are new challenges for health policies in the EU, like "hospital tourism" of patients desperate for better or cheaper treatment, cross-border trade of organs for transplants, and expensive medical equipment for rare diseases which could be used by patients in several EU countries. Yet, on balance, it is very likely that the major elements of health policy, with good reason, will remain within national competence.

Good Intentions and Mixed Results: The Policies on Research, Education and Culture

Few will dispute that 1 billion Euros invested in applied research or educational exchange is a better investment than the distillation of table wines or export subsidies for milk powder. Yet the principles of subsidiarity and academic freedom should require careful policy decisions prior to the launch of EU-wide initiatives in the sciences, education and culture. This is not always the case. Notably when summits fail to achieve agreement on substantial policy progress, substitute action in the "soft" intellectual areas with pious rationales seemingly beyond dispute are being sought to dress up one more "success" for public consumption. It is useful therefore to take a short hard look at the plethora of policy initiatives in the sciences and technologies that have crept up during the last decades.

No doubt, the cradle of modern science lies within the lands of the European Union. They also continue to hold one of the biggest research potentials in the world. Yet there are problems. It is not only in terms of Nobel Prizes, whose jury awards in Stockholm are sometimes curious (not just for literature and economics), but also more importantly in international patents, amongst which the European share tends to lose out massively to the US. Science in Europe is generally seen as "culture" (and is correspondingly under-funded and solitary), while in the US it is organised and financed as a business, which makes a big difference in terms of output orientation and applicability. In Europe also, the heroic days of scientific discoveries of an Alexander Fleming or a Madame Curie are long gone. Contemporary science has an image problem of drudgery and boring unrewarding lab work. In schools it is avoided as a difficult and unattractive subject. As a result there is a shortage of science students and graduates at European universities, and a widespread scientific illiteracy among an otherwise well-educated public. In countries in which scientific education and investments are relatively poor (like in Austria, the Mediterranean and Ireland), the public indulges in a pronounced scepticism towards new technologies. This is not the case in countries like the Netherlands and in Scandinavia, where science education and research are more pronounced.

EU science policies enter only as a pretty late sequence into this picture. Their purpose is to enhance cross-border links of already existing national programmes in order to achieve synergies and a critical mass of pooled research funds and facilities with the common use of data, allowing the comparison of results and the transfer of know-how.

Typically projects are funded which are inter-disciplinary, multi-country and application-oriented. During 1998–2002, the duration of the Commission's "5th framework programme" for research, some 15 billion Euros was spent. As usual, the funds went into a wide variety of worthy causes: in biotech to attempt the mastery of genetics with applications ranging from combating cancer and AIDS, biodegradable waste disposal (like bugs eating up oil pests), and new feed and food. In medicine large epidemological research was conducted into main killers like cardio-vascular diseases, leukaemia, diabetes, and also genetic diseases, viral epidemics and age-induced diseases like Alzheimer's. New forms of radiation therapy against brain tumours were developed. In food technology new methods were found to detect traces of residues of hormone or genetic treatment and new research initiated on "functional foods" to discover new functions of traditional foodstuffs, like for infant nutrition or to combat cancer.

In information technologies the "Esprit" programme was designed to catch up in microelectronics and in software development. "Eureka" implemented GSM standards for worldwide mobile phone use (thus avoiding costly fragmentation). "Semper" introduced electronic safety for online banking. Other IT programmes led to multi-sensors (combining radar and metal detectors) to detect anti-personnel mines, or developed rehabilitation aids after brain injuries. Environmental research covered the chemistry of the stratosphere, climatic change, ocean research and desertification. Within the Mediterranean Sea, temperatures, salinity, plankton density and the effects of inflowing nutrients and waste were measured. Remote sensing of crops was a by-product of the CAP (permitting harvest forecasts and proper acreage payments). New applications monitored desertification, deforestation, forest fires and soil degradation notably in the tropics. Energy research aimed at improved power generation from wind and photovoltaic cells, and at better efficiencies in transport, heating and industrial processes. The JET programme, operating in research facilities in the UK, had developed nuclear fusion, which in difference to conventional nuclear diffusion was safer as it involved neither uncontrolled reactions nor dangerous nuclear wastes. In addition, it is in virtually limitless supply. In the transport sector, research aimed at improved safety features in road transport (material resistance) and at safety structures in railway carriages.

EU research programmes also aimed at the exchange of researchers. "Marie Curie" stipends allowed the dispatch and return of doctoral and post-doc researchers. Some 10,000 Russian former researchers of military technologies (to the extent that they do not yet work in the US) were being "converted" to deal with the civil use of nuclear technologies, advanced aviation and new materials instead. In order to enhance the practicality of academic training and research in technical disciplines, a specific Community programme called "Comett" was initiated. "Comett" mainly covered internships of six months for science and engineering students in high tech companies, working on specific projects often in a cross border context. By the mid-1990s already some 10,000 students and young graduates had gained valuable training experience in project work abroad through this scheme.

What then is the bottom line of the EU's research and technology policy? Its detractors are numerous. Back in the early 1990s, *The Economist* titled its brief as "How Not to Catch Up" (January 9, 1993), claiming that such policies originated more from an inferiority complex, are obsolete in a high-tech world dominated by multinational companies and, in any event, set in too late to improve Europe's poor science education and to excite promising youths to embark on a career in research labs.

While everybody agrees that secondary education in the age of subsidiarity is not the right place for EU initiatives, in the tertiary field a few strategic areas of action are more legitimate — and yield good results.

The starting point is the contemporary career profile. A current graduate will have been born around 1980 and, after a long, happy and ever dynamic career, will retire after 45 years of mostly productive work around 2050. The job profile for qualified work in business or public administration of the first half of the 21st century will be quite different than the one applicable to most such jobs in the century before. Next to the predictable quantities of creativity, dynamism, networking, hard work, long hours and high tech use, professional profiles also include international exposure and multi-lingualism beyond the mastery of Mickey Mouse MBA English. For most EU countries now some 50% of GDP is already generated from revenue abroad, mostly from within the EU, but also from third countries. For most professional careers this implies the need to be able to deal successfully with international customers, requests, inquiries and orders, and with foreign business, legal, cultural and inter-personal issues daily, even in the hitherto most unlikely places, be it local law firms, savings banks, pharmacies and veterinary clinics. Europe's university system, however, as one might have guessed, remains woefully inadequate to prepare most of its students for this perfectly foreseeable challenge. In the past, grants to study abroad were highly selective, allowing only the best and the brightest to study abroad. The EU's "Erasmus" programme was to change all this. Prior to "Erasmus", back in 1986 only 0.5% of Europe's students studied in other EU countries. In 1992, 60,000 students (5% of the total) spent three to 12 months at EU universities abroad. By 1999 their number had increased to 170,000, representing more than 10%. In order to participate, some (obviously not overly demanding) quality criteria had to be fulfilled, including linguistic and cultural preparation for the host country. "Erasmus" students have a fair reputation for partying (which should improve their linguistic and inter-cultural skills at the very least). As future EU taxpayers they should be entitled to some state-sponsored fun prior to their ever-extending working life. Tuition and other fees are waived for Erasmus students and travel grants and a monthly stipend of up to 400 Euros is provided. In order to assure the possibility for serious study, a "European Credit Transfer System" (ECTS) has been set up. Participating universities mutually agree to recognise their students' coursework done at a partner university to count towards the degree back home. Partner universities also develop joint curricula and syllabi, including the use of the regular EU-funded exchange of university lecturers and professors. All of this is no minor feat, given the bureaucratisation of the continental European university scene and each university's firm conviction of being the best, which is most pronounced usually amongst the most mediocre faculties.

Part of the university exchange programmes (codenamed "Socrates" in EU-jargon) is the "Lingua" programme set up to allow current and future language instructors to improve their skills and pronunciation amongst native speakers. "Lingua" also aims at the lesser spoken languages, including most useful international languages like Gaelic and Finnish. With EU enlargement no doubt it will multiply the foreign teaching of Slovenian, Maltese and Estonian. (Unfortunately, Livlandian has just died out; it could have been revived as an official EU language.) There are also school partnerships between EU countries sponsored by a scheme called "Comenius", the exchange of economics graduates and doctoral students supported by the "Spes" programme, and a G24 programme to improve teaching in Eastern Europe called "Tempus" (financed at around 200 million Euros p.a.). At a more practical level "Leonardo" applies. It covers the cross border exchange of trainees — both in post secondary vocational training, for young graduates of technical disciplines and for their trainers and instructors. Some 25,000 youths benefit each year. Finally, about 100,000 youngsters are supported annually when engaged in short term exchange schemes ("Youth for Europe") during their annual vacations.

The statistical sums are quite impressive, notably as regards the more meaningful long term academic exchange: during 1987–2001 one million students participated in "Socrates", and during 1995–1999 alone 40,000 university teachers and 150,000 language instructors benefited from "Erasmus" grants for research and training abroad.

With these schemes the EU succeeded in putting the previously elitist academic exchange schemes ("Fulbright" *et al.*) on a more egalitarian mass base. Having done his/her "Erasmus" has almost become the rule among able-bodied young graduates of the better universities. Those who stayed home will have to find good reasons during future job interviews.

Until 1914 the medieval tradition of "*peregrinatio academica*", the migration of scholars to famous teachers in Prague, Bologna, Paris, Oxford, Uppsala and Heidelberg had been a living tradition. Not by accident this tradition led to the golden ages of European science and civilisation.

The two world wars ended all this. Now, under conditions of mass education in the tertiary sector, the Commission has revived this tradition. In spite of the inevitable room for improvement and criticism there is little doubt that the monies for "Socrates" (meaning "Erasmus" programmes mostly), which during 1995–1999 amounted to 850 million Euros (the same amount was spent for table wine distillation during the same period), was surely well invested. Late in 2002 the Commission announced its new "Erasmus World" programme which starting in 2004 would allow 4,200 post-graduates from third countries to study for two years at EU universities with a monthly grant of 1,600 Euros. In return, some 5,000 EU graduates will be similarly funded to study outside the EU. One thousand grants will also be available for international post-doctoral teaching and research fellowships at EU facilities. "Erasmus World" is budgeted at 200 million Euros. Again, a good bargain, and not only by CAP standards.

Presumably bored by its never-ending action programmes and low technicalities ranging from safe tractor seat provisions to anti-dumping fees for Chinese titanium sponges, the Commission for years now has tended to branch out into the august field of high culture. After year-long debates about its compatibility with subsidiarity the Council then in a moment of weakness typically approves an under-funded programme like "Kaleidoscope" in the past, which raises expectations of EU generosity in the arts scene, which then are regularly frustrated. Current EU cultural initiatives amount to 500 million Euros p.a. This amounts to one Euro and 15 cents per EU citizen, hardly enough to pay him for one pack of popcorn on a movie night. The whole amount is spent on a potpourri of good intentions, promoting the exchange of culture (art works and artists), and nominating an annual "European City of Culture", like the dazzling town of Helsinki, where the usual set of concerts and exhibitions are being sponsored. Then there is the support for audiovisual production (festivals and workshops) called "Media", which surely scares the living daylight out of Hollywood's moguls (if they ever heard about it). There is also the usual stuff about restoring cultural heritage, like training curators and restaurateurs, putting stuff on the Internet, producing multimedia shows which nobody ever watches and modernising museums, mainly by making them look to be of interest to kindergarten children. Similarly worthy is support for life-long learning in inter-cultural cross-border settings. No doubt pottery classes for British housewives in Tuscany are eligible.

The Amsterdam Treaty (which — we may remember — like all other treaties failed to settle a political union) laudably stipulated the respect for national cultures and identifies in all policy areas. But it also stipulates in its Article 13 to combat political incorrectness in all of its contemporary forms of xenophobia, racism, sexism, anti-semitism, etc., which promptly induced the Commission to produce a multi-annual anti-racist action programme running 2001–2006. It clearly favours the minority position of those 20% of EU citizens, which according to Eurobarometer polls favour a *laissez faire* immigration policy with its resulting multicultural mix, while the majority of the 80% which objects (perhaps having the worldwide bloody failure of many multi-cultural societies in mind) is being silenced. The European Union in her first decades had always been a tolerant "open church" with co-existing designs of the left and the right. Since Amsterdam it has perceptively narrowed its political orientation: economically it has adopted the "right" agenda of (ultra-) liberalism and deregulatory privatisations; politically it has moved to the left to advocate multi-culturalism and the ultimately self-destructive dissolution of the already fragile European identity. There is no democratic legitimacy — let alone popular majority — for either decision. The lack of professionalism and of focus of the EU's political correctness offensive (does anybody remember 1997 as the "European Year Against Racism" in any way more intensively than 1991 as the "Year of European Tourism" or similar years for women, children, the old and the demented?) however happily ensures that, as usual, the episode will remain inconsequential, however costly. More significantly the EU's failed aberrations into the minefields of cultural and normative policies are illustrative of an ever increasing dilemma: EU summits failing to solve real issues, yet desperate for "success" get sidetracked into Europeanising issues of secondary importance to the summiteers (like cultural policy), which, however, by any yardstick of subsidiarity should remain in the national, regional, local or best in the private domain of free and unmanipulated personal creativity and freedom of thought.

No Free Lunches:
The Budget, Fraud and Taxation

The curious nature of the political animal that is the EU is clearly illustrated by its fiscal policy constraints. It is neither fish nor flesh. It has no taxation rights, nor can it (luckily) go into deficit. It has to stick to multi-annual spending plans to avoid annual budget conflicts in the Council. Its spending patterns, with their dominance of redistributive agricultural and structural expenditure, are reminiscent of an outsized village economy.

Since the invention of the structural funds accompanying the single market in the 1980s and the cohesion funds as a collateral to the monetary union in 1992, the EU's annual budget has expanded to close to 100 billion Euros. It has since remained just below the threshold of 1.27% of the combined EU GDP which was agreed in 1992. Given the high share of public spending in the EU, although sizeable in absolute terms, the EU budget proper represents just 2.3% of all public expenditure. Per capita it stands at 220 Euros for each EU citizen per year.

The EU budget and its revenues have not been the result of a conscious policy design about policies which should most suitably be financed at the European level, but rather are the predictably skewed and messy result of four decades of unending redistribution battles between member states. First it was agricultural spending, seemingly to compensate French farmers for Germany's industrial market expansion. Then it was the social fund and the European Investment Bank, set up in Luxembourg, to help with Italy's everlasting restructuring and southern development. The European Development Fund (EDF) was set up to aid former French colonies: to this day it is kept out of the EU institutions' decision-making and scrutiny on grounds that it consists of voluntary member states contributions with a relatively large French share. Structural funds were invented when Spain and Portugal joined in 1986, coinciding with the internal market programme.

In 1970 the share of CAP spending stood at 90%. In 1980 it was still at 80%. By 2001 its relative share had shrunk to 46%. But due to the overall dramatic expansion of the EU budget, CAP spending in fact — thanks to "stabilisers" (automatic price cuts) introduced in 1992 — had seen a continued growth in absolute terms. As a result, most of the agricultural sector and the regional economy of large parts of the under-developed regions of Europe (Greece, Portugal, the Mezzogiorno, Southern Spain and East Germany) have become dependent on permanent subsidisation. If proper care is not taken (it probably will not), the same will be in store for the new member states.

In 2001 44 billion Euros were spent on agriculture, 33 billion Euros on regional development, 6 billion Euros on internal policies (like research, education and social spending), 5 billion Euros on external policies (development and food aid mostly), 5 billion Euros on administration (salaries, translations, meetings), and 3 billion Euros on preparing the Eastern accession countries for membership. Apart from the last position, the distribution of the major budget headings were strikingly similar to that of a Soviet *kolchos*. It is recalled this was not a very sustainable profitable institution.

As mentioned, disputes over money dogged EU policy-making almost *ab initio*. Most notorious was the fight over the British budget rebate which raged for one decade (and absorbed most of the EU's political energies at the time) until it was settled at the Fontainebleau summit in 1984. Britain's insistence on a rebate (and Labour's unrealised demands for a renegotiation of entry terms) stemmed from the growing realisation by 1980 that the terms of the CAP, from which the UK's more efficient agriculture had little to gain, were not about to be reformed and that the bulk of the regional funds, originally a British idea, was not about to benefit the UK, but after the Iberian enlargement, instead went to the South (and to Ireland). Given the difficult domestic economic conditions of the 1970s, it was also difficult to argue that British industry — unlike Germany in the

1960s — benefited from EU membership at the time. Two thirds of the British net contribution since have been regularly reimbursed, which leaves Germany as the largest net paymaster in absolute terms high and dry. Largely this is Germany's own fault, and is due also in part to sloppy bargaining. At the 1999 Berlin summit when the financing of the "Agenda 2000" was negotiated, German Chancellor Schröder, whom nobody has ever accused of excessive preparations or negotiation skills, simply seemed to have forgotten to call up from "dear Tony" the reduction of the UK rebate which had been pre-negotiated. So it continued unchanged for the duration of the "Agenda 2000" package (2000–2006).

In order to avoid the annual ritual of budgetary quarrels, the EU in 1988 moved to multi-annual budget plans. They set upper spending limits (like 1.27% of GDP since 1993) and allocated expenditure to major budget headings. The packages "Delors I" (1988/1992), "Delors II" (1993/1999), and "Agenda 2000" (2000/2006) also put the EU budget on a more solid funding base. The earlier major sources of revenue — agricultural import levies and tariff duties — had been in continuous decline, the result of increased food self-sufficiency and reduced external tariffs after the various trade liberalisation rounds.

In 2001, both sources combined accounted for merely 15% of the EU's revenue. More significant are the EU's 1.4% share of member states' total VAT receipts (36% of the budget), and the income from a complicated GDP formula (49%) which better than the VAT reflects member states' differences in economic development. Euphemistically these sources are called the Union's "own resources", but *de facto* they are negotiated membership fees by another name. Jacques Delors had planned (and argued well) for a European energy tax. But, as we know, apart from pious summit talk about re-weighting the tax burden away from labour, these plans have come to naught.

The Commission has long refused to publish balance sheets with receipts and expenditure by member state. They are fraught with methodological problems, like tariff revenues accruing in the major ports like Rotterdam for imports transiting to other countries in the EU, or expenditure going into multi-country projects (as they normally should), etc. Nonetheless, member states, the media and the general public remain incurably fascinated by the subject, as if European integration was a sort of lottery, where, if sensible and lucky, national receipts should be larger than the contributions. This reductionist discussion overlooks the fact that economic and political benefits of integration surely are a multiple of the EU's "own resources" (i.e., the membership fee). People usually don't join a soccer club because they expect to get a higher return in terms of free tickets, free beer or soccer paraphernalia in consequence.

Yet, the net payer/net recipient obsession is a EU reality which dominates the public debate of integration. This includes the silly argument by proponents of integration arguing that integration is a good thing because of cash flows from Brussels into the region or popular local causes. Normally this is more quickly and cheaply done with own funds. And integration does not become any worse when European funds dry up some day, which would spare us the equally tedious and usually acrimonious budget summits (courtesy not exclusively of a certain ill-humoured Spanish Prime Minister).

With all these caveats in mind we arrive at the following net chart of European love and solidarity (1999):

Germany:	− 9.5 billion Euros
UK:	− 3.5 billion Euros
Netherlands:	− 2 billion Euros
Italy:	− 1.2 billion Euros
Sweden:	− 1 billion Euros
Austria:	− 700 million Euros
France:	− 600 million Euros
Belgium:	− 400 million Euros
Finland:	− 200 million Euros
Denmark:	close to nil, marginally positive
Ireland:	+ 2 billion Euros
Portugal:	+ 2.8 billion Euros
Greece:	+ 3.8 billion Euros
Spain:	+ 7 billion Euros

Per head, each Luxembourger pays net 220 Euros, each Dutchman, German, Swede and Austrian around 100 Euros, each Brit, Finn and Belgian roughly 50 Euros per year. In return each statistical Spaniard gets 180 Euros, each Portuguese 280 Euros, each Greek 360 Euros and each Irishman 520 Euros per year. This distribution has obviously become unsustainable after the enlargement of 2004. Thanks to the Spanish Prime Minister, unanimity on budgetary matters will apply in the Council until 2014. This protects the net position of the more militant, old, privileged member class (a position which only Ireland, as a rare success story, is prepared to relinquish).

A closer look at the use of the EU budget reveals that 80% is in fact used for redistribution to member states (agriculture and regional development) and only 20% for genuine European purposes. Instead of going through the arcane formula of the CAP and the regional and social funds and to hope against better knowledge that the funds will reach the deserving addressee, why not go instead for a straight objectivised formula to give unconditional transfers to integration losers? All the political sophistry in the world has not prevented Greece during the long term rule of a Socialist populist, the Berkeley economist Andreas Papandreou (of Mimi fame), to waste most EU funds (accounting for up to 6% of Greek GDP) by nationalising industries and banks and bloating the public sector with hundreds of thousands of his PASOK henchmen.

In federal systems states with a weaker tax base use these transfers usually more responsibly like their own funds, rather than as gift horses to be swindled out of a faraway capital like Brussels and to be wasted on frivolous projects. The case for a slimmed European budget by abolishing the CAP and most Regional/Social Funds is supported by its non-cyclical function. Without means for deficit spending or incentives to save (this happens only involuntarily by the administrative incompetence of certain member states to fill out the proper forms to claim "their" money) it remains largely static regardless of economic cycles: it neither helps in a recession, nor does it push a brake during overheating. Thus there is also a strong economic case for budget downsizing.

This case is also supported by numerous politically harmful problems of management and of principle. Taxation and budget politics should be the sacred duty of parliament. In the EU's *de facto* 2-chamber system, the (unelected) Council does the first (taxation) noisily between (half-) closed doors every five years, and decides the 50% of EU budget to be spent as "compulsory" (meaning agriculture), to be further decided by the agricultural ministers alone (given the clout of the farm lobby over these guys this is akin to letting confirmed alcoholics run a distillery). The elected EP may make proposals on the allocation of this "compulsory" expenditure. And its agricultural committee happily and regularly suggests spending more for its constituency. Yet the Council is free to ignore and to reject this advice. Essentially, the compulsory expenditure is handled by member states' governments. There is no parliamentary involvement or effective control, neither at European nor at national levels. Rather, most administrations during the last 40 years took a distinctly cavalier attitude to the use of the "money from Brussels".

The story is different for the other half of the EU budget, the "non-compulsory" expenditure (mostly infrastructural, social, foreign aid and R&D spending). Here, in case of disagreement, the European Parliament has the edge over the Council.

Within certain set margins the EP can amend this part of the draft budget submitted by the Commission and over-rule with a qualified majority the Council's figures. If the Parliament's ideas are not acceptable to the Council, a special conciliation procedure will take place, followed by a second reading by Parliament. Parliament is also free to reject the entire draft budget *in toto*, which would require the Union to organise its subsequent budget with provisional "twelfths", based on the previous year's monthly expenditure: no doubt a political, administrative and accounting nightmare. Much more popular is for Parliament to put sizeable amounts ("budget lines") "in the reserve": meaning to release them only once the dear friends from Commission or Council have fulfilled certain well-defined conditions.

It is the right of Parliament to refuse the "discharge" of the spent budget, if it feels that overall financial management during the past financial year(s) was not sound. In 1999 the very threat of the EP's refusal led to the downfall of the Santer Commission.

Constitutional reform would have to take a fresh new look at EU finances. Why not supplement the complex revenue side with a straightforward European tax (perhaps a levy on fossil fuel consumption), to be decided by Council and Parliament in a bi-cameral fashion? This would permit Parliament not just to spend money — it usually follows the principle of the more, the better, as savings don't win any political points — but to seriously debate and to be held responsible also for the revenue side in European elections.

EU fraud is a wonderful, big headline-seeking theme inevitably insinuating that greedy overpaid Commissioners and Commission officials have lined their pockets. It is somewhat reassuring however to know that this is the exception rather than the rule.

Fraud to the detriment of the EU happens on the income side (like cigarette smuggling) and on spending. As we saw, member states typically have little incentive to control effectively: their own citizens (often in high places) are involved. Exposure only means problems, embarrassment and repayment of the amounts involved. The Commission believes that only 1.5% of revenues and expenditure are subject to fraud (still representing the hefty sum of at least 1 billion Euros). Bernhard Friedmann, then head of the European Court of Auditors, in 1996 rather estimated the figure of misappropriations to 10% of the budget, implying the staggering amount of 9 billion Euros p.a. Typically, most of the amount has been subject to "irregularities", meaning not pilfered by fraud and corruption, but rather having been spent through incorrect procedures, like for instance insufficiently extensive tendering.

The Court of Auditors is a venerable institution, but it faces two problems — one of abuse of its own privileges (who controls the controllers?), but also the more manifest problem of overworked staff, cumbersome procedures and often less than helpful member state and third country administrations.

Still, the Court's annual reports make fascinating reading. One, for instance, famously describes how Italy's mature olive tree population doubled overnight once an EU scheme to support olive oil production was introduced. Normally it takes two decades for an olive tree to grow fruit. Other reports detail the numbers of gardeners and the size of swimming pools of the Commission's Delegations in tropical lands, or the spending follies of development and regional aid. An evergreen in the reports is the handling and valuation of the CAP's surplus commodities, which, if not exported quickly with expensive subsidies, are often left to rot. Once the report is published, the Commission declares itself shocked and repenting, promising to change its ways, but at the same time blaming (usually correctly) the member states.

The Commission has its own auditing and fraud control systems. They, however, are part of the command chain and cannot operate independently. Typically this has meant that the few internal corruption cases have been dealt with discretely and the culprits punished internally. Naturally this less than transparent procedure has triggered a frenzy of media interest and encouraged self-appointed whistle blowers, like the famous inspector Paul Van Buitenen, to go public. He had compiled a lengthy list of dossiers, some from his own investigations on spending for tourism promotion, the (mis-) management of "Leonardo" programmes and the "ECHO" emergency aids, as well as a couple of old cases which were already subject to year-long investigations. When he felt that his report was given insufficient attention by his superiors, in December 1998, he sent it to a Green MEP who immediately leaked it to the press. The Commission then made all the mistakes it was possible to make: it suspended and sanctioned Van Buitenen, thus giving him an instant martyr and celebrity status. It also declared itself in full solidarity with Mme Edith Cresson, a former prime minister, then Commissioner for Research. She had employed her live-in boyfriend, a retired dentist on a phoney AIDS research contract on which he then travelled to her home town of Castleraugh (where she was the mayor) to attend to her political business. Mme Cresson felt this was standard French practice and remained thoroughly and publicly unconvinced of any wrongdoing. This triggered a media frenzy. Subsequently a series of minor and non-so-minor transgressions [like Commissioner Bangemann accepting an honorarium of 10,000 Euros to speak at an event which his DG had sponsored, or Commissioner Wulf-Matthies accepting gold jewellery from a region (Crete) into which her DG was pouring funds] came into the open.

Half a year later the Santer Commission was dead and forced by Parliament to resign in disgrace. In despair Santer had appointed an independent group of five "wise men" to investigate the allegations of nepotism and corruption and linked his political fate to the conclusions of their report. The findings of the wise men were not particularly dramatic, but their conclusions maintained that due to the complexity of the Commission's decision-making, there was an almost complete absence of a sense of responsibility in financial management in the Commission's ranks. These words proved to be the straw that broke the camel's back. Parliament was in pre-election mood and (royally disregarding their own expense account, wife as assistant, and attendance stipend swindles), faction leaders from all camps outdid each other to ask for the Commission's scalps, which were promptly delivered.

The new Prodi Commission of 1999–2004 was less politically profiled than the old one and soon made internal reform its priority. A few culprits were fired or sidelined into obscurity (typically with a "counsellor" or "principal advisor" title and no responsibility at full pay). Director generals were rotated at no apparent purpose. The organigrams were turned upside down. Administrative units, directorates and directorate generals merged and de-merged. The rule book tightened with threatening sanctions for anybody putting his signature on anything, and two controllers watching each desk officer's every step. It was a miracle, in fact, that as a result of these reforms (reported here only with slight exaggeration) programmes still remained operational, which proves the resourcefulness of the Commission's staff (which as we know by now is paid adequately less for achievements performed than for frustrations suffered). The Prodi and Kinnock reforms, however, in view of this author, failed to address the root cause of poor management. The Commission sitting remote in the administrative towers of Brussels is not made to micro-manage operational programmes. During the politically ambitious (and successful) Delors years, the Commission had taken on board many more operational obligations than it could ever hope to manage effectively with a staff of only 15,000 (for comparison the city administrations of London, Paris, Vienna, Cologne and the Pentagon stand at some 60,000 each).

Just one example: in what turned out to be my worst administrative year at the Commission, overnight I was put in charge of the Union's social and health programmes in Eastern Europe. I had a staff of two, an annual budget of 80 million Euros and some 600 individual projects (ranging from 20 million Euros to 5,000 Euros) in 15 countries from Estonia (no problem country) to Albania (big problem country) to "manage". Five supporting agencies had been contracted to supervise the operations of the projects, which ranged from tourism promotion in Bulgarian villages to AIDS clinics in Poland. The ultimate responsibility lay with me (as I had to sign everything, including hospital equipment delivered from Greece to Albania, with all technical bills in Greek — even a German translation would have been of little help — as "seen and approved" in order to get the payments going). If this sounds like a nightmare, it was one. I was only saved by the efficiency and dedication of my Finnish assistant (he was almost killed by a bunch of Arab thugs — not in Albania, but in Brussels). The purpose of most of the schemes: funding elements of "civil society" in the margins of foreign societies (good and pure intentions!) by remote control from Brussels was a recipe for disasters to happen, and so some did.

Not all allegations were true however. Disgruntled employees denounced the NGOs from which they were fired. An inspection revealed that the contracted village renovation project in the Carpathians was in fact nicely done, and entrepreneurial training seminars in Romania had taken place as stipulated. But one scheme had gone badly wrong. A former British social worker had applied and gotten a 80,000 Euros grant to run a roadside AIDS prevention and consultation centre for gypsy prostitutes in Southern Hungary. As a trained social worker he knew the jargon of political correctness and found the blessing of my predecessor's grant selection board — after all the AIDS street-worker scene is not high society. He soon fell out with his partner organisation, a progressive Dutch hooker association. They informed me that, under the guise of an adoption scheme for gypsy girls, he was in fact selling young women into slavery. An inspection on the spot revealed that his roadside AIDS consulting centre was in fact a whorehouse. I stopped all payments, started reimbursement procedures and asked the Hungarian authorities for a criminal investigation. Some of his street swallows, who had talked too much, disappeared, but a murder investigation yielded no corpses. Inevitably the press got hold of the story. The headline "Briton in Prostitute Aid Scandal" was simply too good to let pass (*Sunday Times*, January 31, 1999). But it is important to note that the EU was the victim of fraud, not its perpetrator. Once the political decision is taken to finance politically correct activities outside the margins of respectable society by remote control from Brussels, such accidents are bound to happen. In this case, once alerted all the right measures were taken; unfortunately the alarm was rung too late.

The conclusion of this and of hundreds of more or less similar stories is simply for the Commission to get out of operational programmes (with all of their inevitable fall-outs and frustrated expectations) and to turn into a purely conceptual and supervisory institution for which its situation at the political apex in Europe (without subordinate administrations) and its staff is uniquely qualified. Fiddling with the organigram and hiring hundreds of accountants and controllers is unlikely to address this fundamental dilemma.

It should be understood that the Commission staff is not corrupt. Not because they are a better people, but pay is too good, controls too strict and sanctions too severe. When on a diplomatic posting in Japan, I was once offered a bribe of 5 million yen (30,000 Euros) "for my troubles". It would have been madness to risk one's career, a horrible investigation, public disgrace and the possibility of life-long blackmail for the equivalent of a few months' salary. (Had it been 500 million yen the story might have been different, and you would certainly not read it here.)

Independently from the EU's "own resources", taxation has become a Community issue. It is obviously central to national sovereignty, not only as source of national revenue, but also as a policy instrument to encourage or discourage consumption, savings, the use of labour, of capital, etc., as well as of societal equity, narrowing the gap between rich and poor, and between cities and the countryside.

The internal market with its mobility of people, goods, capital and services should intensify tax competition. In an ideal European world people and companies should opt for the right mix of the lowest tax and the best public services. The total tax burden is highest in Sweden and Denmark at just above 50% of GDP, and lowest in Greece and Ireland at below 35%, followed by the UK, Portugal and Spain, at just below 40% of GDP. The EU average is at 42.6% (1997), up from 36.7% in 1980, with further tendencies to grow. So much for the fears (of Finance Ministers) and hopes (of tax-payers) for a healthy downward competition on taxes (which, for instance, is very much alive between US states). During the same period the tax burden on labour (23.8%, EU-wide, 1997) increased equally.

Rather, EU Finance Ministers bargain for ever greater tax "harmonisation" notably of indirect taxes (turnover taxes, excise duties) — unfortunately taking the highest levels as benchmarks of harmony. Already in 1977 the value added tax (VAT) was introduced, which is fractionally collected (the previous VAT paid for purchased inputs is deducted from the total payable VAT amount) and ultimately borne by the final consumer at the rate applicable in the country of purchase. Only for cars and mail order purchases does the rate of the country of destination apply. Normal VAT rates vary between 25% (Denmark, Sweden) and 15% (Luxembourg). Excise duties on mineral oil, tobacco and alcohol show even greater variation. In Greece quite reasonably wine is considered as a basic foodstuff indispensable to human health and well-being and therefore untaxed. Unfortunately, in this Greece is not considered a EU role model. Should it ever reach Swedish levels of alcohol taxation, the end of Greek civilisation would surely be nigh.

On occasion some "harmony" in taxation is sensible — like on fuel taxes to avoid, for instance, EU truckers re-routing via Luxembourg to fill their tanks there and take advantage of lower taxation.

Another piece of harmony concerns the withholding tax on capital earnings, which is meant to penalise savings. The Commission and most member states want a minimum withholding tax of 15% or regular reporting to the tax authorities on foreigners' accounts. Luxembourg and Austria have made their agreement conditional upon acceptance of the same conditions by Switzerland, where an estimated 4,000 billion francs of thrifty EU citizens are bunkered. The Swiss are aware that once they render their banking secret to sniffy EU tax inspectors they can return to dairy farming in the high Alps (and Luxembourg bankers start coal mining again, and Channel Islanders return to living on fishing and postage stamps). Hence, their response remains predictable. No doubt new loopholes will be ingeniously invented and properly used. Capital will not have to run to the Caymans and the Bahamas. Only the political capital which the EU's spendthrift finance ministers and Commissioner Frits Bolkestein (1999–2004) have wasted on this mission impossible is amazing. Whether their initiative is legally watertight remains doubtful. Their plans were based on levying taxes on EU foreigners (compared to inlanders). This seems to be at variance with Treaties of Rome provisions and ECJ jurisprudence which outlaws all tax discrimination based on nationality, be it products or taxable citizens.

In conclusion, it would appear that the EU and its citizens are well advised to opt for a low Community budget, for the start of a healthy downward competition on taxation (both direct and indirect) and to resist most attempts at "harmonisation", which in fact seems like a cartel of over-indebted finance ministers trying to peg taxes at the highest possible level, discouraging savings, driving capital away from Europe and ultimately suffocating the economy.

Big Brother in Schengenland: Law and Justice

Europe's integration is a legal construction borne out of treaties, their annexes and their protocols: the Treaties of Rome (1957), the Single Act (1987), the Treaties of Maastricht (1992, in force since 1993), of Amsterdam (1997, in force since 1999), and of Nice (2000, in force since 2002). They and the various accession treaties, once properly ratified by all parliaments, establish EU primary law. The treaties aspire to integration through peace, law, democracy and social justice (unlike the violence of WWII or the Napoleonic wars). They established the fundamental economic freedoms of the internal market and principles of social solidarity, respect national identity, and since a European Council declaration of 1977 have made the "European Convention on Human Rights" (1950) a general principle of Community law.

In line with the spread of political correctness, the Amsterdam Treaty (Article 12) expanded the civic rights provisions to cover anti-discrimination on gender, race, ethnic origin, religion, beliefs, disability, age or sexual orientation. (While the latter is obviously a victory for the gay lobby, it presumably does not cover paedophiles, necrophiles and similar preferences — although surely they constitute a certain sexual orientation. Note that logic has never been a strong point of PC.)

There is however one significant exception to the equal treatment principle: a member state may treat its own nationals worse than EU partners, that is, insist on stricter national standards than those prescribed by internal market regulations. One example: German brewers must stick to the beer purity law of 1516, whilst importers of other EU beers do not need to.

EU secondary law is established by legal acts set by EU institutions based on treaty provisions, as well as by international agreements of the Union. The following legal tools are in use:

- regulations, which apply directly in the entire EU in full;
- directives, which member states need to transpose into national law within a fixed time frame. The objective is binding but it leaves room for interpretation to suit specific national circumstances;
- decisions, which are individual binding acts (typically in competition, state aids cases);
- recommendations, opinions of the Commission, and resolutions, declarations of the Council and EP, which are declarations of intent and goodwill, they may result in legislative and action programmes some day, or maybe not.

Since the 1960s the European Court of Justice in its tradition of case law has ruled that EU was not one of the usual international organisations, but that its treaty provisions restricted national sovereign rights. Hence EU law established a new legal order and took precedence over national law in case of conflict.

While insisting that treaty law cannot be overridden by domestic legal provisions, the Court also made clear that the direct applicability and primacy of EU law only applied to the "first pillar" of Community policies, not to the inter-governmental second and third pillars of foreign and security policy and of justice and home affairs. EU institutions enjoy powers only in policy areas specified in the treaties. Unlike a sovereign state, which can act in whichever policy area it pleases, the EU has no jurisdiction over jurisdiction unless authorised. Sometimes the institutional rules were slightly bent. The European Council, for instance, which has met since 1974 to issue policy guidelines on the EU's future development (and in the process during weak Commission presidencies — meaning all except those of Jacques Delors — usurped more and more of the Commission's right of initiative), only appointed itself as a formal EU institution with the Single Act in 1987.

As we saw, EU powers are far-reaching in agriculture, competition and the internal market, but extremely limited in culture, education and public health. The logic of this historical evolution of competences is sometimes spurious in the light of subsidiarity and common sense. While the EU is legally compelled to act in case of an animal disease like swine fever, it remains impotent if epidemics like hepatitis or tuberculosis threaten to spread from Eastern Europe (where they are currently staging an ugly comeback). The consolidated EU Treaty's new Article 5 defines the subsidiarity principle nicely: the EU must act where objectives can better be attained at Community level. It must not act where objectives can be achieved by individual member state action. A wonderful principle which, due to the incrementalist fashion of European integration, has often been violated.

While the exclusivity of the right of initiative appears to have slipped from the Commission since the mid-1990s, its equally sacred role as "guardian" of the treaties remains. The Commission has the duty to monitor member states compliance and the right to initiate infringement procedures if a member state fails to do so in spite of its legal commitment taken jointly in the Council earlier. First it is asked gently for an explanation and for a date of compliance. If nothing is convincingly forthcoming, a deadline is set. Failing this, ECJ procedures are initiated. Normally this works, as no member state likes being hauled before the ECJ to fight a public battle that is certain to end in humiliating defeat (except for the Germans on beer purity). The Court may even award damages if losses are incurred as a result of a member state's failure to transpose a directive into national law.

But legal challenges before the ECJ can also work the other way round: aggrieved citizens can sue EU institutions (including the Commission) for the failure to act or to request the annulment of EU legal acts when the institution is seen to abuse its competences (like when prohibiting cigarette advertisements).

Who then is the European Court of Justice, that enigmatic ultimate arbiter of all things European residing on the windswept plateau Kirchberg in sleepy Luxembourg? The Court consists of 25 judges, each appointed by his member state for a 6-year term. In their earlier lives they often and ideally had been eminent lawyers or politicians well versed in European law. But as member states are free to nominate anybody they wish, on occasion, you get distinct non-experts, like a feminist labour law professor or a former justice minister as well.

While the Court proceeds along Anglo-Saxon case law, in its proceedings there is also a curious and unique element of French legal tradition, the "advocate general". In the French model he is termed "commissaire du government" in administrative courts without appeal. He issues non-binding proposals for a judgement which the judges then (frequently, but not necessarily always) use as a pre-cooked formula for their own judgement and its reasoning.

The ECJ operates in many functions: as a constitutional court to mediate in arguments between EU institutions, as an administrative court to settle disputes over Community or national decisions, as a labour court to handle social security and labour issues, as a fiscal court to handle taxation and customs problems, as a civil court to award claims for damages, and as a criminal court to review allegations of improper collusion among cartel operators.

Little wonder that the Court is vastly over-worked, with the backlog of unsettled cases piling up. As a sensible, but nonetheless insufficient measure, in 1989 a Court of First Instance (CFI) has been set up in order to allow citizens (including EU officials) recourse against administrative acts of the Commission and other EU institutions.

If we review the institutional arrangements, then the conclusion is quite clear-cut. Although the subsidiarity principle is flouted in a cavalier fashion frequently, at least the institutional provisions of democracy, of parliamentary approval (for 50% of budget and most of the legislation) and of judicial review works effectively on the Community's first pillar issues. This somewhat compensates for the Council's anomaly: an executive that works as a legislature. Unfortunately, democratic proceedings are not respected in the second and third pillars of inter-governmental cooperation.

Curiously there is very little public awareness of the great advances of European integration in the legal field. This could be tragic: law is only effective if it is properly accepted and understood by the citizens. This commonplace wisdom has sadly been neglected by European decision-makers who agreed to organise "justice and home affairs" as the secretive and obscure "third pillar" of European integration. In trying to cut out political (the EP), administrative (the Commission) and legal rivals (the ECJ), Ministers of Justice and Home Affairs, in fact, managed to excise democratic debate and legal control, thus putting the very fabric of European legal culture at risk. The Treaty of Amsterdam transferred some legal issues from inter-governmental treatment ("third pillar") into Community decision-making ("first pillar"), but the basic problem remains.

In 1998 a "space of freedom, security and law" based on the Amsterdam Treaty was announced by the Council. It was to change the "soft law" of lofty but inconsequential recommendations into compulsory provisions.

"Freedom" was defined in both positive and negative terms. EU citizens are to enjoy their basic constitutional freedoms (thank you), freedom of movement, the right to privacy and data protection, but also freedom from discrimination — referring to the PC anti-discrimination codex of gender, race, ethnic origin, religion, ideology, handicap, age or sexual hobbies, without spelling out how conflicts with freedom of opinion, academic freedom, etc., will be resolved. This is of particular importance since democracy and a multicultural society without common values are difficult to reconcile. "Security" is defined, not as one might think as citizens' safety from violent physical attacks or against their property, but foremost with a cross-border touch: as fighting terrorism, trafficking of humans, abuse of children, smuggling drugs and weapons, corruption and cross-border fraud. People threatened in crime ridden metropolitan ghettos would probably set their priorities differently than their interior ministers, but then again they have not been asked.

Finally "law" is defined as access to civil and penal justice, with the approximation of the widely different national provisions as an objective (one can only hope, that the Greek judiciary, Italian legal administrative speed, the impunity of the French political class, and British jail quality are not the benchmark of this approximation). EU cooperation is also undertaken to facilitate the detection and prosecution of criminals — like via "Eurojust", an information exchange and coordination network of public prosecutors.

Schengenland was first invented in the small Luxembourg border town of Schengen in 1985. Then a common visa policy was decided between Germany, France and the Benelux countries. Some rules on police cooperation followed, and the coordination of drugs and firearms laws — the first being lax in the Netherlands and the second in France. With its snail paced dynamism, the hallmark of inter-governmentalism, one decade later in 1995 Schengenland, which encountered what were diplomatically called transitional security problems after the border checks between the countries fell, began to implement common border control provisions and some sort of common visa and immigration policies. Asylum shopping by rejects was abolished after the Dublin Agreement of 1990 (in force since 1997), and a one-stop procedure in the country of entry (if identifiable) was introduced. By the year 2000 Schengenland has expanded to comprise also Austria and the Mediterranean member states. In 2001 the Nordic Union of all Scandinavians, including Norway and Iceland also joined the Schengen empire, but Ireland and certainly the UK are still halfway out. They accept police and legal cooperation, but still insist on proper national border controls although being flooded with asylum tourists and East European gypsies nonetheless.

After years of teething problems, a computerised Schengen Information System (SIS) has been set up linking all police computers and external EU border crossing points. It is a data bank containing wanted people, stolen cars and pilfered art pieces.

Since 1991 plans were around to create a European FBI and in 1995 Europol was set up in The Hague. It still is a far cry from any Eurocop fantasy. Instead of chasing mass murderers and terrorists of the Bin Laden kind, Europol's work mainly consisted of seconded police officers checking their national computer systems to clear up cross-border drug cases. Given the cumbersome ratification procedures of inter-governmentalism, Europol became fully operational only in July 1999. It now also covers trade in stolen cars, nuclear materials, pornography, illegal migrants and prostitutes, money laundering and forged Euros. Europol can only become active if there are indications of organised crime involvement in at least two member states. Then its staff of 350 (2003) will analyse the data available and exchange them with the central national police authority. As national police officers their actions remain subject to national court control. It is planned that in the future, Europol with a larger staff will also deal with more relevant capital crimes and terrorism (once member states have sorted out the small difference between a terrorist and a freedom fighter).

A lot had to be done to improve law enforcement and cooperation in civic and commercial cases between EU member states covering divorces, speeding tickets and bankruptcies. Since 1968 attempts had been made for speedier cross border delivery of legal documents (which normally had to go via foreign ministries, embassies and delivery by bailiffs — taking in my experience, easily eight months between Germany and Belgium, enough time to change one's address and to have it returned to sender, taking another eight months). Since 2000 (note: after 32 years of careful deliberations!) a quicker delivery of court documents has been implemented EU wide. In divorce cases court decisions also involving the custody of children are mutually recognised and enforced (with predictable heart-tearing dramas promptly unfolding in the media). After 2004 this will also apply to commercial and other civil cases. Public authorities between member states since recently can also communicate directly.

In order to obtain a comprehensive picture of the European drug scene, a European Monitoring Centre has been set up in Lisbon (an Amsterdam coffee shop may have been more practical). It is to research into the origins of supply and demand growth and recommend suitable curbs for both, cooperate with third countries (producers and transit), train officials there and plan alternative crops, fight smuggling and supply health information. The observatory is budgeted at some 60 million Euros per year — presumably the equivalent of the monthly intake of a medium sized Turkish or Columbian drug lord.

With Eastern enlargement achieved, plans are afoot to create a joint European border police in order to alleviate the burden on the border countries and to increase the efficiency of patrolling the Eastern land border and the Mediterranean Sea coast which are both equally porous, with illegal mass immigration beginning to threaten the social and cultural fabric of Europe.

The EU and the Rest of the World: Trade First

Once the Customs Union was achieved, it made sense to negotiate trade and commercial issues in unison towards third partners. With a mandate given by the Council then a unified position would also enhance the EU's bargaining strength and leverage. The common commercial policy survived its baptism of fire successfully at subsequent multilateral rounds: "Dillon" (1959–1962), and "Kennedy" (1963–1967). As a more consolidated major player, the Commission then operated at the Tokyo (1973–1979) and Uruguay (1986–1993) rounds, which all helped to reduce tariffs (including the Union's common external tariff) as a significant obstacle to world trade, and to set up multilateral disciplines on a range of non-tariff barriers in order to minimise their harmful effect on optimal global factor allocation.

The EU's commitment to free trade has not always been a linear affair. With Viscount Etienne Davignon as powerful Vice President for Industry and Research at the Commission (1977–1984), the EU in the aftermath of the two oil crises (1973/1974 and 1978/1979) more than toyed with the idea of an interventionist industrial policy using trade policy instruments like anti-dumping charges and "voluntary" import restraint agreements as protectionist tools. Member states watched their inflation and unemployment figures shoot up and saw their car and consumer electronics industries threatened by Japan's neo-mercantilist export offensives. Within the EU then only Germany, Denmark and the Netherlands were in the liberal trading camp, with political Germany as usual too disorganised to resist the French-led majority pushing for interventionist protectionism.

Only when it became apparent that these policies were unlikely to pull Europe out of its technological inertia did the EU switch to a more consistent liberal trade policy, aided by the ensuing success of the internal market programme. Equally, it was quite a few years after Mrs Thatcher came to power that the UK in the mid-1980s began to practise the liberal orthodoxies which are now *de rigeur*.

The development of relations with Japan, as an emerging global competitor, is quite instructive for the increasing professionalism and the policy shifts in the EU's foreign economic diplomacy:

- Until the mid-1970s the Commission had great difficulties in obtaining a bargaining mandate from member states which did not take Japan seriously as an economic competitor out of a mixture of arrogance and ignorance, and thus failed to stop Japan's neo-mercantilist expansion and allowing her markets to remain closed.

- From the mid-1970s to mid-1980s, attempts to fight back the Japanese "invasion" (which had already destroyed the European motorcycle, watch-making and radio set industry) with half-baked measures of temporary export restraint agreements and anti-dumping fees. They were applied when Japanese exports had been sold at prices below production costs and were meant to hurt EU competitors. Japan managed to play masterly one EU country against the other (the UK as self-advertised Trojan horse did not cover itself in glory in this episode).

- From the mid-1980s to the early 1990s, a more sophisticated EU policy attempted to promote EU products actively on the Japanese market (including language and practical business training for European executives in Japan, the famous ETP programme, from which this author also happened to graduate), and to open the Japanese market through negotiations in those uncompetitive sectors of the Japanese economy where an impressive array of non-tariff barriers kept out European products and services. These non-tariff barriers (they have certainly not died out, and were happily copied by Korea) ranged from collusion of the *keiretsu* conglomerates in industrial services (banking, insurance, shipping, road transport, advertising, etc.), to rigged cartels in construction and public procurement, to tax discrimination for liquor and tariff and non-tariff protection for pharmaceuticals, fine chemicals, and for processed foodstuffs and drinks, sometimes quarantining and gassing perfectly healthy quality products for imaginary insects (following standard Australian practice). The most striking example of this twisted protectionist mindset was found in 1995 during the Kobe earthquake when the Japanese customs quarantined 40 Swiss rescue dogs (wonderfully prepared Japan did not have any) for four weeks, until any survivor the dogs might have rescued from the rubble was surely dead. As the reader might sense, this author during 1987–1991 was active on the agro-food, chemicals and transportation front in Tokyo, which was the civilised version of 1914–1918 trench warfare. Once one non-tariff barrier was removed after year-long efforts, a mightier new one promptly popped up. At least it was the EU (and our US friends with their mightier diplomatic artillery and air power) which in the end advanced by a few trenches.

- After 1992 it transpired that corporate and public Japan had burned enough cash on uneconomical investments (in production over-capacities, overheated product cycles, loss-making foreign ventures, corporate palaces, clubs, golf courses and other executive status symbols) to become practically insolvent. As Japan's political elite was too wedded to corporate Japan, the needed hard decisions for restructuring were shelved. Japan's stagnating decline set in and her dreams of economic world mastery imploded. Love and peace began to set into Euro-Japanese relations with lots of energy spent on a wide range of moderately productive cooperative ventures and in-depth political exchanges (like on the situation of Outer Mongolia).

Five years later the Asian crisis of 1997 also deflated the other Asian tigers, revealing yet another case of hyped-up resource misallocation, from which some major actors like Indonesia, the Philippines, Taiwan and Hong Kong, following its annexation by China, had difficulties to recover. The Chinese hyperbole with her unsustainable "miracle" growth based on FDI inflows, but sapped by resource wasting public enterprises, endemic corruption and bankrupt state banks, will no doubt face similar problems.

Hence EU trade policy is well advised to remain level-headed and to reject the regular occurrence of alarmist noises insinuating the need for protectionist miracle cures.

With 6% of the world population counting for 20% of global trade in goods and 26% of trade in services, the EU has a vital interest in a law-based liberal world trading order, which after all has created in the EU tens of millions of higher value added jobs in machinery, car, chemical and aircraft production and in qualified services.

As one of the leading actors in the WTO (since 1995 the successor organisation to GATT) the EU prefers multilateral solutions, like for investment and intellectual property protection, harmonised and/or mutually recognised standards, certificates, testing and customs procedures, rules against uncompetitive practices, effective WTO dispute settlement panels, and predictable enforceable rules governing commercial transactions.

These rules were accepted by China when she joined the WTO in 2001 in return for being granted most-favoured nation treatment by the other contracting parties. With Russia, whose membership is in the pipeline, things will be the same.

After a false start in Seattle (aborted not by fly-in anti-globalisation protesters, but by US incompetence) the new "Doha" Round of trade liberalisation in the EU's view should not just address the "classics", but produce a comprehensive package, covering trade and environment, public procurement, and possibly even minimal social and ethical standards (child labour, prison labour, and even animal rights). This sensible approach was thrown out in Cancun in 2003 by an odd coalition of countries like Egypt, India and Brazil — all suffering from domestic policy induced competitiveness problems. Their wrecking job was promptly applauded by the anti-globalisation lobby in a classic case of inarticulate resentments overtaking possibly better judgement.

Developing countries (India foremost) surely need some convincing that multilateral solutions are also in the interest of their own development. With the ever-declining role of tariff protection, the past EU policy favouring preferential regional arrangements [which the EU maintains with mostly Africa (ACP), the Mediterranean, the

EEA (the European Economic Area, which however includes internal market rules for all) and the accession countries Romania and Bulgaria] and the current fad of bilateral Free Trade Agreements have ultimately outlived most of their usefulness.

In a multilateral trade world facing the US, Japan, China and India, the EU has to speak and negotiate professionally with one voice. The alternative is not to be heard and not to be listened. It took proud national trade ministers a few decades to get the message, but in spite of a few occasional lapses (notably when facing the US skilful divide and rule games), since the mid-1980s the common trade policy has been firmly, professionally and successfully established by the Commission — properly mandated by the Council and controlled by Parliament and the ECJ, as it should be.

Out of Africa: EU Aid

When the EU (then EEC) was founded in 1957, most member states were still proud, if somewhat shaken, masters of colonial empires. France held onto vast territories north and south of the Sahara, Belgium to Congo and to Rwanda/Burundi, Italy to Somaliland and the Dutch to the Antilles. At French insistence these colonies, prior to and after independence, were formally associated with the EU to promote their economic and social development. The Jaounde Association Agreements (1963–1975) then provided limited OAD for Francophone Africa. When the UK entered the common market (with Commonwealth countries fearing for their imperial tariff preferences), most of the rest of Sub-Saharan Africa joined, plus a few Caribbean and Pacific Islands.

With this low performance crowd, then, the classical period of EU/ACP cooperation and development began, governed by successive Lomé Agreements (1975–2000). There were two major components: tariff concessions and grant aid. As a customs policy countries normally practise a system of tariff escalation: import tariffs are highest on processed products, and lowest on the imported raw materials needed for domestic processing, in order to encourage high value added domestically. Courtesy of the Jaounde/Lomé Agreements for ACP countries, the reverse applied for their exports to the EU: the higher the degree of processing, the lower the tariff (normally nil). Except for Mauritius, however, hardly anybody was able to take advantage. There are also EU tariff concessions towards the Mediterranean countries (except for competing Southern agricultural produces) since less far reaching cooperation agreements were concluded with them in the mid-1970s. The more dynamic Asian and Latin American countries are able to benefit from a Generalised System of Preferences (GSP), which since 1971 has allowed almost all of their manufacturers to enter the EU duty free — with the notable exception of textiles (subject to tariff quotas) and foodstuffs (subject to usually prohibitive variable levies).

As the import share of ACP countries into the EU fell from 4.7% (1990) to 2.8% (1994) alone, there was soon agreement on the trade preferences' ineffectiveness. Yet it took a while until they were about to be replaced by asymmetrical free trade agreements with each of the ACP areas of the three continents. Starting in 2006 the EU will eliminate almost all import tariffs. The beneficiary regions will reciprocate between five and ten years later.

The EU grant schemes benefiting ACP countries were to the order of 5 billion Euros p.a. EU aid consists almost exclusively of grants, not credits. Old orthodoxy had it that recipient countries spend credit aid more carefully as they — very theoretically — might have to reimburse it. In reality, there is no difference. Both are wasted. But EU grants at least don't pile up on their debt mountain. There are currently two trends in development aid fashion: one is to move away from work intensive and strategically dubious project aid towards sectoral aid and "macro-economic" (budget) aid for promises of virtuous reforms. The second is a result of the growth of natural and man-made disasters, including the demographic explosion and the proliferation of civil wars: EU emergency food aid and disaster relief already by 1995 amounted to 20% of all EU OAD — run by a fast growing specialist NGO industry — and is expanding rapidly ever since. A ceasefire has hardly been signed but rehabilitation teams are already on stand-by to rebuild shattered and ransacked hospitals, power stations and airports for the use of the surviving warlords and their henchmen (to be retooled from bush fighters into ministers, diamond traders, ambassadors and UN staff).

Reflecting the spirit of the 1980s, which felt worsening terms of trade for commodity producers (compared to higher value added goods) to be "unjust" and in need of compensation and the EU's own expensive (and silly) efforts to keep her agricultural commodity prices "stable", two stabilisation schemes were invented and funded for the benefit of ACP commodity producers. "Stabex" for some 50 agricultural commodities like cocoa, coffee, cotton, etc., important for fertile countries like Ivory Coast, Cameroon, Ghana, Ethiopia and Papua New Guinea . "Sysmin" for the mineral mining of bauxite, aluminium, copper, cobalt, iron, tin, phosphates, manganese and uranium for the benefit of mineral rich countries like Mauritania, Zaire (Congo), Zambia, Niger, Namibia and Guinea. The well meaning logic of those dinosaurs of the era of managed trade and commodity agreements was that single commodity countries' export earnings would slump unjustly and harmfully during the commodity's inevitable period of downswing (remember the pig cycle) and hence should be compensated unconditionally for the shortfall from the rich North. Never mind that the country had pocketed happily the proceeds of excess revenue during the upswing periods and had usually failed to diversify its economy. These schemes were very popular among the recipient governments, as "Stabex" and "Sysmin" funds were paid into their coffers automatically, without strings attached (which must have immensely pleased friendly Swiss bankers, jewellers and real estate agents from Oxford Street to the Cote d'Azur). Instead of doing "justice", tax billions were handed to the corrupted elite of countries privileged by nature in terms of mineral deposits, climate and fertility. Instead of giving incentives to diversify, these funds rather encouraged the opposite, including domestic mismanagement to run down export revenues regardless of global prices. Currently "Stabex" and "Sysmin" (termed "programme aid" in Eurospeak), plus certain support for balance of payment problems and for structural adjustment, have declined to a level of 13% of total EU aid, but they still seem high enough to create mischief.

The objectives of the four different Lomé Agreements (they are actually based on the pretence of having been "negotiated") reflect nicely the fads and follies of the past development decades. Lomé I and II (1975–1985) advocated industrialisation objectives. Lomé III (1985–1990) was passionate about self-sufficiency, food security and rural development. Lomé IV (1990–2000) then proliferated its objectives and instruments to enhance human rights, democracy, good governance, the position of women, the environment and the private sector.

Originally the Lomé philosophy had taken great pride in "equality between partners" (meaning, impossibly, donors and recipients), with their mutual respect for sovereignty, the right of each state to determine its own political system and its social and economic policy options. As most of the ACP clientele consisted (and consists) of fairly unsavoury despots (Idi Amin, Desire Mobutu and Emperor Bokassa were only the more prominent ones), this was fine with them and with their former colonial masters, provided that their extractive industries, plantations and expatriates could operate unhindered and the country did not join the Soviet camp. By 1990 the Soviet option had disappeared and public infrastructure and security had become so disintegrated as to make life increasingly unbearable for expatriate corporations and individuals alike. Whatever the niceties of sovereignty and equality, donors began to insist on and reward basic decency of governance and the semblance of political correctness.

With the end of the Cold War and the changed import needs of modern service economies in the North (with substitute products aplenty, the need for most tropical commodities is much reduced), the only rationale for development aid should be based on the hard realities of global interdependence: preserving the tropical rain forests, arresting desertification, the pollution of air and sea, not to disrupt the world climate, to combat drugs, transmissible diseases and illegal migration, and finally to propagate and facilitate birth control. Unfortunately the naïve belief that the prospects of universal prosperity would reduce population growth automatically has proved fallacious. In Africa, for instance, the population explosion (1960: 270 million people, 1996: 700 million, 2025: 1.5 billion), irrespective of the AIDS epidemic is reversing even the small economic gains made in the few transient national "success stories".

After four failed development decades in Africa the EU's contemporary approach appears more commonsensical: support for structural reforms in LDCs is only sensible if these are internalised by the country and accepted by the elites and the people. The reforms should be socially and regionally compatible. They should be done in a realistic time frame while keeping long term development objectives in sight. Reforms towards a market economy need to be undertaken in a pragmatic fashion, without shock therapies and sudden import liberalisations. Democratic reforms could only work with initiatives and participation of the people themselves. The EU's support should be limited to technical support during elections. EU aid should only be suspended when the democratisation process is brutally stopped (like in Haiti) or if fundamental human rights are systematically violated (like in Sudan).

The case for a common EU development policy is made by the notion of accumulating a "critical mass" of funds to reach sectoral and political results. The 15 old member states' individual activities (which mostly pride themselves in doing well at project work) could be coordinated and targeted towards the larger jointly agreed objectives.

One could equally argue for a conceptual Commission role (like the World Bank) and operational roles for the more abundantly staffed member states and their under-employed tropical embassies. Coordination on the spot is surely commendable (a good idea that does not lose its sparkle even after 40 years of frequently poor implementation), as LDCs typically receive so much excellent and contradictory advice on any of their problems that they can pick and choose with ease the rationale for doing what they would have wanted to do anyway.

The problem of coordination is compounded by the re-emergence of post-Cold War Africa as a low risk playground for hegemonic games of influence between the former colonial powers and the US, as evident during the wars in the Congo Basin and along the Great Lakes. France remains a major player (some temporary disengagement under the prime ministership of Lionel Jospin notwithstanding), with 8,000 well trained Foreign Legion troops and 700 military advisers stationed in six countries from Senegal to Djibouti and with secret provisions in bilateral defense agreements engaging Paris in case of domestic troubles. Where there is oil in Africa, there is also Elf Aquitaine with its special information service. Thus whereas the Danes may improve the rural water supply, the Germans train car mechanics, the Dutch empower marginalised women and the EU delegate hands over his "Stabex" cheque, the quiet French ambassador with his intimate knowledge of the local scene and the right instruments at his disposal proconsul-like will call the shots. The rotating Council presidency may now coordinate.

During 1968/1995, the EU spent (through the Commission's OAD budget, and EIB and EDF funds) 24 billion Euros in Sub-Saharan Africa. Africa's share of EU aid had shrunk from 70% in the early 1970s to somewhat less than 40% in the mid-1990s, reflecting the increased globalisation of the EU's aid policy. The largest amounts were given to Ethiopia, Ivory Coast, Mozambique, Cameroon and Nigeria (some 30% of total aid). Ethiopia alone received 1.4 billion Euros. This was given before and after the fall of the Mengistu regime, which picked wars with Somalia, Eritrea and secessionist tribes in the West, employed famines with genocidal intent against its own peoples and resorted to bloody repression, including the murder of Emperor Haile Selassie and his family. While food aid (prominent in Ethiopia) and project aid, notably in health and education, brings undoubted benefits to the immediate recipients, the overall structural picture of EU aid to Africa is bleak: all key indicators, whether governance, macro-economic health, population control, environment or public infrastructure, all point downwards. There are no success stories — at least none that survive the next regime change or civil war.

On occasion EU aid appears to be outright harmful. No matter how nice environmentally compatible assurances printed on recycled brochure paper might sound, a 2,000 km logging road was built with EU funds through the last remaining rain forests of South Cameroon (*The Economist*, January 12, 2002). Every child in the tropics knows what happens when a logging road is built through a rain forest. Even the World Bank learnt it when it financed roads across the Amazon. Facilitating settlements, timber extraction and slash/burn clearance, it spells the certain end of the entire regional rain forest with all of its wildlife in less than a decade.

In line with more global concerns and shifting strategic interests, EU aid since the mid-1980s has moved to encompass the Mediterranean (from 1.8 billion Euros disbursed during 1986/1990 increasing to 4.1 billion Euros during 1991/1995) and Asia and Latin

America (growing from 2.3 billion Euros to 4.4 billion Euros in 1991/1995). The largest recipients in the first group are Egypt (mostly food aid), Tunisia and Palestine (where the Israelis in 2003 smashed most of the EU funded infrastructure, including schools, government buildings and the Gaza airport). In the second group, the recipients of the greatest largesse were India (1 billion Euros), Bangladesh (700 million Euros), Peru (300 million Euros), and Nicaragua, Bolivia, the Philippines, China and Pakistan at the tune of 260 million Euros each. Interesting that three of them are nuclear powers bullying their neighbours as regional hegemons.

During 1986/1995, Communist regimes also were beefed up. Next to China, these were Vietnam and Cambodia with 150 million Euros each and Cuba with 90 million Euros.

Regardless of the operational short-comings and flawed logic of the much smaller US foreign aid, their strategic purpose in focusing on Israel, Egypt and the Ukraine is crystal clear. In case of Japan, her focus on East Asia and Oceania at least makes geo-political and economic sense. The unfocussed mess of the EU's foreign aid does not make sense by any yardstick: neither strategically nor economically, nor upholding higher morals. A sustained success story still needs to be proven. It is probably an accident — but may not be! — that the world's most successful post-war developing countries like Korea, Taiwan, Singapore and Malaysia never received a cent of EU aid.

As Lord Peter Bauer rightly observed, foreign aid is an excellent method for transferring money from poor people in rich countries to rich people in poor countries. VAT-financed EU aid is no exception.

If one is to search for responsibilities, they lie more with the Commission and Council than with the Parliament. In fact, Parliament only controls and approves 56% of the EU's aid budget that goes through the Commission's books. When it threw out funds intended to benefit Turkey and Syria on account of these countries' persistent human rights violations, Parliament at least proved to be the EU institution to take the often declared human rights objective seriously for once and to face heaps of abuse from the nationalist Turkish media.

About 37% of EU aid consists of negotiated member state's contributions (with a strong share from France) to a special European Development Fund which is earmarked for the ACP countries. It is kept and allocated separately from the EU budget proper without scrutiny from Parliament. About 7% are concessional loans from the government-owned European Investment Bank. MEPs are free to study the EIB's annual report.

In the early 1990s the EU suffered a short-lived reality shock about the situation of its Southern Mediterranean neighbours. It started with the late King Hassan's wish for full EU membership for Morocco and with the Gulf War in 1991. In Algeria in 1992 the Islamists won an election victory which was crushed by the generals, followed by a most cruelly fought civil war. This rekindled fears of general instability among the EU's Southern Islamic neighbours, whose population growth at 2% p.a. showed little signs of abating [projected to grow from 235 million (1997) to 400 million people by 2035] with massive unemployment, social and political destabilisation, mass emigration, crime, drug smuggling and religious fanaticism among restless young men who have nothing to do and feel they have nothing to lose in consequence.

The EU's response was twofold: to expand the free trade area which (by 2000) — with mixed results given the uncompetitive economies of some partners, notably of Turkey — already existed with Israel, Palestine, Turkey and the then accession islands of Malta and Cyprus, to encompass the Mashreg (Egypt, Jordan, Lebanon, Syria) and the Magreb (Morocco, Algeria, Tunisia) countries as well by 2010.

The resulting Free Trade Area would then include the entire enlarged EU and all of the Mediterranean — except for the rough state of Libya (which successfully sneaked out of evil empire status in Washington's demonology). The difficulties for implementation lie in inefficient state-run industries (notably in Algeria and Syria) and in the risk that thousands of so far protected artisan workshops could be swept aside by more effective EU competition. There is also Spanish resistance against the liberalised market access for agricultural products. The lack of farmland water and growing self-supply needs along the overpopulated Southern shores of the Mediterranean did so far little to dissuade Spanish resistance.

In order to prepare for the success of this common economic area of shared prosperity, five-year MED programmes were set up by the Commission. During 1995/1999 they were budgeted at 5.5 billion Euros. Their purpose was to sponsor regional cooperation (on environment, energy, investment promotion, technological research, etc.), to prepare economic structures for free trade and to promote agricultural development. Given the quality of the public administration on the recipient side, implementation of these schemes often leaves much to be desired, but at least the strategic rationale of the MED scheme and the free trade objectives appear to be sound.

A Paper Tiger with Teething Problems: The CSFP

More so than taxation, currency, immigration and justice, foreign and defense policies touch the heart of national sovereignty. Ultimately they need to rely on national consensus and solidarity to use the military, meaning the sacrifice of the lives of young men (and women) to achieve common strategic objectives. To achieve this, the EU has still a long way to go from the piles of mostly inconsequential declarations that stayed unread on the desks of a small army of COREU correspondents in embassies and foreign ministries.

Back in 1954 the draft treaty for a European Defense Community had fallen through. The WEU of 1949 remained an "alliance in the shadows", in spite of having legally a stronger mutual defense commitment than NATO. It endured as a depository for retired Italian admirals conveniently located near good restaurants at the Place Grand Sablon in the heart of Brussels.

The Amsterdam Treaty awards the WEU the role of the European defense arm of NATO. The messy Nice Treaty does so no longer. The WEU's future is therefore unclear. Should it ever be dissolved it would be greatly mourned by the Italian waiters of the Place Grand Sablon.

The origins of the contemporary CSFP reach back to 1969 when at the Hague summit the principles of the European Political Cooperation (EPC) were decided. The EPC rituals were legally consolidated by the Single European Act of 1987. The drama of German unity in 1989 showed unforgettably the depth of friendship which the then leading figures of the UK, France, the Netherlands and Italy (not to forget Poland) entertained towards the German people. Apart from George Bush Sr (who is American after all) and later Gorbachev, it was only

Felipe Gonzales of Spain, who alone among the major European leaders was consistently encouraging and constructive.

Maastricht then created a common currency, but on the CSFP it generated only an ineffective minimalist agreement without the possibility of a rapid deployment of troops. Perhaps this was better so. Once the Yugoslav wars started, France and the UK sided instinctively (meaning rather unthinkingly) with Slobodan Milosevic and the Serbian aggression. Knowing marginally more about Yugoslav realities, Germany and Austria (and the Vatican) sided with Slovenia and Croatia, who defended their right to self-determination.

The Treaty of Amsterdam, like Maastricht, in 1999 further fine-tuned CSFP cooperation and placed its new High Representative, former Spanish Foreign Minister and NATO Secretary General Javier Solana, an internationally well connected and trusted personality, and his small seconded staff of 30 people in the Secretariat of the Council (please note that this was purposefully not the Commission!).

Formally, Mr Solana can only make "proposals" to the Council for common member state action. A lot therefore depended on the strength of his personality, the preparatory work of his staff, the soundness of his judgements and the persuasiveness of his arguments in national capitals. In spite of all odds that the constraints of inter-governmentalism impose, Solana, who concurrently serves as the Secretary General of the WEU, has done remarkably well in his mission impossible (1999–), that is, until the administration of George Bush Jr managed to split the EU neatly into two halves over its war against Iraq.

Solana's work is guided by a "political and security committee", which is composed of the political directors of the member states' foreign ministries. This committee in turn is advised by a "military committee" composed of the member states' chiefs of staff. When they first met in May 2000 their commemorative photo showed a group of jolly potbellied gentlemen posing in ill-assorted uniforms, looking more like an excursion of retired postmasters than the assembly of frightful founder warriors of the future European Army. Remember that such fearsome armies as the Luxembourgers, the Irish, Austrians and

Danes were also represented. The military committee also "guides" the Council's 130 "strong" military staff. Their job is to issue early warnings to the Council, to do strategic analysis, the planning of "Petersberg tasks" (international humanitarian and rescue work, peace-keeping and peacemaking — the military as armed social workers) and the identification of suitable military resources available in the member states.

In December 1999 the Helsinki summit, under the impression of the US-led NATO bombing campaign against Serbia (remember the ignored niceties of international law: no UN mandate and no Serb attack against a country of NATO, an exclusively defensive alliance), decreed that by 2003 up to 5,000 EU policemen from member states should be dispatchable to any place within 30 days to re-establish the rule of law and an orderly administration, and up to 60,000 troops be ready within 60 days for Petersberg tasks at any place anywhere. Although compatibility of equipment and inter-operability (probably meaning effective friend/foe recognition, and decent English lessons for all) was still to be achieved, this was not to be a European Army. The deployment of national contingents still remains subject to sovereign decisions by the member states concerned. Remember that six (Ireland, Austria, Sweden, Finland, Malta and Cyprus) of 25 member states are still formally neutral or non-aligned, though at varying degrees of conviction and seriousness. Although the decision at Helsinki down-scaled initial plans of 100,000 men, 400 fighter planes and 100 warships, the objective remained to be able to react credibly to an international crisis or a crisis in third countries affecting the EU or its aid and cooperation programmes (meaning almost anywhere), if needed also independently of NATO.

In spite of French persistence the latter is still in doubt, as the US formally insists on "no decoupling" and "no duplication" of NATO structures (where they remain in charge). Deeply suspicious of the ever evil designs of her Greek neighbours, Turkey as a NATO member (while claiming to passionately desire EU membership) blocked EU access to NATO planning capacities unless she could formally participate in all CSFP decision-making as a non-EU member.

As an inter-governmental activity, on CSFP decisions unanimity rules. Experience proved even to the most ardent inter-governmentalists involved that nothing except for meaningless notes of concern on trivia in the Outer Hebrides would ever pass the Council. Thus three interesting exemptions were dreamt up to escape from the paralysis of unanimity:

- constructive abstention (a substantial number of member states want action, others don't but could not care less: so they abstain "constructively" in letting the volunteers doing the bloody work while they watch with interest and good wishes);
- QMV on joint strategies, actions and common positions (a veto is still possible nonetheless);
- "enhanced cooperation" (since Nice) between at least eight member states.

Basically it is the Council which decides and acts. The Commission is "associated", may ask questions (whether answers must be given is not stated), and may submit proposals. The EP is consulted, regularly informed (through newspapers mostly), may ask questions and issue recommendations.

It is quite clear that this fragmented structure for decision-making has all the trappings of multiple hybrid compromises with individual member states remaining the key actors. It is not made to withstand the test of a major international crisis. The public impression of a lot of talk and little action is not too far off the mark. Yet the paper work has been impressive. Common strategies were adopted towards Russia, the Ukraine and the Mediterranean. Common positions on issues of concern issued on Bosnia, Montenegro, Haiti, Sudan, Burundi, Angola and Nigeria. Joint actions were undertaken as election monitoring, land mine clearance, support for non-proliferation and dual-use controls. Four special CSFP representatives were appointed, for the Middle East, the Great Lakes, South East Europe and for Macedonia, obviously with mixed results.

Until the war in Iraq of 2003 the division of work with the US followed a rough and not altogether friction-free pattern: the US and their UK sidekick did the bombing (whether in Serbia or in

Afghanistan), and as an economic giant but a political dwarf the EU did the reconstruction. This may be morally gratifying, but politically it is not a very rewarding role distribution.

The war on Iraq and EU enlargement has further dramatised the EU's initial divisions and paralysed its rudimentary capacity to act alone.

First the EU has to sort out its strategic priorities, whether it wants to join the US as a global policeman, or care about its regional "near abroad", mainly ranging from Russia via the Balkans to North Africa, and/or limit itself to territorial defense only. Once a reasoned consensus — not only among the fickle political and cocktail slurping diplomatic classes but more importantly in the European societies at large (on, for instance, the pertinent question: "*mourir pour le Kosovo?*") has emerged, then the re-dimensioning of the member states' armies can begin in earnest. The European NATO member troops are still mostly tank-based mass armies, ready to repulse a Soviet invasion whose planning was based on an amplified repeat of the Soviet conduct of war during 1941–1945 but which luckily never came.

Since the end of the Cold War, the writing is on the wall to move from territorial defense to highly mobile professional troops whose qualification profiles range from military police and armed social workers to mercenaries of the Foreign Legion or Executive Outcomes.

However, there are several constraints in the future set-up of the CSFP:

- public acceptance of military adventures declines rapidly with growing geographical distance from the EU's borders;
- finding consensus within the Council regresses the closer external conflicts are located to the EU's borders (it is fairly easy to agree on the bad guy in East Timor, but much more difficult to do the same in Bosnia);
- the frequency of armed regional conflicts is set to grow with larger populations competing for scarcer resources in degrading environments with the inflammatory messages of religious and ethnic fanaticism spreading ever more widely and quickly;

- the costs of external interventions in terms of finance and lives lost will often spiral out of control, and the purpose and sustained "success" of these operations become ever more elusive;
- US unilateralism is likely to become more aggressive until inevitably reaching the natural limits of "imperial overstretch".

All of the above speaks for a very much restrained regional security role of the EU. But also this role needs to be achieved at a level of political credibility and military effectiveness. Credible deterrence, after all, is the surest way to preserve peace, to settle conflicts without war and thus to save lives. Continued inter-governmentalism is certain, however, never to reach this reasonable objective of strategic constraint and effective European regional security.

CHAPTER 23

Scenes from a Marriage: The US and the EU — Common Destiny and Drift

The script is a nightmare for any director short of the talents of an Ingmar Bergman. There is little prospect for a box office hit. It is not a pretty sight. An old quarrelsome couple of no particular sophistication (no Richard Burton, no Elizabeth Taylor), suburban lower middle class at best. He is resourceful, tough, bossy, insensitive and ignorant beyond his immediate concerns. She is from a better family, with little current achievements to show, resentful, nagging, disorganised and full of unachieved aspirations. There is an unending series of petty quarrels, culminating in periodic fits of hysteria and noisy threats, which however inevitably recede without consequence in sullen silence and daily routines. A divorce is not imminent. There is no visible unfaithfulness and little risk of Latin lovers, Russian or Oriental brides eloping with either of them. Yet fault lines are visible which are deeper than the usual wear and tear of an old couple. Incantations of the past ("When we did postwar reconstruction", "when we were in Korea together") won't help. Can there be a happy ending? You are the marriage counsellor, what do you do?

The global power equation at the outset of the third millennium is straightforward enough. Having won the Cold War, there is only one superpower left which can project its military superiority on a global scale. There are four regional powers: the EU, Russia, China and India, with superpower potential, but constrained by serious political and/or economic limitations to the pursuit of regional interests at least for the decade to come. Then there are sub-regional powers, like Japan, South Africa and Brazil, and local powers like Pakistan, Nigeria, Turkey and Israel, and finally the familiar crowd of mischief makers: North Korea,

Iran, Libya and Cuba (the latter now in retirement). The world's major danger spot (the odd tin pot dictator like Kim Jong-il apart) quite clearly lies in that major fault line of civilisation, so perceptively identified by Samuel Huntington, which separates the Islamic world from the rest. (In the words of Johannes Rau, Germany's former president, not by accident a pacifist Protestant lay preacher by origin: "Huntington must not be right." If you preclude the likely truth as politically inadmissible, then the rest of your analysis, conclusions and actions is certain to be based on twisted logic. Of course it is inconceivable that the earth is anything but flat). From Indonesia to Morocco this fault line, which sits on the world's largest fuel deposits, is the result of an explosive amalgam: persistently high population growth, exploding cities teeming with unemployed, restless and poorly educated youth, failure of state centred development ("Arab socialism") with discredited repressive and corrupt ruling elites, and the spread of Saudi sponsored aggressive Islamism that is murderously totalitarian in its fundamentalist seriousness. As Lee Kuan Yew puts it, it may take up to two decades until Islamist theocracy, the *khalifat*, in view of its inevitable earthly failure, loses its mass appeal, like among the educated youth of Iran. In their terrorist pursuits, which aim at the extermination of infidels and traitors, Islamist fundamentalists are aided by the lawlessness in the expanding number of failed states, like the Taliban's Afghanistan, the Sudan, Yemen and Somalia, with much more populous Pakistan and Bangladesh, which also show signs of becoming increasingly ungovernable, appear to be going the same slippery road downhill. (N.B.: State failure is not limited to the Islamic world. It is, in fact, more common in Black Africa and threatens to proliferate into parts of Eastern Europe and Latin America.) In difference to earlier forms of international terrorism (Carlos and the likes), the new Islamist terrorism of a messianic figure like Osama is helped by the communication, mobility, finance and technologies of globalisation and by the protection accorded to his henchmen by safe heavens and undisturbed recruitment of Islamic militants in the shadow of the mosques and madrashas in the West.

To defeat Islamic terrorism, to dry up its root causes (including the reconstruction of the multitude of failed states) and to fight the various evil axis members one by one visibly strains the resources of the one remaining superpower. Taking on Saddam and the (much more dangerous) regime in Pyongyang at the same time would have already proved too much. The US (in difference to Europe) have the advantage to orient their actions to the big (global) picture and to long-term scenarios. Although often erratic (following changes of administrations — and sometimes within — friends might turn into foes, neglected sideshows into theatres of strategic priority, and vice versa), contradictory at times, too strongly wedded to oil, Israeli and other parochial interests, and when galvanised into action (like after 9/11) pursuing a too simplistic manichean ("good" versus "evil") propaganda, which it then tends to believe in, still the Pax Americana with its "benign selfishness" (Bill Emmott) at least has a sense of purpose (to spread free trade, market economies, democratic governance and to curtail arms of mass destruction). Basic features of current US foreign policies are roughly consistent with these objectives: to expand NATO, to stabilise Eastern Europe and to increase the pool of volunteers for global pursuits, to treat the EU as a somewhat troublesome junior partner, to maintain a friendly distance from Putin's Russia, to keep a watchful eye on China's regional designs, assuring her nervous neighbours (including Taiwan), to finish rough country despots off one by one (Milosevic 1999, the Taliban 2001, Saddam 2003, perhaps Kim Jong-il in 2005) and to set up a National Missile Defense (if it ever works) against their desperate aggressions. So much for the big picture.

More close up, the actionist impatience and self-righteousness germane to US political culture and the perceived need to act quick and decisive (without too much consultations with awkward and indiscrete allies) on selective interventions in the US interest, then to everyone else appears like unilateralist bullying running roughshod over legal niceties. US action then conveniently seems to suppress facts which do not fit preconceived notions (like the ones which ultimately led to disaster in Indochina 1964–1975) and happily enters into contradictions which seem perhaps obvious only to outsiders: free trade rhetoric is matched by flagrant protectionism in steel, agriculture and public procurement. A war on terror is transformed to one for regime change in Baghdad. NATO, a defensive alliance, was used to run an unprovoked, and undeclared bombing war against Belgrade. There is insistence on the extra-territoriality of US sanctions (on Iran, Libya, Cuba), while rejecting the jurisdiction of the international criminal court for US nationals.

There is also a fundamental ambivalence towards European unity. Having helped behind the scenes (like the Vatican) to put European integration on track in the 1950s (and to discourage British attempts at sabotage), this reflected the wish not only to prevent the rest of Europe from falling into Soviet hands, but also to gain a reliable junior partner for, if possible, permanent global support, like a sort of magnified UK. Since the days of Henry Kissinger's *realpolitik*, these American hopes were regularly disappointed and triggered an avalanche of public criticism. Yet, at the same time, whenever the EU — egged on by the French — attempted to establish its own defense identity, to beef up the toothless WEU and to straighten its awkwardly-constructed CSFP which is based on cumbersome inter-governmental cooperation, the US saw the emergence of a potential rival power, and true to form slammed the brakes themselves or encouraged the British to block most of the exercise — only to bemoan European disunity and its lack of effective capacities soon after.

The persistence of US lobbying for Turkey's EU membership is an interesting case study for the subservience of European integration to US strategic interests in the Middle East and in the Central Asian great game. Turkey, an economically bankrupt ally to the US (and Israel) with on occasion fairly aggressive designs of her own in the neighbourhood, fits into the EU about as nicely as does Mexico (a much more peaceful and, after all, culturally more compatible Christian country) into the US. Obviously Turkey's political class — now dominated, in PC-speak by "moderate Muslim fundamentalists" (as much an oxymoron as the State Department's consideration of Mao Tse Dong as a moderate land-reforming Stalinist until 1947) — and its military harbour grand ambitions for fellow

Turk people in Central Asia with their untapped oil wealth in the Russian backyard. EU funds associated with membership are seen as the panacea to reform the socially and regionally torn semi-continent, to shape up its corrupt and incompetent elites and administration and to finance its ventures abroad. The grand Turko-US plan has only the minor drawback of not being matched by realities. The Turkish economy is in no shape to withstand competition in the EU's single market, the Turkish administration patiently unable (and probably unwilling as well) to implement EU law, and the Turkish elites — both military and civilian — seem perfectly unaware of the sovereignty sharing principles of European integration. The EU similarly appears unable to accommodate Turkey, a country with a population of 63 million growing at 2% p.a., to finance her huge development needs, to integrate her intemperate uncompromising nationalism and to accommodate the Islamic values of Turkish society (with significant differences ranging from *habeas corpus* to religious freedom, freedom of expression, rights of women and of minorities). This accession adventure, based on mutual misunderstanding and on external pressure, would do neither Turkey nor the EU any good. The latter surely would not survive. Yet, probably against better knowledge, Washington's pressures were incessant, unrelenting and — successful.

The EU with its inter-governmental decision making in foreign affairs is rather driven by regional concerns. Some member states (UK: the Commonwealth, France: Sub-Saharan Africa, Spain: Latin America) have inherited larger political interests, but basically with the consolidation of the CSFP (and its trade and aid instruments) since the early 1990s has a clear regional focus, covering Eastern Europe including Russia, with Polish accession also the Ukraine, and the Southern shores of the Mediterranean. As a fragmented regional power, the EU has learnt to see its external environment as largely given. It can be influenced and stabilised at best and accommodated at worst. Unpleasant long-term developments (so dear to the US strategic community) like the proliferation of nuclear and other nasty arms, Islamic fundamentalism and the demographic time bomb ticking in and around Europe are happily ignored. The use of military tools out of area are abhorred on most of the continent, given its unhappy history, the thoroughness of anti-militarist re-education, the absence of strategic interests and the lack of projective capacities of Europe's military. Europe's armies — both East and West — are still geared and trained towards tank and mass conscription based territorial defense (re-fighting the German-Soviet war of 1941–1945).

Rather the skills of smooth diplomacy, well tuned by 50 years of progress on integration, are preferred in Europe's near abroad. On occasion this appears like a caricature of contemporary German diplomacy: buy yourself out of trouble and then naively assume to become everybody's sweetheart. Yet, frequently based on more solid empirical research and more extensive information networks than the broad stroke sketches made in Washington DC (the French, for instance, having experienced Maghreb terrorists before, had the clearest grasp of Bin Laden's evil network prior to 9/11, but in the US — and everywhere else — nobody cared to listen), the combination of soft incentives (diplomatic shows, trade concessions and straight cash disguised as aid) have often proven to be the more effective tools.

Instructive is the comparison of US and EU relations with Russia and with China. Both Western allies share an interest in market reforms, effective democratisation and a civilised foreign policy for their counterparts. Yet the US keep a sceptical greater distance to Russia, which as a remaining nuclear power has declined to second order status. For the EU she is foremost a potentially dangerous neighbour (with a common border running east of Finland and also, since 2004, east of Estonia and Latvia and around the Königsberg/Kaliningrad exclave of Northeast Prussia) if destabilised. Hence generous financial and managerial support is extended (and human rights violations in Chechnya conveniently ignored), an approach which the US with good reasons views as a moral hazard. The US sees China as a regional rival in East Asia that actively disrupts US designs. Hence they are eager to demonstrate the limits to Chinese power (regarding the Spratlys, the international sea lanes and the Taiwan Straits). The Europeans, with no strategic interests left in the Far East, just act like salesmen in Beijing (albeit with a bad conscience for not having mentioned human rights loudly).

Europe also manifestly suffers from the junior partner's syndrome, cultivating its resentment of US unilateralism (regardless whether this was born out of arrogance or out of desperation). This inferiority complex is fed from many sources. Partly, it stems from popular resentment against globalisation, structural adjustment, modernisation (for which US capitalism is blamed), or against the notion of Pax Americana. Partly, it is a also a highly enjoyable intellectual past-time (not requiring much mental effort) to criticise US bigotry in matters like Israel and oil, to ridicule their Manichean world view and the international ignorance of the US public in general and their media and politicians in particular, and to lampoon the current President, who in his first term acquired his office by third world means. There is a lot of gratuitous criticism from the sidelines whenever the US takes more or less unilateral action (or no action). Any amount of concern is voiced beforehand. If things go wrong (collateral damage, US losses, objectives not reached), they lend the morally gratifying sentiment of having been right. If US action is successful (like their decisive support for German unity), it is quickly discounted and taken for granted. At the same time, within Europe this mentality of dependency safely assumes that if things go wrong (either within the EU or with the EU's neighbours), ultimately it will hopefully be the US who will sort them out.

By historical standards the current international environment is still mercifully benign. Out of some 180 nations only 2% are ruled by externally aggressive dictators, and in some 6% normal government functions have collapsed, with the law of the land being exercised by armed thugs. About 5% of mankind suffer the misrule of such regimes. In the 1930s, in consequence of the disruptions of WWI, the badly designed Paris peace treaties of 1919 and the world economic crisis, more than half of humanity was subjected to Communism, fascism and warlordism.

Yet, even under current conditions, the US political and military might, as impressive as they appear, is threatened by imperial "over-reach", that classical cause of death of all empires (Paul Kennedy), if it was required to deal with all deviant cases of governance from Venezuela, Belarus, Myanmar to Sierra Leone, to disarm the handful of rough states, and to contain one or two uncooperative regional powers (China, Russia or India) at the same time or even successively. The number of reliable partners for a global division of labour is obviously small. By elimination it is only the EU which shows any promise and potential to size up to this role of equal partnership — not just in financial burden sharing and post-war rehabilitation (the US bombs and the EU rebuilds) — but in real policy and joint military decisions (which, *nota bene*, by necessity do not always have to correspond in full to US economic and strategic objectives: the art of compromise has already been invented, even the most belligerent think tanks might want to take note). In a logical first step the EU would have to take charge of its near abroad: Eastern Europe and the Mediterranean, with relations with Russia and the Middle East handled in joint partnership. It would hence be in the US national and global interest to encourage the EU's autonomous military and foreign policy capacities (and to discourage divisive and dysfunctional special relationships with individual member states, whatever their possible sentimental value).

Europe also needs the US, less for global adventures, but for strategic support and solidarity in case of serious trouble in the EU's volatile near abroad — from Russia to the Balkans and North Africa. And almost more importantly just by "being there", available, but hardly ever invoked, as the ultimate arbiter should the internal balance of power in Europe's perennial coalition of nations once again threaten to turn seriously skewed. The US has intervened three times (1917–1919, 1942–1945, 1948–1989) to reset the scale and to rescue the continent's liberty. Freed from the constraints of the Cold War, Europe immediately saw the resurgence of old power coalition games in 1989 when France (Mitterand), the UK (Mrs Thatcher), the Netherlands (Luebbers), Italy (Andreotti) and Poland (Mazowiezki) briefly tried to block German unification — in vain, courtesy of George Bush Sr and the Baker boys. The same happened during the first Serbian wars (1991–1996), when in a strange reflex world war alliance patterns resurfaced, like a more nostalgic than rational British-Franco-Greek pro-Serbian bias, which Slobodan Milosevic was able to exploit successfully for too long a time.

The strategy for a partnership of equals does not need new transatlantic rhetoric, new institutions, symposia or pompous new EU embassies in Washington DC. It rather requires to reinforce systematically the classical channels and existing fora for substantial cooperation (notably within NATO), based on a new sense of joint purpose based on common perceptions, on identical objectives and shared external threats, and to define a complementary division of labour between the two. Exhortations are not sufficient. Real efforts and discipline are needed on both sides (we are now back to our marriage analogy!).

The EU would have to straighten its decision-making on foreign and security matters towards qualified majority voting in bi-cameral procedures (Council and Parliament), that is, put them out of the realm of finnicky inter-governmentalism with 25 cooks spoiling the porridge, to a sphere of Community competence (in clearer US language: federal jurisdiction). This would apply to a European Army (consolidating the 60,000 men of the Petersberg contingents), a beefed-up Europol operating as a European FBI, and a future European border guard with a strong naval component. The US should not view this development as a threat but rather turn supportive (and massage their British and Polish friends accordingly). The US should also give up their fixation with relegating the European side to a junior role in almost any joint venture (some welcome change is now visible in the Balkans). In the war on terror, as an immediate step joint policing, intelligence sharing, coordinated immigration policies and concerted financial sanctions should apply to dry out fundamentalist milieus supportive and sympathetic to terrorism. This should also include coordinated repatriations (done successfully by an Islamic country like Malaysia in 2003).

Intellectual analysis should turn from a dialogue of the deaf (or worse: public diplomacy by megaphone) to two-way exchanges.

Europeans should begin to take long-term strategic thinking seriously (even when conclusions threaten to turn unpleasant or politically incorrect). Americans should start to take empirical European country and area studies (including those revealing embarrassing internal weaknesses of their strategic friends in the Middle East, Turkey, the Ukraine, etc.) seriously as well. The US should stop pushing for the EU membership of Turkey (and other new Eastern European and Middle Eastern "candidates"), and the EU in turn will not incite Mexico, Haiti and Colombia to become future US states (even though this might equally "stabilise" the Americas).

Both sides should work hard to solve their perennial economic and trade disputes — the sadly familiar tales of bananas, hormone meat, GM food, steel duties, agricultural and aircraft subsidies, anti-merger rules and Buy-America acts — as what they are: low politics, technical issues to be resolved in a consensual, depoliticised and pragmatic fashion, much in the way that intra-EU economic disputes are defused and resolved. After all, trade and investment are much more balanced across the Atlantic than between any other continent. There are no losers, only winners.

Limits to Growth: Big Bang Enlargement and Its Aftermath

In December 2002, the Copenhagen summit concluded four years of accession negotiations with eight Central/Eastern European countries and two Mediterranean islands, the capitals of which some EU heads of governments perhaps had difficulties in identifying, let alone in spelling. Bill Clinton could be forgiven when in 1999 during his visit to Ljubljana he confused Slovenia with Slovakia. But when Hans van den Broek, then Commissioner in charge of Enlargement, got Poland and Hungary mixed up during the official opening of the accession talks back in March 1997, this was more auspicious. In spite of differentiations, as promised by the Commission and demanded by the Council, in subsequent treatment by the Commission (most visible once Guenter Verheugen took over the enlargement portfolio in 1999) a large convoy was assembled from which only the heavily limping and obviously unprepared Bulgarians and Romanians were decoupled.

The enlargement by the ten after all referenda and parliamentary votes on the ten accession treaties turned positive on May 1, 2004 increased the number of member states by 33% (to 25), the EU population by 25% (to 440 million) and its GDP by a mere 330 billion Euros (+2%), the equivalent of that of the Netherlands. These few indications alone suffice to illustrate the EU's new self-inflicted institutional and policy dilemma. They are bound to lead to a "crisis", for the resolution of which solutions need to be found. A solid and enduring approach of subsidiarity oriented federalism with a downsized European public function would surely appear a sensible one.

The original design and outlook for the accession talks had been one marked by toughness, objectivity and differentiation. "Sweat saves blood" is not by accident the motto of successful US military instructors. The benchmarks for future members were set high at the Copenhagen summit of 1993: they were to be democracies with the rule of law, protecting their minorities, with effective market economies able to withstand the competitive pressures of the internal market and to have the administration and legislation in place ready to implement EU law in full on day one of membership (except for the very limited transitional arrangements negotiated in the accession treaties).

The need for such detailed conditions and monitoring of compliance was unique in the previous history of enlargement negotiations, but necessary given the candidates' huge inherited developmental gap and the dramatic burden left by 40 years of Communist mismanagement of their economy, the public administration, the human resources and the environment.

Every year since the initial "Opinions" of 1996, the Commission has published progress reports which documented in earnest detail the candidates' advancements sector by sector, starting out with fairly summary clean bills of health in the political field, then giving a standard macroeconomic review of the achievement of a market economy and its competitiveness, and finally and most extensively, the legislative and administrative preparations in each field of EU policy competence: agriculture, competition, social policy, energy, telecoms, etc. Each report states briefly the gist of the *"acquis"* in each sector, reviews what the country has promised, what it delivered and what still needs to be done. Over time, some of the latter lists showed significant reductions, both in terms of sheer quantity (some 20,000 EU legal acts totalling 80,000 pages had to be "transposed" into national law) and in terms of importance, as the directive on tractor seat standardisation might have a somewhat lesser importance than a banking directive (except to tractor seat manufacturers). After a few years of sustained efforts, the more motivated countries had only a few marginal directives left on their "to be done" lists. The progress reports do not really make very exciting reading (for those with serious sleeping disorders they are more effective than pills or alcohol), but they fulfilled three useful functions:

- giving candidate countries a fair assessment of where the Commission thought they stood in the complex preparatory process: they could compare themselves to their neighbours or within sectors (e.g., when the Ministry of Commerce did a lot to implement EU law, while the Ministry of Agriculture or the Customs Service promised a lot but did little during the annual review period);
- showing member states and their citizens that the Commission was attentively monitoring progress and was not taking anything (like forged Romanian statistics or grand Polish promises) for granted;
- targeting of the EU's "Phare" funds earmarked for accession preparation at the policy areas of greatest need (typically training of public administration, police, judges, customs people, the set up of regional planning bodies, competition offices, food hygiene labs, environmental inspectorates and other aspects of a more decentralised institution building replacing the inherited centralised ministry structure of old apparatchiks). They also served for a while as a useful differentiator of countries. Some, like (Greek) Cyprus and Malta had very little problems to begin with (except for money laundering and a problematic shipping registry). Others, like Hungary, Estonia and Slovenia, followed by Latvia, made great and impressive progress to address the economic and administrative problems inherited from the decades of Communist misrule. With other countries, like Poland, Slovakia and the Czech Republic, the record was decidedly more mixed. Areas of progress contrasted with significant fields (like competition, trade and industry policy, public procurement, telecom liberalisation) in which progress was often delayed and displayed the ambivalent attitude which parts of the (changing) political elites maintained towards European integration and a non-discriminatory market economy.

With the advent of Guenter Verheugen, who soon after his arrival confided to a German newspaper (*Die Welt*, December 2, 1999) that he had rewritten the reports' conclusions, this "objectivity" (and the incentive to reform for the laggards) was pretty much diluted. Czechs and Poles henceforth were to be as good (or almost as good) as any front-runner. Only Bulgaria and Romania, whose Communist period was worse and who suffered from lost years of post-Communist cleptocratic rule by the old nomenclatura and hence with the delay of real reforms, did not manage to catch up even with the best of the Commissioner's intentions. But still the Copenhagen summit of 2002 promised them 2007 as membership date. Yet it may still be difficult for both to achieve economic competitiveness and administrative preparedness. (This is certainly more likely for Romania, ruled until 2004 again by Ion Iliescu, leader of the old pro-Moscow faction of the Communist party. He had Nicolae Ceaucescu, the genius of the Carpates and his lovely wife Elena tried and shot after a Communist palace coup in December 1989, then usurped power in the ensuing turmoil engineered by the Securidate secret service.)

The negotiation process itself was a decidedly unexciting exercise ploughing with each candidate country through 29 chapters of the "*acquis*". If a country had no difficulty with the "*acquis*" — like, say, Hungary and the Czech Republic on fisheries on account of their long coast line — then the chapter was closed "provisionally" (until the final negotiation session at Copenhagen). When there were misgivings, transition periods limited in time and scope were negotiated. These were raised either due to demands of the candidates for political reasons — like, for instance, Polish, Czech and Hungarian insistence on discriminatory restrictions on farm and forestry land purchases for EU citizens — or because costs for compliance were too high, like for waste water treatment and pollution control from stationary sources (power stations, etc.). In a few instances, it was the Union and its member states who insisted on transition arrangements, like countries close to the Eastern border (read: Germany and Austria), requesting seven years of reduced access to most of their labour markets. Then real negotiations set in to find transition arrangements for a transition period of X years after accession as a compromise until full compliance. This then is the iron rule of accession talks: there are no permanent exemptions (except, as it turned out, for Maltese real estate) from EU rules, even when the rules appear as silly or unsuitable for the country. If a country does not like to comply with the rules of membership, it is free to stay outside. The less the number of requests for transition arrangements (like by Cyprus or Estonia) the smoother obviously the accession negotiations. The more frequent they were, the bumpier was the process (unless, as usual, gentle Mr Verheugen intervened and made his candidates happy again, thus reducing their need for tougher and speedier adjustment measures, and a new insufficiently prepared potential troublemaker announces his imminent arrival on the expectant Community scene).

Typically during enlargement negotiations the final session, in which senior politicians get directly involved for the first time, is one of confusion, nervousness and drama, with ultimately a happy ending under the limelight of TV cameras. The subjects are a handful of highly politicised "leftovers" from the technical accession talks, the institutional representation of the future member states and estimates of their budgetary contributions and the EU's expected receipts. At Copenhagen in 2002 touchy issues like the freedom to take up employment (for Easterners) and the right to buy real estate (for Westerners) had already been "successfully" restricted for transitional periods in the concerned countries. And the representation of the accession countries in the EP and the Commission and their voting rights in the Council had already been unilaterally settled in the Treaty of Nice. Hence only cash remained as an essential issue. The Commission and the Danish Presidency had offered the ten future member states 40.4 billion Euros as gross receipts during 2004/2006, which Polish last minute bargained then succeeded to up by 430 million Euros (+1.06% of the total) for all. As these are gross amounts, deducting their own contributions to the EU budget, a net amount of 12 billion Euros remains available for transfers. As much of the actual funding depends on national co-financing (e.g., for regional development and direct farm aids), and given their own proven record of poor "absorptive capacities" of EU "Phare" funds in the past, the actual net amount will be rather closer to 9 billion Euros or less.

Yet, the consequences of the 5th enlargement are likely to be more complex and potentially crisis-inducing than any previous enlargement round.

In terms of economics the story is fairly clear-cut. Most accession countries are growing healthily at rates of 4–6% p.a., having overcome the worst of their transformation crisis. They are likely to catch up sooner or later (meaning in up to 30 years) in due course, thus potentially replicating the long term success stories of Ireland, Spain and Portugal. In order to modernise — and modernisation needs are huge, starting from airports and hospitals to housing renovation and consumer durables — big trade deficits are regularly run up towards all of the EU's 15 old member states. The higher the purchasing power in the accession countries, the higher their import demand for goods and services from the old EU 15, which is surely welcome economic news given their mostly stagnating domestic demand.

After the initial investment phase to secure market access for consumer products, EU investors have, since the mid-1990s, moved increasingly towards a genuine pan-European division of labour in supplying the capital, technical and managerial know-how and matching them with a skilled low cost Eastern labour force in car manufacturing , consumer electronics, wood processing, textiles and construction materials. This aided European competitiveness in the world market, and facilitated export earnings, qualified employment and know-how transfer for the accession countries. The Europe Agreements of the mid-1990s, which provided association and free trade between the candidate countries and the EU, have already established this win-win situation. Full EU membership will be further supportive, strengthen legal certainty and recourse to EU law for foreign investors, and help to modernise infrastructure with EU funds and easier access to international credit. It is not very far-fetched to forecast the emergence of a new sustained growth area stretching from Tallinn in Estonia down to the Adriatic shores of Slovenia and Croatia. Some high growth pockets are already visible along Baltic seaports: Tallinn, Riga, Danzig, Stettin, and also in the greater Prague area, Bratislava, Western Hungary and the West of Slovenia. Prior to their annexation by the Soviet Union in 1940 Estonian per capita income was higher than Finland's, and prior to 1946 the Czech lands' industrial output exceeded those of neighbouring Austria and Bavaria by far. Poland in the 1930s was at an income level on par with Spain, while today Spanish incomes are four times higher. Historical comparisons may be distorted as at the time Eastern Europe benefited from large German and Jewish populations and a local bourgeoisie which have since been murdered or expelled. They underline, however, a residual strength of human capital, of industrial traditions, and of advantageous locations in the heart of Europe which are about to be put to good use again.

Once Bulgaria and someday even Romania have achieved their economic competitiveness, similar mutual advantages can be expected. With Turkey the situation is more difficult. The country has always been a market economy of sorts, albeit with strong import protection and a sizeable state sector and one run for the benefit of the military. Once a customs union was set up (at Turkey's request) between the EU and Turkey in 1995, the Turkish economy sucked in more competitive EU imports, but failed to use her export potential in textiles and other labour-intensive products. Economic hardship was the inevitable result as wishful political thinking had overruled economic reality and common sense.

Politically, the enlargement story is less clear-cut for the EU. Given their developmental gap and the promises made during their referenda of 2003 with EU membership being sold to the electorate as the short-cut to riches and prosperity, continued demands for the higher redistribution of funds will figure high on the EU's future agenda. At the same time, current net beneficiaries under Spanish cheer-leadership are unlikely to accept smaller transfers in the medium term, the Eastern have-nots led by Poland clamour for higher transfers (to rectify all sorts of past and current wrongs), and the net payers led by Germany, the new sick man of Europe, are fiscally unable to resort to cheque book diplomacy of old. Welcome to the Ecofin and European Councils, starring the 25, which have started in 2004 already and certain to climax in 2006, when the "Agenda 2000" financial allocations run out.

If Poland and company have not yet been able to bankrupt the EU's transfer mechanism with her five million farmers by the time the transitional limitations on direct CAP payments end in 2008, then Romania, not to mention Turkey, both large developing countries, will spell their definite end. In addition, with the new member states' limited absorptive capacities and frequently corrupt administrations, financial scandals (Poland, Slovakia, Romania and Bulgaria have already had their fair shares of a "Mister 10%/20%" taking his cuts of EU aid at national or regional levels in the pre-accession stage) will proliferate and expose the EU's weak financial management even further.

There are quite a few policy fields, like environment, social and food standards, in which the accession countries have enormous difficulties in catching up with existing EU legislation. It is difficult to fathom them endorsing any more tough new EU standards or new substantial EU legislation in these areas. Ditto the EU's foreign aid schemes: the enthusiasm for aid transfers to countries in Asia or Latin America with similar or even higher per capita incomes will understandably be very limited.

More significant will be the accession countries' basic attitudes to integration. Not only had they to suffer through some 40 years of foreign occupation and the forceful incorporation into a Russian or Serbian dominated multi-ethnic empire with a totalitarian ideology, but earlier they often also had to forego national sovereignty. Prior to the Berlin Congress of 1878 the map of Eastern Europe, which is now home to some 22 independent nations, showed the colours of just four empires: the Russian Empire, the German Empire, Austria-Hungary, and the Ottoman Empire. Many countries achieved national awareness only late in the 19th century. National independence for Estonia, Latvia and Lithuania was exercised only between 1919 and 1940. Slovakia was independent only during the war, and Slovenia for the first time ever only since 1991. Little wonder that an exuberant nationalism abounds and the notion and the symbols of national sovereignty are held in high esteem. Whether the national elites and the general public in all new member countries are really eager and aware of the need to share sovereignty voluntarily in a federally structured Europe remains very much in doubt. In some countries with a more self-assured national consciousness like Hungary or Estonia this may be the case: in Poland, the Czech Republic, and Romania, probably not. During the EP elections of June 2004 most electorates in the new member states demonstrated their disinterest with very low participation rates, most strikingly so in Slovakia (17%) and in Poland (20%). In ultra-nationalist Turkey the very notion of supra-nationality is too absurd to be considered seriously. It very much appears that the Community of 25 plus will only survive with stronger internal differentiation: a two-tier Community of a federated core, with a more loosely structured internal market plus some selective policies around it, in which most of the newcomers (plus the usual suspects among the old members) would find their comfortable place. This would look very similar to the concept of the old EU 12 surrounded by a "European Economic Area" (which today only consists of Norway, Iceland and Liechtenstein), a notion which Jacques Delors had entertained back in 1992.

This dilemma can also be spelled out for the Union's future foreign and defense policies, the core of sovereign high politics. After enlargement the European Union, with its almost doubled membership, will be a very different animal on the world scene. With a population of 550 million (including Turkey), twice the size of the US and half that of India or China, its global role for better or worse is bound to increase, particularly so in the field of international economic relations, in which its competence and decision-making structure are relatively the most cohesive and least threatened by fragmentation.

This will be different for the Union's nascent common high politics foreign and security policies. The historical orientations and security interests of the 12–14 newcomers (if we include Turkey as a recognised candidate and Croatia as a new serious applicant) differ even more widely than those of the old EU 15 between Finland and Portugal, and Greece and Ireland (to mention only the outer perimeters of geopolitical perspectives and interests).

In terms of formal accession talks, the negotiation chapter on CSFP was certainly one of the least problematic with plenty of lofty, well intentioned exhortations and with piles of resolutions ranging from Colombia to East Timor, the further away the more morally correct: a lot of "soft *acquis*", but little substance. Hence the CSFP chapter was quickly "provisionally closed" and ticked off for all 12 applicants, including countries with such divergent security interests as Lithuania, Bulgaria, Cyprus and Malta. If we compare voting behaviour in the UN, then the ten Central and Eastern European accession countries already since years vote regularly and reliably along pre-agreed EU lines, more so than certain EU member states. Only the Mediterranean countries (Cyprus, Malta and Turkey) rather followed their own foreign policy agenda.

Defense interests, in spite of a common recent NATO membership among the new Eastern members, are potentially equally diverse as are those of the old EU member states. Among the new NATO members, Poland is most committed to the Atlantist view of muscular deterrence. Hungary appears to be more in the continental camp. The Czech Republic, due to the absence of perceived external enemies, like the good soldier Sveijk and their Austrian neighbours, seems curiously disinterested in a serious defense policy. The Baltic nations, traumatised by Stalin's attempt at genocide, share the Polish view of their big Eastern neighbour, and cultivate their links to Kiev and even to Beijing. Perceptions of Russia are more positive in Bulgaria, as her historical liberator from Ottoman despotism, and in Slovakia where Russia was seen as the pan-Slavic protector against forcible Magyarisation in the late 19th century.

Cypriot foreign policy, understandably, is focused on attempts to overcome the division of the island, the result of Turkey's traumatising invasion of 1974. As a result, and similarly to that of Malta, Cypriot foreign policy followed in many ways its previous non-aligned pattern, cultivating friendships in the Arab world and in Moscow. An enlarged EU 25 is clearly more diverse. This is a hindrance for common action, but also an asset in terms of additional know-how on Eastern European and Middle Eastern realities, which sometimes was conspicuous in its absence from past policy decisions.

Turkey, as Asia Minor and as a continent of its own, plays in a different strategic league. Its population of currently 62 million with 2% annual growth will double in less than 30 years. In the US-inspired "great game" over control of access to the expected oil resources around the Caspian Basin, and as a stepping stone to the Persian Gulf, Turkey is expected to play a pivotal role as a regional hegemon, a role that the US had designed previously for other promising partners like Iran or Pakistan in the Middle East.

Turkey is supposed to cooperate closely and to export its "secular Muslim" model of development to fellow Turk-speaking peoples like the Azeiris, the Kasachs, the Kirgizs, the Turkmen and the Uzbeks, who gained independence in 1991, but also to the Tatars, Bashkirs and the North Caucasian peoples in Russia and possibly even the Uigurs, the repressed nationality of Sinkiang in North West China. Turkey, which historically was oriented more towards Arabia, the Balkans and the Black Sea, is supposed to rediscover its ancient ethnic cousins. The US-sponsored pipeline project from Baku to Ceyhan at the Turkish Mediterranean coast serves evidently less commercial but strategic interests, putting the transport of an increasing proportion of Central Asian crude oil and possibly later also of natural gas out of Russians or Iranian reach.

Yet Turkish influence, due to the lack of resources and also to the fading appeal of Kemalism back home, has been minor in Central Asia compared to the efforts of Iranian and Saudi-sponsored fundamentalists or to continued Russian influence working through the local nomenclatura and state security and resource business interests.

Turkey is also seen as a check against Iran and the radical Northern Arabs, Syria and Iraq, against whom it is able to withhold the flows of water of the Tigris and Euphrates by means of a complex system of giant dams which is currently being completed. Potential territorial disputes over the Sanjak of Alexandrette, the province of Hatay, loom with Syria, which maintains a claim to this north-western coastal land that was handed by French colonial authorities back to Turkey in 1939.

At almost annual intervals the Turkish military undertook massive military incursions at the strength of several infantry and tank divisions against suspected PKK bases across the border to Northern Iraq. Even under US occupation since 2003 violent tensions reoccurred. The border to Armenia is closed following the Russian-supported Armenian occupation of a large part of eastern Azerbaijan. Bilateral relations are still burdened by the memories of the genocide committed against the Armenian population in Eastern Anatolia during and after 1915.

Similarly, relations with Cyprus (and by extension with Greece) have been traumatised since the Turkish invasion ordered by Premier Ecevit in 1974 divided the island, with the Greek population of North Cyprus remaining expelled and Turkey regularly threatening to formally annex its occupied areas.

Turkish relations with all of its neighbours are latent or overtly conflictual. An enlarged Union would inherit these adversarial relations equally with those of a more amicable nature held with many Turk peoples and with Turkey's ally Israel.

Even more significant will be Russia's perception of encirclement. If the EU's enlargement (in difference to NATO's) has so far raised few eyebrows in Moscow, with Yeltsin during his past presidency even declaring to favour Russia's accession itself, the membership of Turkey for declared geopolitical and strategic reasons in a stratagem subservient to the Clinton administration's past objective of a *cordon sanitaire* around Russia, will generate defensive reflexes. Russia would then see herself physically cut off from potential allies in Northern Arabia, Iran, India and (partly) China; she would feel herself locked in not only in the Black Sea. But then the Baltic Sea situation could be perceived in a similarly adversarial light.

It is clear then that EU's current foreign policy mode of least common denominator and trying to be everybody's darling cannot be maintained with the addition of a regional hegemon who appears determined to follow its own geopolitical agenda with strong US support. The accession of the other new member states has just added the "normal" complications — sufficient "only" to render the unanimity principle on CSFP matters finally unworkable. Turkish membership, however, would put the EU before very hard (and, for most, unacceptable) consequences: to become supportive of a course of foreign policy adventure, which actually has no interest or benefit for anybody in the EU, but as a consequence of which all would bear the costs of Russian, Armenian, Iranian and Arab hostility.

It appears curious that no serious thought has been given to the consequences of Turkish EU membership, not just on the likely demise of the CSFP, but also to most other EU policies ranging from agriculture to the internal market and to internal security, which could no longer be maintained should an essentially non-European major developing country with an overcharged public administration join. This confirms a strong Turkish suspicion that the European Council's invitation is not meant seriously after all.

The Pursuit of Happiness and Frustrations: Careers in Europe

The scene may be familiar to any travelling missionary on European integration matters: while you drone on and on about the win-win situation of shared sovereignty, your student audience inevitably dozes off (except for the unavoidable handful of Europhobics who remain on high alert), and after a while not even your incessant attempts at cracking Euro jokes (a rare species!) will wake, let alone cheer them up. It is only when you casually mention job prospects "in Europe" at the end of your over-long speech, that everybody suddenly gets jolted into high attention. Attractive girls put on their most winning smiles and ask for your telephone number when inquiring about "stage" prospects in the Commission. Prospects of easy riches, generous expatriate packages in a stimulating international work environment, with wide discretionary powers at a young age over a whole continent emerge. This and plenty of global business travel will surely compensate for the Brussels rain.

A dream job within reach. True or false? Yes and no. There are colleagues who love their Commission (and other EU institution) jobs and happily trot to their offices (almost) every day, throwing in unpaid overtime and weekend work without complaint. Yet there are others who are deeply unhappy, living through escapist daydreams, and who stick to their jobs, for which they have suitably minimised the workload, only by the lack of employment alternatives. So it all seems to depend... On occasion, in your professional biography you experience both situations successively.

The Commission has some 15,000 permanent officials. The other Community institutions (the administrations of the Council, Parliament, Court of Justice, Court of Auditors, Committee of Regions,

Economic and Social Committee, affiliated specialist EU offices, foundations and institutes) employ an additional 10,000 people.

The EU staff is typically sorted into a (nonetheless fairly upwardly open) caste system of four professional grades: A: university graduates doing managerial and analytical work; B: qualified grammar school graduates working on routine administrative tasks; C: middle school graduates working as secretaries or doing other qualified clerical work; and, finally, D: elementary school graduates doing manual work, like as ushers, drivers or in the mail office.

There are about 6,000 A grades working in the Commission, half of which are however full-time translators ("LA"). Of the remainder, 300 are diplomatic staff at the Commission's external Delegations in third countries. About 2,700 work in headquarters in Brussels or Luxembourg. This means one A grade professional officer per 150,000 of his fellow EU citizens; indeed, in spite of all Eurocracy mythology, a very lean European administration (too lean, in fact, to do its politically acquired current budget and project work overload properly). It is about as thinly spread as the district officers of the Indian civil service in British India. Compare to this the number of federal employees in supposedly anti-big government US: three million in pre-Department of Homeland Security days.

Recently, Neil Kinnock's business school inspired reforms have transformed the French inherited A/B/C/D caste system into a linear, overlapping scale (with the increased scope for individual up and downward movements). But the differentiation of job contents and career prospects according to academic qualifications will remain essentially. There is a case to be made for such a meritocracy-based mandarinate: a university graduate in the social sciences with some post-graduate experience will normally write better policy analysis than even a clever inspector without any tertiary experience (who in turn is surely stronger in executive operations). A sensible upwardly mobile flexibility is in place. Remember that among the two most successful Europeans, Jean Monnet had only elementary school training (he could have become a security guard in the Commission), and Jacques Delors only finished secondary school (which would have qualified him to manage the Commission's print shop as a career highlight).

An ideal first exposure to the inner workings of European integration is offered by the Commission's internships ("stage") of five months' duration. They are best suited to recent graduates who have either finished a thesis on European integration or who contemplate a dissertation or a future career in the same field.

"Stages" start every year on March 1 and October 1 for some 600 trainees from all member states and a few from the rest of the world (*"les nouvelles stagiaires sont arrives"*). They are poorly paid at 500 Euros per month, or volunteer to be not paid at all (which helps one to be selected, but not to survive).

They often have applied to interesting-sounding directorate generals, like those for environment, culture, social affairs, development and external relations [which in some cases have no work to do (culture), spread mainly boredom (social affairs), or often deal with issues too confidential to be handled by *stagiares*]. Only very few cognoscenti apply to substantial policy DGs like agriculture, competition, internal market or regional development, where in view of the overworked staff, they can do a lot of real and interesting work during their internship. It obviously helps to contact heads of units or senior desk officers in one's area of interest to gain acceptance. There are about twice as many applications as places available.

Once accepted, there are two types of *stagiares*; those who party and network full-time and those who want to gain useful work experience at least during the daytime. There are also two types of jobs — some which entail work and others which are just empty desks with a telephone. Ideally jobs and work motivation should match. There should be a superior (*"counseiller de stage"*) around who allocates useful and feasible tasks, but this does not always work. Often a workaholic and resourceful *stagiaire* can rescue his *stage* by volunteering to make himself useful and in fact, in spite of his short stay, may make historical work on a piece of European policy (and himself an attractive recruit to the professional EU scene around the Brussels institutions).

Indeed the EU-related employment opportunities outside the EU institutions proper are a multiple of those provided by the institutions proper. Hundreds of business associations, trade unions, professional bodies, state and regional governments, foundations, religious organisations, management consultants, PR companies, translation offices, law firms and other auxiliary services are around and eager for young, EU-knowledgeable and multilingual graduates ready to work long hours for initially very low wages.

Yet again, many *stagiares* are more interested in relaxing after their stressful university studies in a multinational atmosphere of young mid-twenties. Their "stage" will remain a nostalgic episode of fun and parties, but of little consequence (unless they get married in the process).

There are three ways to get into the mainstream professional career (A) track in a Community institution. First, by competitive mass entry examination for most (more about this later), or second, by special appointment into a cabinet position of a Commissioner or some other well connected special temporary posting for a lucky few to be regularised later by "*concours bidon*", a phony entry competition. It is this second group which has given proof of higher social intelligence and hence, on strength of cabinet-based connections, rises faster to the top than the first group, which is gifted more with analytical intelligence. The result is an ambivalent structure in which sometimes clever senior desk officers and heads of units are managed by politically well connected half-wits whose management experience in the cabinet may have been limited to reacting to the prevailing political winds and to picking up the phone and barking: "The Commissioner wants by tomorrow morning ... ".

Finally, the third recruitment path is an even more elegant, rare and refined method: it leads straight to the top. Formally it is done by a very restricted "*concours sur titres*", a CV-based evaluation, followed by interviews. A senior Commission or Council post is not filled by promotions from within "the house" but offered to member states, who then pull all political levers (telephone calls from Prime Ministers/Chancellors are a favourite method) to push for their native sons (and a few native daughters), on occasion those they want to get rid of. New member states are allowed to use the same system to fill the senior posts of their quota based on "regional balance".

In case of Spain, back in 1986 many of her senior positions were taken up by young Socialists (then all in their late twenties) from Andalusia. And, if they have not stumbled over corruption charges, they are still around in their director posts, now in their late mid-life crises. Austria in 1995, in spite of the noisy warnings of this author, still managed to export her "red/black" proportional patronage system (then a dying, discredited model back home) to EU institutions.

With post-Communist parties back in power in many Eastern accession countries, we can expect the vigorous pursuit of partisan career placement of the nomenclatura's offspring into life-time EU positions. Poland has already publicly laid claim to no less than 2,000 posts.

Back to the mainstream *concours*: it is a major undertaking organised bi-annually for the major recruitment categories like external relations generalists (my entry), statisticians, economists, EU lawyers, customs people, vets, agriculturalists, translators, etc. The dates and particulars are published in politically correct advertisements (nicely illustrated with a bunch of models, including two attractive ladies, one black and one white, in leadership roles; never seen such a thing in two decades of real EU life) in the major quality dailies (like the *Guardian* and the *Financial Times*; don't look for it in the *Daily Mail*). The particulars are also accessible on the Commission's (and other EU institutions) web-pages. The formal criteria for A level entry (A8/A7) competitions are minimal: to have graduated from a real university, to have completed one's military service (wherever still compulsory), to know a foreign EU language, and to have had at least two years of professional post-graduation experience if wishing to enter at A7 level. In real life, however, it is highly advisable to apply only if one has studied seriously abroad for at least one year, is fluent in English, French or German (in addition to one's own mother tongue), and has done a fair amount of EU-related studies, including if possible a "stage", to be able to pass.

The conditions of the exam (in the tradition of French and Italian public service entry examinations) are ferocious. Sometimes soccer stadia are rented, holding up to 50,000 candidates out of which some 200 may pass and report to the next hurdle, the oral entry exam. The written exam consists traditionally of three elements:

a) A multiple-choice test with a lot of general knowledge, current affairs and factual EU questions.
b) The submission of a bunch of fictitious documents which are to be synthesised into a briefing paper for senior hierarchy.
c) A dialectical essay on a theme like: "Is a common commercial policy preferable to national trade policies, and if so, why?" (I hope the attentive reader is by now able to answer this one).

There is a rich folklore about cheating at these exams, ranging from people using cell phones in toilets, to bribing Italian (why always Italian?) ushers to supply advance copies, or organising collusive conspiracies for exam paper corrections (a version very virulent in Austria back in 1995). But very few stories in circulation have been found to be true. And when they were, the exams were cancelled, repeated and the culprits punished.

The multiple-choice test (a US speciality, since kids over there don't know how to write coherent sentences any more) is currently under fire: Brits and women fail in inordinate numbers. In the days of political correctness, it is certain to be replaced. Nobody should be put at a disadvantage because his knowledge of current and past world affairs is shaky, or because she is unable to take risky informed decisions in a limited time.

The 0.5% who pass the written part of a general *concours* about six months later will be told to present themselves for an oral exam. A jury of Commission officials will ask the candidate a battery of factual questions, some in his preferred foreign language. He will also give a short presentation on a pre-set topic (with his brains as the only reference source). This time only some 60% flunk. The winners will be put on a "reserve list" from which Community institutions will invite people for interviews for those vacant posts for which they do not find suitable internal candidates.

Sometimes this is because they want fresh thinking, unspoiled characters to fill certain work and brain-intensive posts, sometimes the posts (like in accounting or anti-dumping) are so awfully boring and dead-end that no internal candidate will ever present himself voluntarily. In the interviewing stage, the head of units and directors will check out the candidates' social skills and their presumed ability to blend into their multinational European work teams.

Those who on that occasion sport nose rings, tattoos or who tell their future bosses how their departments could be better run, or that they cannot stand Germans or Greeks will probably wait for a telephone call for a long time.

The reserve lists are valid until the next *concours* two or three years later yields new eager laureates. Those who have not been called up from the reserve list may reapply for the next *concours*.

There is a wide range of public and commercial programmes offering courses (for a lot of money) claiming to teach how to pass the *concours*. The *concours*, however, deviously have been designed that only clever, informed graduates pass, not those who have taken "how to" cram courses. When I was posted to Vienna during Austria's accession process, I was frequently invited to contribute to training seminars for aspiring Austrian EU officials. Yet back in Brussels unfortunately I saw only very few of my past disciples having succeeded (in spite of much improved pass rates for a new member state entitled to fill her quota of "national balance", which for Austria stood at around 2% as her share of the EU's population). Personally, my own tried and tested recipe for success back in 1982 consisted of a good night's sleep and some strong cups of coffee prior to the exam, so as to be able to remain driven and focused during its duration of four long hours.

You join an EU institution by signing up to the "statutes", which for want of an employment contract stipulate the rules and regulations, the rights and duties of the official and his institution. Most importantly, an official must guard his independence towards outside instructions and insinuations from his home country and from interested lobbyists. The usual obligations of loyalty and secrecy apply, including fairly medieval censorship provisions on officials' publications. As the statutes are up for revision it is hoped that these pre-democratic remnants will cease to exist in compliance with the European Charter of Human Rights.

Young A grade officials typically enter as junior desk officers grade A8 (without post-graduate professional experience) or A7 (with at least two years of professional experience) and can reasonably expect to reach grade A4 (principal administrator, section chief or deputy head of unit) by the end of their careers at 65. They are supposed to change their posts within their institution every three years to give prove of their mobility: which is wonderful, except that it prevents living institutional memories (which bureaucratic organisations also need in order to avoid repeating past mistakes). A typical unit of the Commission, say of relations with Japan, consists of one head of unit (A3 or A4), one deputy (A4 or A5), four more junior A grades, three B grades to handle executive tasks and two secretaries and now rather scarce office managers (C) to work for the entire team.

There are, however, also those whose ambition in life is to rise above the position of deputy head of unit in the Commission's Japan division. They compete with those who either have cultivated the right connections with the right national, political or social networks or those who have been recruited into the Commissioners' offices ("cabinets") and are landed into cushy managerial posts ("parachutage") once their Commissioner's job is drawing to a close. For these senior positions like Director General (A1), Director (A2) and Head of Unit (A3), the principle of "geographical balance" applies. In their most primitive and blatant form ("reserved for a Frenchman", for instance), they were outlawed by the ECJ back in 1993. But they are a continued practice in more subtle forms (added on by gender *desiderata*) nonetheless. This surely makes an "unequal opportunity employer" (*The Economist*, March 20, 1993). But it is the price to pay for pan European political correctness.

Back in 1986, together with a colleague and friend, Malcolm Colling, I did a study of the Community institution's then senior management based on their biographical submissions to a specialist Who's Who. At the time, we arrived at the following conclusion (published in *Courier du Personnel*, No. 489, 1987):

> "The Who's Who data we analysed, however sketchy and unsatisfactory they often are, have given a clear indication of a European meritocracy emerging, whose elite positions are clearly based on

personal achievement and individual merit with all indications —
except for gender — pointing to achievement by performance and
not to ascribed or inherited factors.

Administrative top management show a fairly even spread in
birth places and nationalities [though there remains a slight bias
against the enlargement nations (then: Spain and Portugal) and
the Dutch].

Almost all have university training, normally in law, economics, politics or a combination thereof to the Master's level
and frequently beyond. They more often than not studied at the
better-known European universities (with a relative preference for
Oxbridge and the Sorbonne) and have a fair share of study experiences abroad (usually in a neighbouring European country).

While graduating in their mid to late 20s, many, typically in their
mid 30s published — partly extensively — academic, professional
and/or EC related works.

When analysing pre-EC careers, it becomes apparent that future
A1/A2s join the Community institutions at a later stage in professional life than do future A3s or below. The former typically have
a background in politics, banking, central government service and
international organisations.

They have their fastest start when joining a cabinet and then
with preference work in the Commission's external relations DGs,
or serve in further cabinet positions. Another preferred entry
route for a top level Community career involves experience as a
party official (but not as an MEP!) in the European Parliament's
structure.

Obviously then, good political contacts to one's capital are fairly
essential to a successful top level Community career.

The A1/A2 office holders also appear as distinct from their A3
colleagues in terms of more accelerated mobility. After their initial, fairly lengthy, posting they tend to move around at 3–4 year
intervals, spiralling themselves speedily upwards. Thus, mobility has increased considerably during the subsequent "generations" of top EC officials, with those who joined the Community

institutions during the founding decade being promoted typically at earlier ages, but usually staying longer in their positions.

Obviously hard work needs its antidote of hard play. Top Community officials enjoy an impressive array of off-duty pastimes with active sports (tennis, skiing, swimming, horse riding) being clear front runners ahead of the more leisurely or cultural pursuits.

In meeting the Euro-elite, we encounter a meritocracy of diverse national and regional backgrounds, well-educated, and particularly in its top bracket, with entry into Community institutions often furthered by good political ties to the national capital. Job mobility prior to and after joining Community institutions is also a common characteristic of the Euro-elite's top level.

The situation of A3 office holders, who on average have done longer service in Community institutions and have held fewer cabinet and pre-EC career positions, thus appears to be different from the above A1/A2 pattern.

The message emerging from our data is fairly obvious: what may be good for the Community institutions (namely to keep good political and personal ties to the national capitals in offering promising career opportunities and to maintain a healthy diversified administrative elite), may not always be beneficial or motivating to the able and dynamic junior and middle level European officials, who increasingly may see themselves deprived of the chance of joining the European meritocracy through truly European service."

What we could not cover in our study were the classical affinities of certain nationalities: the French had traditionally strong influence over agriculture, the legal service and the budget, the Germans over competition and the Brits over transportation.

Below the top level of director generals, it was fairly evident that middle management positions held by French officials frequently commanded fairly strategic units. The Germans managed those of a technical or legal nature, and the Italians local procurement. The larger the EU expanded the more these traditional affinities became diluted, since within units also some national balance needs to be maintained. This also applies to external relations: Spaniards should not always work with Latin America, Frenchmen not exclusively with Francophone Africa, Brits with the Commonwealth . . .

The work style of the Community institutions has successfully accommodated the different national administrative styles of the 25 member states, bridging also the big intra-European cultural divide between the Germanic and the Latin work styles, the first of which, according to Richard Lewis, being "linear-active", and the second "multi-active", with the Finns and Estonians preferring a "reactive" work and communication style. This diversity is accommodated with a great tradition of target orientation by giving latitude of tolerance to operational ways and work styles to achieve these shared objectives. Multinationally mixed European teams also have an excellent ability to draw directly on different national policy experiences and to relate to their capitals for factual and policy inputs (not only useful to prepare sensible policy drafts, but also essential to gain acceptance in the Council and in Parliament later on).

At a more senior level the differences in leadership styles, notably between Germanic and Latin management cultures, inevitably begin to show. The former are typically used to flat hierarchies, more open information exchange (including admission of mistakes), less power distance and autocratic behaviour than the latter. Exceptions on both sides, as usual, confirm the rule.

Part of a relaxed, friendly and cooperative work style are open office doors, a widely practiced informality and a benign neglect of job titles, formal job descriptions and of administrative procedure (including inevitably sloppy archiving).

Attempts at formalising procedures inevitably fail. This started with the rule that officials should identify themselves when relying on the phone. The army of Franco-Belgian secretaries simply changed from "*Oui*" to "*Allo*" to demonstrate their reform-mindedness. Linguistically the rules are clear: according to the EU language charter every citizen has the right to correspond with EU institutions in his own national language. Within the institutions, however, English (45%), French (40%) and German (6%) are most used, with an ever-growing share of Euro-Pidgin English (which however due to its limited vocabulary and multilingual abuse — including nonsensical Americanisms — becomes increasingly useless for precise drafting).

Approval systems for spending decisions have always been cumbersome and complicated, with dozens of signatures needed to get contracts and payments approved. With all anti-corruption and pro-transparency measures introduced, the situation has turned from bad to worse, as counter-checks, audits, reporting requirements, interventions and delays have multiplied.

How does the Commission deal with delinquent and dissident staff? Dissidence and whistle-blowing are not really appreciated. As long as they are not leaked and do not become public, such drafts simply go into waste bins, with their authors similarly sidelined. In case of disciplinary problems, the Commission also prefers a discreet approach. People are rarely fired or publicly sanctioned. They are usually shifted into a quiet place (*"limogé"*, literally means "sent to Limoges", a place to be exiled in the French provinces) with silly work or none at all. Only in rare instances, when a case is bad or public enough, a slow but ruthlessly working machinery is set in unstoppable motion to expedite the exit of the culprit into the outside world, possibly even stripped of his pension rights.

Following the resignation of the Santer Commission, one of its surviving members, Neil Kinnock in the subsequent Prodi Commission (1999–2004), embarked on a large scale reform effort of internal structures and proceedings. Organigrams were turned upside down twice a year and directorate generals rotated (as if an excellent agriculturalist also qualified as a top diplomat, and vice versa). Wonderful new business school hype was brought in by an overpaid army of business consultants to supersede the rigid, but typically bypassed, rules of French-style meritocracy. Laudable intentions apart, the new rules seem to reduce administrative autonomy even further and make directorate generals ever more depended on the whims of their political masters, the Commissioners (who, it is recalled, caused their own downfall back in 1999; it was not their officials). The fact that large parts of the Commission have been absorbed by self-referential introspective reform attempts has certainly cost political capital in the current crucial public debate over future governance in Europe.

It is no secret that pay conditions for Eurocrats are better than for national public servants — but the latter can stay home, remain integrated in local and national society, work in their own language and legal system and remain intellectually less challenged.

EU pay conditions, however, compare unfavourably to those of member states' diplomats stationed in Brussels, to NATO staff and to expatriate managers of private companies. All of the erstwhile diplomatic perks for Commission staff, like the famously low-priced Christmas liquor parcel (*"collis"*) of tabloid fame, sadly vanished long ago. Yet if one manages monthly revenues wisely, a comfortable upper middle class lifestyle in the better suburbs of Brussels is possible. The children are taken care of pretty well in multilingual European schools. Senior ranks who owe their promotion to their Socialist party tickets may, on occasion, suffer from cognitive dissonance, should they reminisce that their suburban villas and Mediterranean vacation homes are paid for from the VAT contributions of the toiling working classes, but this does not seem to disturb Socialist politicians elsewhere unduly either. It is less the taxman than the self-inflicted ill fortune of multiple divorces that can thrust a long serving Eurocrat into poverty.

There has been a perceptible generational change in the make up of the European civil service in the last decade. The founder generation of Euro-pioneers, which had fought in the last war, has vanished years ago. It was made up of characters with a sense of mission and commitment. Whether they remained idealists — or often, in the absence of useful work induced by Council blockades in the 1960s and 1970s, turned culinary hedonists — they remained impressive characters, well versed in European languages and history.

Today's staffers at almost all levels are hardworking organisation men and women. They are doing a job, frequently well and highly motivated, but only rarely following a European vocation. With the Commission's changed profile, there are more and more budget technicians, contract administrators and accountants than creative policy analysts or intellectual visionaires. Their lunch breaks consist of sandwiches with mineral water. Gone are the long booze-ups with lobbyists. As a young official back in the 1980s, I used to despise the old lazy officialdom. With the wisdom of hindsight I now have to ask for their forgiveness. With conformist staffers, some of whom have even begun to outsource their strategy papers, and streamlined promotion profiles, the Commission might risk to degenerate into a glorified and then probably overpaid Council secretariat. This would be a pity for all of Europe.

Brussels, Europe's Unfinished Capital

What is a capital? Niamey is a capital and so is Ulan Bator. There were transitional capitals like Bonn or Vichy. There are also artificial ones like Canberra and Brasilia, or currently still more fictional spots like Abuja (Nigeria) or Astana (Kazakhstan).

Yet typically one does ascribe capital functions to definite global cities with an imperial past, with an impressive urban heritage, of great cultural standing and a continued continental, if not global role, like London, Paris, Berlin, Rome, Madrid, and also Tokyo, Moscow, Washington DC, etc.

With all due respect you would not normally list Brussels among them. No doubt it is a serious capital. It is pretty and likeable in many of its *quartiers*. When asked about the advantages of Brussels, most ex-pat residents will quickly cite its convenient location to reach Paris, London or Amsterdam. On the other hand you will find few people in London or Paris who will list their town's closeness to Brussels as a major advantage.

Yet Brussels until the late 19th century was a pleasant medieval town like the centres of Ghent, Bruges, Antwerp and Louvain today. Leopold II with his Congolese funds imposed elements of neo-classicist grandeur on a restive populace and on its parochial local politics. The medieval town perished and so did many of the 19th century constructions.

The 1960s and 1970s attempted the imitation of a functional and car-oriented city, in trying to look like Dallas or St Louis. The slums of Anderlecht and Schaarbeek appear to complement the picture of an imperfect European imitation. Impressive suburbanisation occurred in the Flemish North-Eastern to Southern fringe. Supranational corporate and military headquarters and suburban shopping malls dot the major outgoing arteries. Windswept skyscrapers popped up west of Gare du Nord. The monofunctional European HQ around the Schuman area is similarly sterile (and attractive only at its undeveloped fringes: Place du Luxembourg, Place Jourdan and at Merode, where it meets real Belgium).

Hence Brussels represents a curious symbiosis: vestiges of the medieval, symbols of short-lived imperialism, a fairly neglected public infrastructure, and the partly already very run down and discredited modernisation of the last decades, coexisting happily with the residual communal spirit and initiative of Brussels almost anarchist burghers and of those of its foreign residents who were willing and able to integrate. Is this the capital of Europe? Yes, it is.

With all its contradictions it adequately describes the current halfway state of European integration. We are beyond Luxembourg or Bonn, so to speak, but surely are not yet (and probably shall never be) in the London or Paris league. Hence Brussels is fine and fair for Europe at the moment. But there are a few things, besides fixing pot holes and the long-suffering sewage system, which should be done with urgency as sound urban management, including upgrading the metro, its stations, regional public transport and the railway stations (the stench of urine around Central Station has unfortunately become a most memorable impression for shocked first time visitors); banning gangs of armed thugs, mostly ill-adjusted immigrant youths from the inner city, with an effective policy of zero tolerance; enlarging public parks and green spaces (instead of parking lots) in the inner city; and regenerating urban spaces in the greater Schuman ("European") area.

These are undramatic and inexpensive but hopefully effective fixes that would make Brussels a cleaner, livelier, safer and more urban capital for the present needs of Europe.

But how about the capital of a hopefully more democratised, federal Europe, which should also comprise some 100 million new citizens from Central/East Europe?

Let's begin at the top. The elected President of the democratically controlled European Commission should not reside on the 15th floor of the Breydel (or the refurbished Berlaymont), but in a "White House" with its own identity, say the Bibliotheque Solvay. He and his state guests are not protected by gum-chewing private security guards, but by uniformed Euro-Cops or members of the Euro-Force. One could even think about a changing-of-the-guard ceremony.

Federal symbolisms are important. There should be a monument to the unknown European soldier of the European civil wars of the last century, containing the bones of victims of the battles at Ypres, Verdun, the Isonzo, Stalingrad and Tobruk. (Unfortunately there is no shortage of suitable sites.)

More important is civic culture. For visitors wishing to see Europe, there should be full access and transparency to all EU institution proceedings, to witness Parliament, Council and Commission debates — not just a "St Schuman Day", but a regular feature on a walk-in basis with briefings by well-informed information officers supported by a well-stocked public library with Internet access and televised monitors on all ongoing European affairs.

The promotion of an intellectual capital should follow: think tanks, policy-oriented research institutes (beyond the narrow confines of "European lobbying studies"), a greater European dimension of local and international universities, the establishment of genuine European media — both print and electronic — in Brussels.

In terms of urbanisation, improvements could include redesigning Rue de la Loi and Rue Belliard from current inner-city race tracks to tree-lined boulevards; upgrading inner city life within *les ceintures* by rehabilitating the rich architectural heritage, animating urban qualities, attracting private capital, corporate headquarters and upper-class residences; expanding attractive pedestrian shopping and leisure areas by linking Brussels' three most attractive urban sites, Grand Place, Mont des Arts/Les Sablons and Avenue Louise; redevelop the Gare de Midi area by inducing corporate headquarters to move from sterile greensite "corporate villages" to a vibrant and then also safe inner-city location, and, last but not least, preserving traditional Brussels *quartiers*, ensuring that they are not destroyed by developers or by "ethnic invasions", creating slums and lawless no-go areas.

Possibly Brussels local politics (witness the last four decades) may be unable or unwilling to deliver. If the communal tax base proves too weak and intercommunal fragmentation too strong, perhaps a "Brussels DC" unified and quadrilingual European metropolitan might be an option. For the time being, however, in the typical time-honoured incremental fashion of European integration, let's give the current local authorities their chance.

---

*This chapter was originally published as "Meeting European Integration Half Way" by the *European Voice* — certainly the world's most well-informed weekly on European affairs — on September 13, 2001 in response to an essay competition on the future of Brussels. My intellectual labour won me a crate of champagne (which was subsequently consumed by my mother-in-law and our Polish cleaning lady).

BIBLIOGRAPHY

Peter Altmaier *e.a. Finanzkontrolle und Betrugsbekaempfung in der EU*. St. Augustin: Konrad Adenauer Stiftung. 1996.

Asia Europe Roundtable (ed.). *Regions in Transition*. Singapore: Asia-Europe Foundation. 2001.

Graham Avery and Fraser Cameron. *The Enlargement of the European Union*. Sheffield: Sheffield Academic Press. 1998.

Ian Bache. *The Politics of EU Regional Policy*. Sheffield: Sheffield University Press. 1998.

Baerbel-Maria Baerlach *e.a.* (eds.). *The New Public Health Policy of the EU*. Munich: Urban & Vogel. 1999.

Timothy Bainbridge. *The Penguin Companion to European Union*. 3rd Edition. Harmondsworth: Penguin. 2002.

David Baker and David Seawright (eds.). *Britain For and Against Europe*. Oxford: Clarendon Press. 1998.

Michael J. Baun. *A Wider Europe*. Lanham, MD: Rowman and Littlefield. 2000.

Gilles Bertrand *e.a.* Scenarios Europe 2010. Brussels: European Commission Working Paper. Forward Studies Unit. 1999.

Alistair Blair. *The European Union Since 1945*. London: Longman. 1999.

Dieter Blumenwitz *e.a.* (eds.). *Fortschritte im Beitrittsprozess der Staaten Osteuropas zur EU*. Koeln: Verlag Wissenschaft und Politik. 1999.

Klaus-Dieter Borchert. *The ABC of Community Law*. Luxembourg: OPOCE. 2000.

Shaum Breslin and Richard Higgott. "New Regionalisms in the Global Political Economy". *Asia Europe Journal*. 1/2003. 167–182.

Martin J. Bull and James L. Newell (eds.). *Corruption in Contemporary Politics*. Houndmills, Hants: Palgrave Macmillan. 2003.

Rolf Caesar *e.a.* (eds.). *Die Zukunft Europas im Lichte der Agenda 2000*. Baden-Baden: Nomos. 2000.

James A. Caporaso. *The European Union. Dilemmas of Regional Integration*. Boulder, CO: Westview Press. 2000.

Paolo Cecchini. *The European Challenge 1992. The Benefits of a Single Market*. Aldershot: Gower. 1988.

Philippe Chenaux. *Une Europe Vaticane? Entre le Plan Marshall et les Traites de Rome*. Brussels: Editions Ciaco. 1990.

Clive H. Church and David Phinnemore. *The Penguin Guide to the European Treaties*. Harmondsworth: Penguin. 2002.

Michelle Cini (ed.). *European Union Politics*. Oxford: Oxford University Press. 2003.

Arthur Francis Cockfield. *The European Union. Creating the Single Market*. Chichester: Wiley Chancery Law. 1994.

Richard Corbett. *The European Parliament's Role in Closer EU Integration*. Houndmills, Hants: Macmillan. 1998.

Aidan Cox and Antonique Koning. *Understanding EC Aid*. London: Overseas Development Institute. 1997.

Roy Denman. *Missed Chances. Britain and Europe in the Twentieth Century*. London: Cassell. 1996.

Roy Denman. *The Mandarin's Tale*. London: Politico's Publishing. 2002.

Desmond Dinan. *Ever Closer Union: An Introduction to European Integration*. Boulder, CO: Lynn Riener Pubs. 1999.

Francois Duchene. *Jean Monnet. The First Statesman of Interdependence*. New York/ London: W.W. Norton. 1994.

Andrew Duff. *Reforming the EU*. London: Federal Trust. 1997.

Christiane Duparc. *The European Community and Human Rights*. Luxembourg: OPOCE. 1993.

Ali M. El-Agraa. *The European Union: Economics and Politics*. 6th Edition. Upper Saddle River, NJ: Prentice Hall. 2000.

Klaus Emmerich. *Europa neu: Das Konzept des Praesidenten der EU Kommission Jacques Santer*. Vienna: Ueberreuter. 1995.

Bill Emmott. "A Survey of America's World Role". *The Economist*. 29.6.2002.

Ernest Enzelsberger. "Die Euregio Bodensee und die EU". *Die Union*. 2/1996. 37–54.

European Central Bank. *The Monetary Policy of the ECB*. Frankfurt: ECB. 2001.

European Commission. *Panorama of EU Industry*. Volumes I and II. Luxembourg: OPOCE. 1997.

European Commission. *Regions. Statistical Yearbook 1996*. Luxembourg: Eurostat. 1997.

European Commission. *The Competitiveness of European Industry*. Luxembourg: OPOCE. 1997.

European Commission. *The Demographic Situation of the EU*. Luxembourg: OPOCE. 1995.

European Commission. *The Future of North-South Relations*. Brussels: Cahiers of the Forward Studies Unit. 1997.

Pascal Fontaine. *A New Idea for Europe. The Schuman Declaration 1950–2000*. Luxembourg: OPOCE. 2000.

Pascal Fontaine. *Europe in Ten Lessons*. Luxembourg: OPOCE. 1992.

Pascal Fontaine. *Jean Monnet, a Grand Design for Europe*. Luxembourg: OPOCE. 1988.

Stephen George. *An Awkward Partner. Britain in the European Community*. Oxford: Oxford University Press. 1998.

Hella Gerth-Wellmann. *Die Lome Politik der Europaeischen Gemeinschaft*. Munich: Weltforum Verlag. 1984.

Leslie Friedmann Goldstein. *Constituting Federal Sovereignty*. Baltimore, MD: Johns Hopkins University Press. 2001.

David C. Gompert and F. Stephen Larrabee. *America and Europe*. New York, NY: Cambridge University Press. 1997.

Charles Grant. Delors. *Inside the House that Jacques Built*. London: Nicholas Brealey Publishing. 1994.

John Green. *Energy and the Environment in the EU*. Brussels: Friends of the Earth. 1998.

A.J.R. Groom and Paul Taylor (eds.). *Functionalism*. London: University of London Press. 1975.

Richard N. Haass (ed.). *Transatlantic Tensions*. Washington, DC: Brookings Institution Press. 1999.

J.P. Hayes. *Making Trade Policy in the European Community*. Houndmills, Hants: Macmillan. 1993.

Stanley Henig. *The Uniting of Europe*. London: Routledge. 1997.

Wilhelm Henrichsmeyer *e.a.* (eds.). *Auf der Suche nach europaeischer Identitaet*. Bonn: Europa Union Verlag. 1995.

Simon Hix. *The Political System of the EU*. New York: St. Martin's Press. 1999.

Martin Holland. *European Community Integration*. London: Pinter Publishers. 1993.

Eric Holm. *The European Anarchy*. Copenhagen: Copenhagen Business School Press. 2001.

Rudolf Hrbek *e.a.* (eds.). *Die Europaeische Union als Prozess*. Bonn: Europa Union Verlag. 1998.

Reinhard Hummel (ed.). *Ein Markt — eine Waehrung*. Vienna: Signum. 1995.

Samuel P. Huntington. *The Clash of Civilizations*. New York, NY: Simon and Schuster. 1996.

Thomas Jansen. Reflexions sur l'identite europeenne. Brussels: European Commission Working Paper. Cellule de Prospective. 1999.

Jean-Claude Junker. *Europe: A Vision for the 21st Century*. Singapore: Asia Europe Foundation. 1998.

Helmut Karl *e.a.* (eds.). *Europaeische Raumordnungspolitik*. Bonn: Europa Union Verlag. 1996.

Ferdinand Kinsky. *Foederalismus: ein gesamteuropaeisches Modell*. Bonn: Europa Union Verlag. 1995.

Romain Kirt. "Der Euro — die Einfuehrung einer einheitlichen Waehrung". *Die Union*. 2/1996. 33–36.

Romain Kirt (ed.). *Die Europaeische Union und ihre Krisen*. Baden-Baden: Nomos. 2001.

Romain Kirt. *Kleine Nation, grosse Union*. Echternach: Editions Phi. 2000.

Max Kohnstamm and Wolfgang Hager (eds.). *A Nation Writ Large?* London: Macmillan. 1973.

Arnold Kopicek and Brigitte Marcher. *Der Concours der EU*. Vienna: Verlag Oesterreich. 1999.

Gerd Langguth. "Die Europapolitik von Franz-Josef Strauss". *Die Union*. 2/1995. 26–29.

Jacques Le Goff. *Das alte Europa und die Welt der Moderne*. Munich: Verlag CH Beck. 1994.

Anton Leicht (ed.). *Regierungskonferenz 1996*. Vienna: Signum. 1996.

Philip Lynch *e.a.* (eds.). *Reforming the EU — from Maastricht to Amsterdam*. Harlow, Essex: Pierson Education. 2000.

Gary Marks *e.a.* (eds.). *Governance in the European Union*. London: Sage Publications. 1996.

John McCormick. *Understanding the European Union*. Houndmills, Hamps: Macmillan. 1999.

Steve McGriffen. *The European Union: A Critical Guide*. London: Pluto Press. 2001.

Reinhard C. Meier-Walser (ed.). *Die USA und Europa. Politische Studien.* Special Edition. 4/2000.

Yves Meny and Vincent Wright. *La crise de la siderurgie europeenne.* Paris: Presses Universitaires de France. 1985.

Nicholas Moussis. *Handbook of EU.* 4th Edition. Rixenart: European Study Centre. 1997.

Philomena Murray. "An Asia Pacific Response to the European Union: Australian Elite Perceptions". *Asia Europe Journal.* 1/2003. 103–119.

Beate Neuss. *Geburtshelfer Europas?* Baden-Baden: Nomos. 2000.

Sir William Nicoll and Trevor C. Salmon. *Understanding the European Union.* Harlow, Essex: Pearson Education. 2001.

Juergen Noetzold (ed.). *Wohin steuert Europa?* Baden-Baden: Nomos. 1995.

Peter Norman. "The State of the Union". *Studies in International Relations.* 23/2002. 229–268.

Christian Noyer. *The Euro: Impact on Asia and the World.* Singapore: Asia Europe Foundation. 1999.

Neill Nugent. *Government and Politics of the European Union.* 5th Edition. Houndmills: Palmgrave-Macmillan. 2002.

Chris Patten. *East and West.* London: Macmillan. 2000.

John Peterson and Elizabeth Bromberg. *Decision Making in the European Union.* Houndmills, Hants: Macmillan. 1999.

John Peterson and Michael Shackleton (eds.). *The Institutions of the European Union.* Oxford: Oxford University Press. 2002.

John Pinder. *The Building of the European Union.* Oxford: Oxford University Press. 1998.

Horst Reichenbach *e.a. Integration: Wanderung ueber Europaeische Gipfel.* Baden-Baden: Nomos. 1999.

Carolyn Rhodes (ed.). *The EU in the World Community.* Boulder, CO: Lynn Riener Pubs. 1998.

Moritz Roettinger and Claudia Weyringer (eds.). *Handbuch der europaeischen Integration.* Vienna: Manz'sche Verlagsbuchhandlung. 1991.

Ben Rosamund. *Theories of European Integration.* Houndmills, Hants: Macmillan. 2000.

Glenda G. Rosenthal. *The Men behind the Decisions: Cases in European Decision Making.* Lexington, Mass.: Lexington Books. 1975.

Wilfried Roth *e.a.* (eds.). *Walter Hallstein. Der vergessene Europaer?* Bonn: Europa Union Verlag. 1995.

Albrecht Rothacher. "Consumer Protection in Central and Eastern Europe and EU Accession". *South East Europe Review.* 2/1999. 187–190.

Albrecht Rothacher. "Die Struktur- und Regionalfoerderung der Europaeischen Union". *Gemeinwirtschaft.* 6/1994. 7–17.

Albrecht Rothacher. "Die Tuerkei in der EU? Eine kritische Laenderstudie". *Jahrbuch der Freiheitlichen Akademie.* Vienna. 2001. 160–202.

Albrecht Rothacher. "Die Verkehrspolitik der EG und Oesterreich". *Oesterreichische Zeitschrift fuer Verkehrswissenschaften.* 3/1993. 1–5.

Albrecht Rothacher. "Eastern Enlargement of the European Union". *Journal of Social Sciences.* 14/1998. 131–136.

Albrecht Rothacher. *Economic Diplomacy between the European Union and Japan.* Aldershot, Hants: Gower. 1983.

Albrecht Rothacher. "EU Accession and Political Change in Austria". *Journal of European Integration.* 19/1995. 71–90.

Albrecht Rothacher. "Europaeischer Umweltschutz als Ueberlebensfrage". *Conturen.* 3/1993. 104–121.

Albrecht Rothacher *e.a.* (eds.). *Oesterreichs europaeische Zukunft.* Vienna: Signum. 1996.

Albrecht Rothacher. *Im Wilden Osten. Hinter der Kulissen des Umbruchs in Osteuropa.* Hamburg: Reinhard Kraemer Verlag. 2002.

Albrecht Rothacher. "Nationale Identitaet und Demokratie in der Europaeischen Gemeinschaft". *Jahrbuch fuer politische Erneuerung.* Vienna. 1994. 476–487.

Albrecht Rothacher. "Social Realities and EU Social Policy in the Accession Countries". *South East Europe Review.* 3/2000. 21–27.

Albrecht Rothacher. "Zum Elend der EG-Kritik der Alten Linken und Neuen Rechten". *Oesterreichische Monatshefte.* 1–2/1993. 17–22.

Albrecht Rothacher and Malcolm Colling. "The Community's Top Management: A Meritocracy in the Making". *Courrier du Personnel.* No. 489. 10/1987. 10–25.

Jacques Santer. "Christdemokraten und die europaeische Integration". *Die Union.* 4/1995–1/1996. 43–46.

Philippe C. Schmitter. *How to Democratize the EU … and Why Bother?* Lanham, MD: Rowman & Littlefield. 2000.

Heinrich Schneider. *Rueckblick fuer die Zukunft. Weichenstellungen fuer die europaeische Einigung.* Bonn: Europa Union Verlag. 1986.

Hagen Schulze. *Staat und Nation in der europaeischen Geschichte.* Munich: Beck. 1994.

Andrew Shonfield. *Europe — Journey to an Unknown Destination.* London: Allen Lane. 1973.

Andrew Shonfield. *Modern Capitalism.* London: Oxford University Press. 1969.

Larry Siedentop. *Democracy in Europe.* Harmondsworth: Penguin. 2001.

Brendan Simms. *Unfinest Hour. Britain and the Destruction of Bosnia.* London: Penguin. 2002.

David Stanners and Philippe Bourdeau (eds.). *Europe's Environment. The Dobris Assessment.* Copenhagen: European Environment Agency. 1995.

Rudolf Strohmeier (ed.). *Die Europaeische Union. Ein Kompendium aus deutscher Sicht.* Opladen: Westdeutscher Verlag. 1994.

A.J.P. Taylor. *The Struggle for Mastery in Europe.* Oxford: Oxford University Press. 1971.

Paul Taylor. *The European Union in the 1990s.* Oxford: Oxford University Press. 1996.

Christian Tomuschat (ed.). *Der Ausschuss der Regionen.* Bonn: Europa Union Verlag. 1995.

Jose I. Torreblanca. *The Reuniting of Europe.* Aldershot, Hants: Ashgate. 2001.

Frank Vibert. *Europe: A Constitution for the Millennium.* Aldershot, Hamps: Dartmouth Publishing. 1995.

Hans von der Groeben. *Deutschland und Europa in einem unruhigen Jahrhundert.* Baden-Baden: Nomos. 1995.

Hellen Wallace and William Wallace (eds.). *Policy Making in the European Union.* 4th Edition. Oxford: Oxford University Press. 2000.

Helen Wallace and Alasdair R. Young (eds.). *Participation and Policy Making in the European Union*. Oxford: Clarendon Press. 1997.

Graham Watson and Joanna Hazelwood (eds.). *To the Power of Ten*. London: Centre for Reform. 2000.

Werner Weidenfeld (ed.). *Europa Handbuch*. Guetersloh: Verlag Bertelsmann. 2002.

Werner Weidenfeld (ed.). *Europa oeffnen. Anforderungen an die Erweiterung*. Guetersloh: Bertelsmann. 1997.

Werner Weidenfeld and Wolfgang Wessels. *Europe from A to Z*. Luxembourg: OPOCE. 1997.

Michael Welsh. *Europe United?* New York: St. Martin's Press. 1996.

Martin Westlake (ed.). *The EU beyond Amsterdam*. London: Routledge. 1998.

Georg Wiessala. *The EU and the Asian Countries*. London: Sheffield Academic Press. 2002.